# THE ULTIMATE SOUTH PARK AND PHILOSOPHY

The Blackwell Philosophy and Pop Culture Series
*Series editor: William Irwin*

A spoonful of sugar helps the medicine go down, and a healthy helping of popular culture clears the cobwebs from Kant. Philosophy has had a public relations problem for a few centuries now. This series aims to change that, showing that philosophy is relevant to your life—and not just for answering the big questions like "To be or not to be?" but for answering the little questions: "To watch or not to watch *South Park*?" Thinking deeply about TV, movies, and music doesn't make you a "complete idiot." In fact it might make you a philosopher, someone who believes the unexamined life is not worth living and the unexamined cartoon is not worth watching.

Already published in the series:

**24 and Philosophy: The World According to Jack**
*Edited by Jennifer Hart Weed, Richard Brian Davis, and Ronald Weed*

**30 Rock and Philosophy: We Want to Go to There**
*Edited by J. Jeremy Wisnewski*

**Alice in Wonderland and Philosophy: Curiouser and Curiouser**
*Edited by Richard Brian Davis*

**Arrested Development and Philosophy: They've Made a Huge Mistake**
*Edited by Kristopher Phillips and J. Jeremy Wisnewski*

**The Avengers and Philosophy: Earth's Mightiest Thinkers**
*Edited by Mark D. White*

**Batman and Philosophy: The Dark Knight of the Soul**
*Edited by Mark D. White and Robert Arp*

**Battlestar Galactica and Philosophy: Knowledge Here Begins Out There**
*Edited by Jason T. Eberl*

**The Big Bang Theory and Philosophy: Rock, Paper, Scissors, Aristotle, Locke**
*Edited by Dean Kowalski*

**The Big Lebowski and Philosophy: Keeping Your Mind Limber with Abiding Wisdom**
*Edited by Peter S. Fosl*

**Black Sabbath and Philosophy: Mastering Reality**
*Edited by William Irwin*

**The Daily Show and Philosophy: Moments of Zen in the Art of Fake News**
*Edited by Jason Holt*

**Downton Abbey and Philosophy: The Truth Is Neither Here Nor There**
*Edited by Mark D. White*

**Family Guy and Philosophy: A Cure for the Petarded**
*Edited by J. Jeremy Wisnewski*

**Final Fantasy and Philosophy: The Ultimate Walkthrough**
*Edited by Jason P. Blahuta and Michel S. Beaulieu*

**Game of Thrones and Philosophy: Logic Cuts Deeper Than Swords**
*Edited by Henry Jacoby*

**The Girl With the Dragon Tattoo and Philosophy: Everything is Fire**
*Edited by Eric Bronson*

**Green Lantern and Philosophy: No Evil Shall Escape this Book**
*Edited by Jane Dryden and Mark D. White*

**Heroes and Philosophy: Buy the Book, Save the World**
*Edited by David Kyle Johnson*

**The Hobbit and Philosophy: For When You've Lost Your Dwarves, Your Wizard, and Your Way**
*Edited by Gregory Bassham and Eric Bronson*

**House and Philosophy: Everybody Lies**
*Edited by Henry Jacoby*

**The Hunger Games and Philosophy: A Critique of Pure Treason**
*Edited by George Dunn and Nicolas Michaud*

**Inception and Philosophy: Because It's Never Just a Dream**
*Edited by David Johnson*

**Iron Man and Philosophy: Facing the Stark Reality**
*Edited by Mark D. White*

**Lost and Philosophy: The Island Has Its Reasons**
*Edited by Sharon M. Kaye*

**Mad Men and Philosophy: Nothing Is as It Seems**
*Edited by James South and Rod Carveth*

**Metallica and Philosophy: A Crash Course in Brain Surgery**
*Edited by William Irwin*

**The Office and Philosophy: Scenes from the Unfinished Life**
*Edited by J. Jeremy Wisnewski*

**South Park and Philosophy: You Know, I Learned Something Today**
*Edited by Robert Arp*

**Spider-Man and Philosophy: The Web of Inquiry**
*Edited by Jonathan Sanford*

**Terminator and Philosophy: I'll Be Back, Therefore I Am**
*Edited by Richard Brown and Kevin S. Decker*

**True Blood and Philosophy: We Wanna Think Bad Things with You**
*Edited by George Dunn and Rebecca Housel*

**Twilight and Philosophy: Vampires, Vegetarians, and the Pursuit of Immortality**
*Edited by Rebecca Housel and J. Jeremy Wisnewski*

**The Ultimate Harry Potter and Philosophy: Hogwarts for Muggles**
*Edited by Gregory Bassham*

**The Ultimate Lost and Philosophy: Think Together, Die Alone**
*Edited by Sharon Kaye*

**The Walking Dead and Philosophy: Shotgun. Machete. Reason.**
*Edited by Christopher Robichaud*

**Watchmen and Philosophy: A Rorschach Test**
*Edited by Mark D. White*

**X-Men and Philosophy: Astonishing Insight and Uncanny Argument in the Mutant X-Verse**
*Edited by Rebecca Housel and J. Jeremy Wisnewski*

**Superman and Philosophy: What Would the Man of Steel Do?**
*Edited by Mark D. White*

**The Ultimate Daily Show and Philosophy: More Moments of Zen, More Moments of Indecision Theory**
*Edited by Jason Holt*

**The Ultimate South Park and Philosophy: Respect My Philosophah!**
*Edited by Robert Arp and Kevin S. Decker*

Forthcoming:

**Ender's Game and Philosophy**
*Edited by Kevin S. Decker*

**Sons of Anarchy and Philosophy**
*Edited by George Dunn and Jason Eberl*

**Supernatural and Philosophy**
*Edited by Galen A. Foresman*

# THE ULTIMATE SOUTH PARK AND PHILOSOPHY

## RESPECT MY PHILOSOPHAH!

Edited by
**Robert Arp and Kevin S. Decker**

**WILEY** Blackwell

Wiley-Blackwell is an imprint of John Wiley & Sons, formed by the merger of
Wiley's global Scientific, Technical and Medical business with Blackwell Publishing.

*Registered Office*
John Wiley & Sons, Ltd, The Atrium, Southern Gate, Chichester, West Sussex, PO19 8SQ, UK

*Editorial Offices*
350 Main Street, Malden, MA 02148-5020, USA
9600 Garsington Road, Oxford, OX4 2DQ, UK
The Atrium, Southern Gate, Chichester, West Sussex, PO19 8SQ, UK

For details of our global editorial offices, for customer services, and for information about how
to apply for permission to reuse the copyright material in this book please see our website at
www.wiley.com/wiley-blackwell.

The right of Robert Arp and Kevin S. Decker to be identified as the authors of of the editorial
material in this work has been asserted in accordance with the UK Copyright, Designs and
Patents Act 1988.

*Library of Congress Cataloging-in-Publication Data*
The ultimate South Park and philosophy : respect my philosophah! / edited by Robert Arp,
Kevin S. Decker.
       pages    cm – (The Blackwell philosophy and pop culture series ; 83)
   Includes bibliographical references and index.
   ISBN 978-1-118-38656-9 (pbk.)    1.  South Park (Television program)    I. Arp, Robert.
II.  Decker, Kevin S.
   PN1992.77.S665S68 2013
   791.45′72–dc23
                                                              2013006624
A catalogue record for this book is available from the British Library.

Cover image: Background © Roman Okopny; spacecraft © Sven Herrmann;
city © Murat Giray Kaya (all istockphoto); boy © Tim Kitchen/Getty Images.
Cover design by www.simonlevy.co.uk

Set in 10.5/13pt Sabon by SPi Publisher Services, Pondicherry, India
Printed in Singapore by Ho Printing Singapore Pte Ltd

1   2013

# Contents

# Introduction
## "Well, I'm Afraid It's About to Happen Again"
## Introducing *The Ultimate South Park and Philosophy*

*Robert Arp and Kevin S. Decker*

We're convinced. *South Park* is one of the most important series on TV.

Why? Because the show isn't afraid to lampoon the extremist fanatics that are associated with any social, ethical, economical, or religious position. This is extremely important and necessary in our diverse society of free and autonomous persons who hold a plurality of beliefs and values. Why? Because someone who thinks they have the "corner on truth" can become fanatical. Fanatics usually stop thinking issues through and, ultimately, they're primed to cause harm to others through their actions. We want to be critical thinkers, and part of thinking critically means that we're committed to having beliefs that aren't treated as *so* sacred that we never, ever doubt them—or laugh at them. In other words, we need a healthy dose of skepticism about any belief, and this is one of the important lessons that *South Park* teaches us.

Unfortunately, even philosophers have caved in to the temptation to be "dogmatic" about their beliefs. But in the long, long dialogue that is philosophy, every dogma has its day, and other philosophers sweep in to point out the extremist (if not very fanatical) views of their predecessors. This can be done in a number of different ways, each equally interesting. The American pragmatist Charles Sanders Peirce (1839–1914), for example, pounced on the fact that all our

*The Ultimate South Park and Philosophy: Respect My Philosophah!*, First Edition.
Edited by Robert Arp and Kevin S. Decker.
© 2013 John Wiley & Sons, Inc. Published 2013 by John Wiley & Sons, Inc.

thinking is done through the medium of signs, and that the meaning of every sign is incomplete since it has been shaped by previous thinking—earlier signs—each of which is even less complete. Although you would never confuse him for Peirce, the French deconstructionist Jacques Derrida (1930–2004) wrote that all our concepts are defined negatively by what they're *not*—that is, by their difference from other concepts. For Derrida, thinking is the "play of differences" that presents alternative possibilities, rather than hard realities. The penetrating insights of Peirce and Derrida provide excellent case studies in the healthy type of skepticism that *South Park* affirms.

There are other important lessons to be gained from *South Park*, and the chapters in this book are a testament to this fact. First, and foremost, we need to laugh. We need to laugh at the extremist fanatics not just because their ideas are usually, well, *extreme* and *fanatical*, but because when their reasoning is exposed to sunlight, it withers. Critical thinkers need to be fair-minded, pragmatic, and balanced in their recognition that people's perceptions of the truth are just that, people's perceptions. The creators of *South Park* intend their show to poke fun at the "kooks" of any position, and, according to Parker in an interview with Charlie Rose, "What we say with the show is not anything new, but I think it is something that is great to put out there. It is that the people screaming on this side and the people screaming on that side are the same people, and it's OK to be someone in the middle, laughing at both of them."[1]

There's been a lot of laughter *and* philosophy that *South Park* has offered us over the years. In 2006, the book *South Park and Philosophy: You Know, I Learned Something Today* was published, and in that pioneering book, philosophers tackled issues like whether it's morally appropriate to laugh at the nurse with the dead fetus attached to her head, or the fact that Scott Tenorman has just been fed his own parents, or that Mr. Garrison's parents did *not* molest him when, apparently, they should have. A big part of us says no, this isn't appropriate, but another part affirms a joyous yes! (Take that, Nietzsche!) Other issues they took on included Cartman's "authoritah" and the source of the binding force of laws; whether a robot can understand; the ethics of capitalism; the fear and question of death; arguments for the existence of a divine being; how people are objectifying, or turned into things; and what makes you who you are—the question of *identity*. Such is the depth and breadth of *South Park* that the earlier book needed to dive into disciplines like sociology, psychology, and political science, as well as philosophy.

This book is such a bigger project that it required taking on an additional editor and several consignments of Chef's Salty Balls to keep up the pace of writing and editing. It's made up of wholly new chapters and some of the best chapters, revised in the face of new philosophical problems and fresh *South Park* heresies, from the earlier book. We think you'll find it's equally engaging a read, for sure. For example, along with Kevin Murtagh, whose chapter deals with blasphemous humor, you might cringe at the thought of a statue of the Virgin Mary bleeding out of its vagina. But you might also agree with Murtagh that there is value in metaphorically "hitting people over the head with a sledgehammer" to get them to start thinking. Philosophers will often do that simply by introducing philosophical ideas to students for the first time. Still, if you look at Willie Young's chapter, you'll likely agree with him that the claim that *South Park* corrupts people is "a lot of hot air."

Religious fanatics get hit pretty hard by the creators of *South Park* and rightly so. The kind of connection between fanaticism and harm we mentioned already is most obvious in the countless examples of terrorist actions committed in the name of some god throughout history. As Henry Jacoby says in his chapter, this link between fanaticism and violence can be blatant or it can be subtle. And the point Jacoby makes through the words of the famous philosopher and mathematician, William K. Clifford, is that you're intellectually "wrong," as well as morally wrong, when you think you've got the corner on truth with little or no evidence. However, in another chapter, Jeffrey Dueck argues that it's possible to be a rational, reflective individual and still be a believer in some god. "It's good to beware the Blainetologists of our world," Dueck thinks, "but we should also be careful about surrendering rationally justifiable ways of life that may help to define us."

These days, when you think of fanatics the next thought that comes to mind is the religious right and its connection to American politics and government. In his chapter, John Scott Gray considers recent American politics as discussed in the *South Park* episode, "Douche or Turd." Did we really have a decent choice in the 2004 presidential election? Religious fanaticism and politics make another appearance in Jacob Held's chapter about those "faggots who want to get married" but *still* face a social "glass ceiling" many places in the world.

As you'll see throughout this book, philosophy deals with the love and pursuit of wisdom, and this quest makes us ask what kinds of things really exist, what we're justified in believing, what we ought to do, and how we ought to be living, among other things. In the context of this book, it also forces us to face whether the threat of Manbearpig is real or not, or whether the greater threat is an Al Gore unleashed on the world. The authors have skillfully deployed characters, events, and situations in *South Park* episodes in order to drag important and interesting philosophical issues, kicking and screaming, into the light. Our hope is that (if you are, in fact, able to read), you'll have indeed "learned something today" as a result of your reading the following chapters. So, let's go on down to *The Ultimate South Park and Philosophy* and meet some philosophical friends of mine ... *ours*, really, since there are two of us editing this book.

## Note

1. *The Charlie Rose Show*, September 26, 2005.

# Part I

# DOING PHILOSOPHICAL THINGS WITH SOUTH PARK

# Flatulence and Philosophy

## A Lot of Hot Air, or the Corruption of Youth?

### Willie Young

In the episode "Death," Kyle's mother leads a boycott of the boys' favorite cartoon show, *Terrance and Phillip*, because of its continuous farting, name-calling, and general "potty humor." While the parents are up in arms over this supposedly "moral" issue, the boys wrestle with the problem of euthanasia and Stan's grandfather, something none of the parents will discuss with them. "Death" brings together many central issues that have made *South Park* successful and controversial—vulgarity, the misplaced moral concerns of American culture, the discussion of controversial moral topics, and the criticism that *South Park* itself is a "disgusting" show. Since "Death" that criticism has only grown—getting even bigger than Cartman's fat ass—drawing fire for its obscene language, making fun of religion, and emphasis on freedom of speech.

Like the parents protesting *Terrance and Phillip*, critics of *South Park* make claims that are strikingly similar to those that have been leveled against Western philosophy since its beginnings. Philosophy, it's been charged, also mocks religious beliefs, leads younger folks to question accepted authority and values, and corrupts our children and culture. These condemnations formed the basis for Socrates' (470–399 BC) trial and execution in Athens.[1] So in this chapter we'll explore the heretical possibility that people perceive *South Park* as dangerous precisely because it is a form of philosophy. The "danger" *South Park* poses has to do with its depiction of dialogue and free

*The Ultimate South Park and Philosophy: Respect My Philosophah!*, First Edition.
Edited by Robert Arp and Kevin S. Decker.
© 2013 John Wiley & Sons, Inc. Published 2013 by John Wiley & Sons, Inc.

thought. In the end, we'll have learned something: like Socrates, *South Park* harms no one. Philosophy and *South Park* actually instruct people and provide them with the intellectual tools they need to become wise, free, and good.

## Oh my God! They Killed Socrates! You Bastards!

In Plato's (427–327 BCE) *Apology*, Socrates defends himself against two charges: impiety, or false teachings about the gods, and corrupting the youth of Athens. Socrates probably had as much chance of winning his case as Chef did against Johnny Cochran's "Chewbacca" defense! What is most important about Socrates' own defense, though, isn't so much *what* he says as *how* he says it. He defends himself by questioning his accuser, Meletus, leading him through a process of reasoning. For example, Socrates refutes the charge of corrupting the youth like this:

> SOCRATES: You say you have discovered the one who corrupts them, namely me, and you bring me here and accuse me to the jury … All the Athenians, it seems, make the young into fine good men, except me, and I alone corrupt them. Is that what you mean?
>
> MELETUS: That is most definitely what I mean.
>
> SOCRATES: You condemn me to a great misfortune. Tell me: does this also apply to horses do you think? That all men improve them and one individual corrupts them? Or is quite the contrary true, one individual is able to improve them, or very few, namely the horse breeders, whereas the majority, if they have horses and use them, corrupt them? Is that not the case, Meletus, both with horses and all other animals? … It would be a happy state of affairs if only one person corrupted our youth, while the others improved them. You have made it sufficiently obvious, Meletus, that you have never had any concern for our youth; you show your indifference clearly; that you have given no thought to the subjects about which you bring me to trial.[2]

Through the analogy with horse training, Socrates shows that the accusations against him are quite illogical. Just as most people would injure horses by trying to train them, and only a few good trainers improve them, so too it's likely that a few teachers improve the virtue of the youth, while many others corrupt them. Socrates argues that he's the one teaching Athens' youth about virtue, while many others—including the idiots sitting before him—corrupt them. (As you can imagine, this did not go over well with the jury.)

While showing that the accusations are groundless, this "apology"—a word that in this case mean "defense"—demonstrates why Socrates got the death sentence of drinking hemlock. Socrates is famous for saying "I know that I don't know" and, actually, this is a wise insight. For Socrates, philosophy was the love and pursuit of wisdom, and this required questioning others to find out what they did or didn't know. Unfortunately, people often believe they're wiser than they are. By questioning them, Socrates would show them that they don't know what they believe they know: "I go around seeking out anyone, citizen or stranger, whom I think wise. Then if I do not think he is, I come to the assistance of the god and show him that he is not wise."[3] What makes Socrates wise is his recognition of his own ignorance. Many powerful people in Athens saw him as dangerous because they believed the debates he carried on would undermine their bases for power.

In the town of South Park, people in positions of power also believe they're teaching the children wisdom and virtue. However, as in Athens, most "teachers" in South Park seem to make the children worse, not better. For example, Mr. Garrison "teaches" the children creationism before switching to an unflinching Darwinism; Mrs. Broflovski always goes to crazy extremes with her "moral" outrage; Uncle Jim and Ned teach the boys to kill harmless bunnies and squirrels in "self-defense"; and the mayor panders shamelessly to voters. None of the townsfolk really *talk* to the children, except Chef (R.I.P.), who taught the art of making sweet, sweet love to a woman. Blindly following the crowd, the parents of South Park protest *Terrance and Phillip*, boycott Harbucks, and—yes—bury their heads in the sand to avoid watching *Family Guy*. And they corrupt the children far more than a television show ever could. As in "Something Wal-Mart This Way Comes," their mindless consumption leads to an unrestrained cycle of economic and mob destruction. Like the Athenians, the adults don't know as much as they believe they know. Ultimately, if television does corrupt the children, it does so because they are left to passively absorb it by their parents, with no one to educate them about what they are seeing. Of course, there are also cases where parents and people in powerful positions *do* try to discuss issues and ideas with the children. In these discussions, though, the adults usually sound like bumbling idiots. Socrates might even say that since this treatment systematically harms the children, there's evil at work in South Park.

## Cartman Gets a Banal Probe

One of the most memorable philosophical reflections on evil in the twentieth century is Hannah Arendt's *Eichmann in Jerusalem: A Report on the Banality of Evil*, a study of the trial of Adolf Eichmann for his role in the deportations of millions of European Jews to concentration camps during the Jewish Holocaust. Eichmann just followed the law of the land, whatever it happened to be, and when Hitler was making the laws, Eichmann simply carried them out.[4] In the words of Arendt, Eichmann was an unreflective person, unable to think for himself and *definitely* unable "to think from the standpoint of somebody else."[5] What was really monstrous about Eichmann was not his vicious cruelty, but the fact that he wasn't that different from so many Germans who, under Nazism, accepted and supported laws that were obviously evil and believed that they were doing what was right. Eichmann's banality—the fact that there's nothing distinctive or exceptional about him—is *precisely* what makes him evil. He was "one of the crowd" who *didn't* walk to the beat of a different drummer and *didn't* rock the boat. He was a compliant citizen under a dictatorship, which speaks *for* its subjects and, thus, cuts off their reflective and critical thought.

Thoughtlessness leads to evil, as Arendt says, because it doesn't let us see things from others' perspectives. By blindly following orders, Eichmann didn't think about what his actions were doing to others, or even what they were doing to him. By saying he was "following the law" and "doing his duty," he ignored how his actions sent millions to their deaths and, despite his protests, made him a murderer. Thinking, according to Arendt, requires taking another's standpoint, reflecting on how you might be harming others, and asking if you can live with what you're doing.

While the adults in South Park blindly follow the latest fad or what they are told, it's the children who point out the absurdity and potential harm that lurks in this thoughtlessness. To be more accurate, it's usually Kyle or Stan who are the reflective ones, while Cartman's mind is as empty as the Cheesy Poofs he devours daily. He's often sadistic, cruel, and evil. Like Eichmann, Cartman is probably evil because, when it comes to "authoritah," he lacks reflection and critical analysis. (And like Eichmann, he has a Nazi uniform that he's sported on occasion.) Cartman sings the Cheesy Poofs song so well because he just imitates what he hears on television. His evil is an *imitation* of the evil characters of our culture, as prepackaged as his afternoon snacks. Cartman consumes evil and imitates it as blindly and thoughtlessly as Eichmann—even when feeding Scott Tenorman his own parents (like Medea in Greek tragedy), trying to kill Kyle and Stan on a lake (like Fredo in *The Godfather*), or torturing Muslims with his farts (like Jack Bauer in *24*) to find the "snuke." Most importantly, because of this thoughtlessness, Cartman is unable to see things from anyone else's viewpoint, as we see most clearly in his manipulation of his mother. Arendt says that such thoughtlessness is precisely what allows evil to emerge in modern society, and Cartman's mindless consumption is as thoughtless as it gets.

## Friendship Kicks Ass! The Dialogues of Kyle and Stan

Part of what makes *South Park* philosophically interesting is the contrast between Cartman's evil stupidity and the nonconformist, reflective virtue of Kyle and Stan. Philosophers like Plato and Aristotle (384–322 BC) have noted the importance of how critical reflection leads to harmony or balance and helps us to avoid extremes. After all, the "extremes" of thinking and acting often lead to mistaken beliefs and harmful behavior. Following Plato's lead, Aristotle offered the idea that *virtue* is concerned with striking a balance or hitting the mark between two extreme viewpoints, ideas, beliefs, emotions, or actions.[6] *South Park* addresses moral issues through a discussion and criticism of established "moral" positions, both conservative and liberal, which are found to be inadequate. Kyle and Stan come to a harmonious position, in part, by negotiating and listening to these views before reaching their own conclusion through questioning and reason. Frequently, their conclusion recognizes that there's truth in each position, but that a limited perspective is still dangerous. For example, it's true that hybrid cars are more environmentally responsible than gas-guzzling SUVs. But when an air of moral superiority clouds one's judgment, this "smug cloud" creates hostility and pollutes society in other ways.

*How* Stan and Kyle reach their conclusions is more significant than the conclusions themselves. Think of how they talk about whether it's wrong to kill Stan's grandpa, who wants to die. Like Socrates, they question others, seeking people who are really as wise as they believe themselves to be. Their parents, Mr. Garrison, and Jesus won't discuss or touch this issue "with a 60-foot pole." What Kyle and Stan ultimately realize—with the help of Stan's great-great-grandfather's ghost—is that they shouldn't kill his grandfather, because the action would change and harm them. As it turns out, Stan's grandfather is wrong in asking them to do this vicious action. Note that the boys reach this conclusion through living with each other, recognizing their differences, and engaging in debate. Stan and Kyle—unlike Eichmann and Cartman—learn to see things from others' perspectives, through their ongoing conversation.

In the *Apology*, Socrates makes the astounding claim that a good person cannot be harmed by the actions of others. This seems false. After all, aside from being a cartoon character, what could prevent Cartman from punching out the Dalai Lama? But what Socrates means by "good" is something different than we often realize. Goodness means being willing to think about your actions and *being able to live with what you've done*. Despite any *physical* harm— torture, imprisonment, exile, or death—that may come a person's way, no one could "hurt" a virtuous person by making them *do* something bad. Cartman, for example, couldn't make the Dalai Lama punch *him*. Socrates, for his part, refused to execute an innocent person, or to try generals for "crimes" beyond the laws of the city. And Socrates would rather die than give up the thinking and questioning that he sees as central to philosophy:

> Perhaps someone might say: But Socrates, if you leave us will you not be able to live quietly, without talking? Now this is the most difficult point on which to convince some of you. If I say that it is impossible for me to keep quiet because that means disobeying the god, you will not believe me ... On the other hand, if I say that it is the greatest good for a man to discuss virtue every day and those other things about which

you hear me conversing and testing myself and others, for the unexamined life is not worth living for man, you will believe me even less.[7]

Arendt thinks likewise about goodness. Ethics, for those who resisted the Nazis, was being able to look back on their lives without shame, rather than adhering to a rigid set of questionable rules:

> Their criterion [for goodness], I think, was a different one; they asked themselves to what extent they would still be able to live in peace with themselves after having committed certain deeds; and they decided that it would be better to do nothing, not because the world would then be changed for the better, but simply because only on this condition could they go on living with themselves at all. Hence, they also chose to die when they were forced to participate. To put it crudely, they refused to murder ... because they were unwilling to live together with a murderer—themselves. The precondition for this kind of judging is not a highly developed intelligence or sophistication in moral matters, but rather the disposition to live together explicitly with oneself, to have intercourse with oneself, that is, to be engaged in that silent dialogue between me and myself which, since Socrates and Plato, we usually call thinking.[8]

Thinking, for Arendt, is a twofold process: it involves seeing things through another's eyes through dialogue and reflection, as well as asking what you can live with for yourself. It is, then, both an internal and an external dialogue, and only through this dialogue can critical reflection and goodness become real. Whereas Eichmann and Cartman don't critically reflect upon the consequences of actions, nor put themselves in another's shoes, thoughtful dialogue makes us attentive to others around us, lets us live with them, and helps us attend to our own goodness. Such dialogue allows us to live with ourselves—even when, like Socrates or those who resisted the Nazis, this means we must die.

Of course, in South Park there's no Socrates to teach philosophy or help us engage in dialogue. Surrounded by ignorance and violence, the boys are on their own. While the four are friends, *South Park* makes its compelling points in philosophy and ethics through the friendship of Kyle and Stan. For instance, in "Spookyfish," where the "evil" Cartman (who is good) arrives from a parallel universe, an evil Kyle and Stan arrive *together*. Their friendship—thinking from one another's perspective—is what helps them to be good, both for themselves and for others. In Arendt's words, to live well is to "be plural," so that the good life is never simply one's own.[9] This probably is why Plato wrote about important philosophical issues in dialogue form, so that it becomes clear that debate and discussion of ideas is essential to intellectual and moral growth.

For all their faults, Kyle and Stan still debate and discuss whether certain actions are wrong. On his own, Stan sometimes just goes along with the crowd, though he develops a general refusal to do harm over the show's history.[10] After the boys throw toilet paper all over the art teacher's house, Kyle can't live with what he's done. Through their conversations they learn goodness and engage in the "thinking" Arendt describes. Friendship, then, helps us to examine our lives. In the episode "Prehistoric Ice Man" Larry says that "living is about sharing our ups and downs with our friends," and when we fail to do this we aren't really living at all. If thinking and goodness only arise through real dialogue with others—through critically questioning and examining *our own* views—then we need more friendships like the one Kyle and Stan share.

## An Apology for South Park: Getting in Touch with Your Inner Cartman

If good friendships help us to critically examine our lives, then perhaps it's no accident that the critical voice of *South Park* has been created by two friends—Trey Parker and Matt Stone. In the *Apology* Socrates likens himself to a gadfly, an annoying pest that goes around "stinging" people with his challenging questions and critical reflections to keep them intellectually awake and on their toes. *South Park*, too, serves as a gadfly, trying to wake American culture from its thoughtlessness and ignorance. The show generates discussion and debate and leads many people to discuss ethical issues that would otherwise be passed over in silence. For a show that supposedly corrupts, it has a more intense focus on religion, ethics, and democracy than its critics would like to admit. But, of course, we could still ask if the *way* that *South Park* presents these issues is really necessary. For example, is it philosophically wise and necessary to use the word "shit" 163 times in one show? Or have so much, farting, vomiting, and violence? What philosophical goal can such vulgarity serve?

The vulgarity and crudeness of *South Park* is often defended on the grounds of free speech. However, a different issue is also in play. *South Park* often says what is not socially or morally acceptable to say; that is, in terms established by Sigmund Freud (1856–1939), what must be *repressed*. According to Freud, our thoughts and actions are shaped by "drives," including emotions, desires, and hostile or consumptive energy. (Freud would have a field day with Cartman's twisted little mind!) These drives are part of our embodied being, yet, since they are dangerous and often violent, we try to control and even silence them. This control is a form of repression, but it can often have unintended consequences. Repression of a drive can lead to other sorts of unconscious, violent behavior, and suppressed wishes like these form the content of dreams, our "unconscious" life.[11] Repression, or internal censorship, redirects but doesn't diminish our aggression. In spite of our intentions, this unconscious aggression often shapes who we are, how we think, and what we do.

What Freud discovered with psychoanalysis was that talking about our dreams may serve as a way to address this repression and its associated violence. When we talk these ideas and feelings out, the repression is broken and, through the realization, we can come to terms with the desire and shape it through thinking. Representing desires lets them be expressed, and this helps us to integrate them into the structure of our lives.[12] By bringing to light what had been unconscious, dream interpretation lets us think through these aspects of ourselves.

Freud also thought that jokes work like dreams. When one person tells a joke, its spontaneous and unexpected word-form breaks through another person's repression. Laughter is a "release of energy" that had been blocked; this is why many jokes have a vulgar or obscene dimension. As Freud points out, jokes only really work when the person telling them doesn't laugh, so that the surprise can make others laugh.[13] There is pleasure in laughing at the joke, and in telling it, as well as pleasure in freeing others from their repression.

Through its vulgarity, *South Park* verbalizes the drives and desires that we often repress; and, it allows us to laugh so as to reveal these inhibitions. This is what makes the show's crudeness essential. Showing us "Token" or the conjoined fetus nurse, or saying *shit* over and over brings out the aggression and desire that we can't express on our own. And, for things that really *shouldn't* be said, Kenny says them in a muffled way, and the other boys comment. By verbalizing these drives, the show lets us begin to think them through. It's then possible to analyze them and, by doing this, distance ourselves from them. For instance, many episodes address how outsiders are berated and subjected to racist or xenophobic slander. By working through these incidents, the show demonstrates that such slander is used among friends as well. Verbal sparring, when so understood, needn't lead to violence or exclusion. It doesn't justify such speech, but it does create a space in which the hostility can be interpreted and analyzed.

Likewise, there's a reason for all of the farting on *Terrance and Phillip*. At least two interpretations of this show-within-the-show are possible. First, there is the issue of why the boys love such a stupid show so much. It's not that they wish they could fart all the time. Rather, when they fart, Terrance and Phillip do what's forbidden: they transgress parents' social prohibitions. This appeals to the boys because they wish they could be free from parental control and regulation too.

Second, regular viewers (some of them my students) have noted that *Terrance and Phillip* is self-referential, a way for *South Park* to comment on itself. The opening of *South Park* tells us that, like *Terrance and Phillip*, the show has no redeeming value and should be watched by no one. The stupidity and vulgarity of the cartoon is better understood, however, if we look beyond *South Park*. Is *Terrance and Phillip* really more vapid, crude, and pointless than *Jerry Springer* or *Wife Swap*? Is it more mindless than *Fox News*, *The 700 Club*, or *Law and Order*? When we see Kyle, Cartman, Kenny, and Stan watching *Terrance and Phillip*, this is a reflection of the fact that television fulfills our wish for mindlessness. What offends the parents in South Park—and the critics of *South Park*—is not that the show is vulgar and pointless, but that it highlights the imbecility of television in general.

Both interpretations show that censorship can be questioned at multiple levels. On the one hand, censorship looks at vulgarity, choosing what can and can't afford to be seen based on social norms. *South Park* questions this sort of censorship, saying what can't be said and challenging social forms of repression. But, if part of *South Park*'s message is the need for thinking, then it also questions how television, by fulfilling our wish for mindlessness, represses active thinking. Of course, brainlessness can't simply be blamed on parents or television corporations or two doofusses from Colorado who can't draw straight. Like the mindless Athenians who were to blame for their own ignorance, or Eichmann's responsibility when he thought he was just obeying the law, if we really hold a mirror up to ourselves, we'll find that our own mindlessness is the heart of Wal-Mart. Like Socrates, *South Park*—and Kyle and Stan specifically—present us with a way to reflect on what *we think* we really know, and through reflection move beyond our mindlessness.

## The Talking Cure for Our Culture

By ceaselessly testing the limits of our tolerance, *South Park* asks us to examine the things we think we know, why certain words and actions are prohibited, what we desire, and what we're teaching our children. It provocatively asks us to think about what's truly harmful, and what issues we really should be outraged about. Breaking the silence of our culture's repressions could be the starting point for a Socratic dialogue that helps us to think, analyze our desires and aggression, and become better people. If we take the opportunity to discuss the show, why it's funny, and what it tells us about our culture and our own desires, then *South Park* need not be seen as mindless, vulgar, or corrupting, but rather as a path to thinking that helps us to live with one another, and with ourselves.[14]

## Notes

1. Plato, *Apology, in Five Dialogues: Euthyphro, Apology, Crito, Meno, Phaedo*, trans. G.M.A. Grube (Indianapolis, IN: Hackett Publishing, 1981). Also see Xenophon, *Recollections of Socrates, and Socrates' Defense Before the Jury*, trans. Anna Benjamin (Indianapolis: Bobbs-Merrill, 1965).
2. Plato, *Apology*, 30.
3. Ibid., 28–29.
4. Hannah Arendt, *Eichmann in Jerusalem: A Report on the Banality of Evil* (New York: Viking Press, 1964), 135–150.
5. Plato, *Apology*, 49.
6. See Plato, *The Republic of Plato*, trans. David Bloom (New York: Basic Books, 1991); Aristotle, *Nicomachean Ethics*, trans. Terence Irwin (Indianapolis, IN: Hackett Publishing, 1999).

7. Plato, *Apology*, 41.
8. Hannah Arendt, "Personal Responsibility Under Dictatorship," in *Responsibility and Judgment* (New York: Schocken, 2003), 40–41.
9. Arendt, "Some Questions of Moral Philosophy," *Responsibility and Judgment*, 6–7.
10. I owe this insight to Kyle Giroux.
11. See Sigmund Freud, *The Interpretation of Dreams* (New York: Avon Books, 1965), 156–166.
12. For more on this issue, see Jonathan Lear, *Love and Its Place in Nature: A Philosophical Interpretation of Freudian Psychoanalysis* (New York: Farrar, Strauss, and Giroux, 1990).
13. Freud, *Wit and Its Relation to the Unconscious*, trans. A.A. Brill (New York: Dover, 1993), 261–273.
14. My thanks to Kyle Giroux for his work as a "*South Park* consultant" and his suggestions for ways to update this version. Additional thanks to Keith Wilde and Nicole Merola for their comments and suggestions on this chapter, and to numerous students from Endicott College for their discussions of an earlier version of it. Errors remain my own.

# You Know, I Learned Something Today

## Stan Marsh and the Ethics of Belief

*Henry Jacoby*

*A wise man, therefore, proportions his belief to the evidence.*
—David Hume

People believe all sorts of things for all sorts of reasons; sadly, few people pay attention to reasons based on logic, rules of argumentation, theory, or evidence. And the inhabitants of South Park are no different. But why should we think critically and rationally? Why does it matter? What harm is there in believing something if it makes you feel good, provides you with comfort, or gives you hope? If evidence is lacking, so what?

In his essay "The Ethics of Belief," W.K. Clifford (1845–1879), an English mathematician and philosopher, explained the potential harm of believing just anything. "Every time we let ourselves believe for unworthy reasons, we weaken our powers of self-control, of doubting, of judicially and fairly weighing evidence," he wrote, concluding that it's "wrong always, everywhere, and for anyone, to believe anything upon insufficient evidence."[1]

Amid the exaggerated craziness and illogic of the citizens of South Park, we're sometimes treated to flashes of insight and well thought-out ideas that surprise us. Stan shows off his critical thinking skills as he takes on TV psychics, various cults, and unsupported religious beliefs

*The Ultimate South Park and Philosophy: Respect My Philosophah!*, First Edition.
Edited by Robert Arp and Kevin S. Decker.
© 2013 John Wiley & Sons, Inc. Published 2013 by John Wiley & Sons, Inc.

in a way that would've made Clifford proud. In this chapter, we'll examine how Stan exposes the frauds and the harms they bring, while defending scientific thinking and a healthy skepticism.

## Belief and Evidence

We acquire our beliefs in various ways, most notably by observation and authority. The kids believe that Mr. Hankey exists because they see him, but what we see isn't always trustworthy. Cartman, after all, sees pink Christina Aguilera creatures floating around, but they aren't real. Often, our beliefs come on the authority or the testimony of others. The parents believe the children have ADD because that's the conclusion reached by school psychologists. Such a belief may sometimes be a reliable one, but not when it comes from the South Park testers, who are fools. Further, we must be careful when relying on authority figures. Maybe Scientologists believe that there were once frozen alien bodies put in the volcanoes in Hawaii because their leaders say so. But this is nonsense that should be rejected by any sane person.

We see, then, that rational belief requires evidence. The more outrageous the belief, the more evidence is required. As Stan told the Mormon family in "All About Mormons," "If you're going to say things that have been proven wrong, like the first man and woman lived in Missouri and Native Americans came from Jerusalem, then you better have something to back it up!" Stan's pointing out here that Mormon beliefs should be rejected unless they can be defended, since they're implausible in the face of accepted facts. The Mormons have *the burden of proof*; that is, the obligation is on them to provide the evidence to back up their claims.

Sadly, for most of the crazy claims made in South Park, that obligation is never met. But there are exceptions. In "Pandemic" one of the imprisoned members of a Peruvian flute band makes the seemingly preposterous assertion that their music (annoying though it may be) is the only thing keeping away "the furry death." We later learn that he is correct, as giant guinea pigs wreak havoc in the bands' absence. Sometimes what seems absurd can be defended after all! But extraordinary evidence is required. So if you're going to suggest that an alien wizard is causing sexual addiction in some kids ("Sexual Healing"), or that the first pope was really a rabbit ("Fantastic Easter Special"), you'd better have compelling reasons.

Returning to "All About Mormons," two villagers are talking about Joseph Smith. One of them says, "He claims he spoke with God and Jesus." The other one asks, "Well how do you know he didn't?" Is this a fair question? Should unproven claims be accepted when it appears that they can't be disproved? No. A request to disprove something isn't a request that needs to be answered. This is because the burden of proof always lies with the person making the additional claim, not with those who doubt its truth. If this were not the case, then we would be required to entertain *any* belief, no matter how absurd. I can't disprove the existence of alien souls inhabiting our bodies, but that doesn't mean I should consider this Scientologist claim to be likely. Or to take another example, when Cartman suggests ("Jewpacabra") that the Jewpacabra is real and coming for them, the leaders of Sooper Foods reluctantly cancel the Easter egg hunt since they can't prove that no such creature exists. Kyle has it right here, as he tells Cartman, "There's no reference of it anywhere on the known species webpage," and anyone who says otherwise "is either lying or stupid." We shouldn't fall into the "disproof" trap. If our beliefs can't be supported, then they should be rejected, or at least put aside until further evidence comes about.

Believing things without sufficient evidence hardly seems like a good way to lead a successful life. It's difficult to understand how making decisions without evaluating the available evidence would work in the long run. Imagine picking a college, a career, a place to live, a mechanic, a doctor, or anything, for that matter, without reasoning and examining the facts involved. Imagine going through your life merely guessing whenever a decision is to be made, or going by how you feel at the moment, or basing decisions on what's said by someone who may not be reliable.

Take as an illustration the time when Kyle became very ill and needed a kidney transplant ("Cherokee Hair Tampons"). Instead, his mother took him to the new "Holistic Healer" in town, Miss Information. At her shop, the townspeople lined up to buy all sorts of useless products. Her employees, introduced as Native Americans, must surely know all about healing! Fortunately for Kyle, these "Native Americans" (who turned out to be Cheech and Chong) were honest enough to convince Mrs. Broflovski that Kyle was really sick and should be taken to a real doctor. Stan, who realized from the start that the "healers" were frauds and their methods unscientific, had been urging this all along. He later tricks Cartman into giving up a kidney, so everything works out well for Kyle in the end. Often though, when we start with beliefs that have been uncritically accepted, the outcome isn't so fortunate. When the *South Park* version of the company BP (the one which caused the oil spill in the Gulf) continued drilling without carefully examining the potential risks, it proceeded to create an even worse disaster by ripping a dimensional hole in space allowing the evil Cthulhu to cause great devastation ("Coon 2: Hindsight").

What's at stake is not just having correct beliefs. As we've seen, having incorrect beliefs can have dire consequences, but notice, too, how closely beliefs are tied to action. In "Trapped in The Closet," Stan tells Tom Cruise that he's not as good of an actor as Leonardo DiCaprio, Gene Hackman, or "the guy who played Napoleon Dynamite." This causes poor Tom to become depressed, and he locks himself in the closet. Now, why should a famous actor care what a little boy thinks of his acting skills? Well, he *should* care if he was a Scientologist and believed that that little boy is the reincarnation of Scientology founder L. Ron Hubbard. And Mr. Cruise believes *this*, because the current Scientology leaders told him. So his illogical actions are motivated by a ridiculous belief that's held, not on the basis of any testable evidence (well, they did test Stan's "body thetans" with their "E-Meters"—more unsupported nonsense), but solely on the basis of authority. And the "authority" here is hardly reliable or objective; in fact, later the leading Scientologist admits to Stan that it's all made up and he's doing it for the money.

## Faith, Self-Interest, and Evidence

Many people say their beliefs, especially their religious beliefs, are based on faith. What does this mean? And is this a good idea? First, let's be clear what is meant by *faith* in this context. Sometimes faith means a kind of confidence. In "Scott Tenorman Must Die," Cartman was confident that his friends would betray him, and they did. This allowed his plan for revenge on Scott to work perfectly. Cartman, we might say, had faith that his plan would work.

Now this kind of faith isn't opposed to reason and evidence. Cartman reasoned that he could accurately predict what his friends would do based on their past actions. This is perfectly reasonable. If, on the other hand, Mr. Garrison had faith that his students would all work hard on their homework assignments, his confidence would be misplaced. He has no good reason to think so. So faith in the sense of being confident may be reasonable or not, depending on one's evidence.

Talking about religious faith, however, we usually don't mean confidence based on reason. This kind of faith is in fact *opposed* to reason; quite simply, it is belief without good evidence. After hearing the story of Joseph Smith, a story that Stan points out is unsupported and contrary to known facts, Stan says, "Wait: Mormons actually know this story, and they still believe Joseph Smith was a prophet?" The reply, of course, is "Stan, it's all a matter of faith." So, faith appears to be a kind of fallback position we can take when we can't support our views. But this shouldn't be encouraged, for it would render any belief whatsoever acceptable.

Does a belief have to be supported by evidence in order for it to be a rational belief? Can there be *reasons* that justify believing something besides just evidence? Let's make a distinction between *prudential* reasons and *evidential* reasons. The difference between them is easy to illustrate with an example. Suppose that I tell you that John Edward— the self-proclaimed psychic whom Stan puts in his place—really can communicate with the dead. Since you watch *South Park*, you know that John Edward is the "biggest douche in the universe," so you don't believe my claim for a second and you demand proof. Suppose I tell you that if you do believe it, I'll give you lots of money (I show you the full briefcase); but if you don't believe it, you get nothing. Now you have a reason to believe that John Edward is not a fraud, and it's a *good reason*. But you still don't have a shred of evidence. Your reason, instead, is prudential: it's in your best interest to believe.

Blaise Pascal (1623–1662), a French mathematician and philosopher, attempted to justify religious belief in exactly the same way. His argument has come to be known as "Pascal's Wager."[2] Pascal urges us to think of belief in God as a bet. If you wager on God existing (if you believe in him) and God exists, you win. God rewards believers with eternal joy and happiness. But if you don't believe and God exists, then you lose. God punishes non-believers with eternal suffering and pain. What if God doesn't exist? Well, in that case the non-believer has the truth and the believer doesn't; but whatever positive or negative results emerge are negligible in comparison to what happens if there is a God. The point is, if you have *any chance at all* to achieve eternal peace and avoid eternal damnation, you're a fool not to go for it. Prudential reasons reign: it's in your best interest to believe in God.

Notice a few things about Pascal's Wager. First, he's not trying to prove that God exists. If we could prove that there is a God, then the Wager would be pointless (the same would be true if we could prove that there is no God). Pascal starts by assuming that we don't know either way. Second, Pascal isn't arguing that we should simply go on faith alone. He's instead arguing that religious belief is *reasonable* because it's prudential. There have, however, been many criticisms of the Wager that show that it's not a very good argument for religious belief. Let's look at two of these, as they are nicely illustrated in *South Park*.

First, you might wonder why God would choose to torture someone for all eternity simply because they don't believe in him. Isn't God supposed to be perfectly good? Why would a good being wish pain and suffering for anyone? In the episode "Cartmanland," Kyle wonders the same thing. Cartman inherits a million dollars and buys an amusement park, while Kyle suffers from hemorrhoid pain. Kyle begins to lose his faith as well as his will to live. If there were a God, he reasons, He wouldn't reward someone like Cartman (who's evil) while allowing me (who's good) to suffer. He says: "Cartman is the biggest asshole in the world. How is it that God gives him a million dollars? Why? How can you do this? There are people starving in Alabama, and you give Cartman a million dollars? If someone like Cartman can get his own theme park, then there is no God. There's no God, dude."

Kyle's parents, in an attempt to restore his faith, tell him that God sometimes causes us to suffer, perhaps to test our faith, and they read him the story of Job. (Incidentally, the idea of God testing us makes little sense; if he is all-knowing, he would already know what we would do, rendering any test pointless.) But the story horrifies Kyle: "That's the most horrible story I've ever heard. Why would God do such horrible things to a good person just to prove a point to Satan?" Kyle reasons here that if there really were a God, there would be justice in the world. God wouldn't reward someone like Cartman and neither would he allow people like Job and Kyle to suffer.

We can see how all of this applies to Pascal's Wager. Imagine someone who's a really good person—loving, honest, helpful, kind—yet she doesn't believe in God. She thinks she ought to be moral to make the world a better place, let's say, not because God says so or to get some personal reward. Does it really make sense to think that God (who is supposed to be supremely good, remember) would allow such a person to be tormented for all eternity?

A second—and much worse—problem for Pascal's argument is that he assumes that we *know* the possible outcomes of our wager. Pascal says that God rewards believers and punishes nonbelievers. But this is just an assumption. If we had proof of this, we would already know that the religious view of things is true, and we wouldn't need a prudential argument. Remember, the point of the Wager is to convince us to believe when we have no evidence of God's existence or non-existence. Without evidence, there are lots of possibilities to consider. Perhaps God rewards everyone, or maybe there's no afterlife at all. Maybe God values reason and punishes those who believe blindly without any evidence. There are endless possibilities.

Even if we could show that only religious believers get rewarded (and how would we prove that without making the Wager pointless?), we still have the problem of *which* religious beliefs to have. In "Do the Handicapped Go To Hell?" we're treated to a bunch of religious folks who, to their horror, find themselves in hell. They are told that they have *the wrong religious beliefs*, since only the Mormons go to heaven!

## What's the Harm, Dude?

*Those who can make you believe absurdities can make you commit atrocities.*

— Voltaire

Maybe Pascal's Wager doesn't show us that we *should* believe in God, but still, we might ask, what's the harm? Perhaps we should only have beliefs based on reasons, but what's wrong with prudential reasons? In "All About Mormons," Gary tells Stan, "Maybe us Mormons do believe in crazy stories that make absolutely no sense. And maybe Joseph Smith did make it all up. But I have a great life and a great family, and I have *The Book of Mormon* to thank for that. The truth is, I don't care if Joseph Smith made it all up." And in "The Biggest Douche in the Universe," John Edward tries to defend himself to Stan when he says, "What I do doesn't hurt anybody. I give people closure and help them cope with life." So, echoing Gary, Stan's Mormon friend, we could similarly say we don't care if Edward is a fraud, as long as what he does makes people feel good. Again, what's the harm?

But this is only part of the story. For one, as we've already seen, unsupported beliefs can lead to harmful consequences. In "Timmy 2000," the belief that Timmy has ADD (that he is not mentally disabled) eventually causes a wild spread of unnecessary prescription drugs and, worse, a belief that the music of Phil Collins is actually good. In "Super Best Friends," some of the followers of magician David Blaine blindly follow him and commit suicide, believing they will go to heaven. In both of these cases, the believers feel good about their beliefs; they provide hope or comfort. But they're still extremely dangerous.

A second sort of harm here is mental weakness and laziness. As Clifford said, "Every time we let ourselves believe for unworthy reasons, we weaken our powers of self-control, of doubting, of judicially and fairly weighing evidence." His point is that even if a person's unsupported beliefs cause no immediate harm (as in the examples from *South Park*), it still weakens the mind. Stan's dad even gives himself cancer so he can get medicinal marijuana ("Medicinal Fried Chicken"), and, like him, we get used to accepting ideas uncritically, growing mentally lazy, and this encourages others to do the same. Just like Randy Marsh, most of the citizens of South Park rarely use their critical faculties. This makes them easy prey for every cult, fad, or con that comes to town. Think of just about any episode of *South Park*, and you'll find many examples of this mental weakness and laziness.

## Inquiry, Hard Work, and Progress

To understand a final reason why uncritically accepting unsupported beliefs—however hopeful they might make us feel—is not such a good thing, we turn to Stan at his best. Again, from "The Biggest Douche in the Universe," John Edward challenges Stan: "Everything I tell people is positive and gives them hope; how does that make me a douche?" Stan's reply is brilliant: "Because the big questions in life are tough; why are we here, where are we from, where are we going? But if people believe in asshole douchy liars like you, we're never going to find the real answers to those questions. You aren't just lying, you're slowing down the progress of all mankind, you douche." He follows this up with another terrific speech, this time to the members of Edward's believing audience:

> You see, I learned something today. At first I thought you were all just stupid listening to this douche's advice, but now I understand that you're all here because you're scared. You're scared of death and he offers you some kind of understanding. You all want to believe in it so much, I know you do. You find comfort in the thought that your loved ones are floating around trying to talk to you, but think about it: is that really what you want? To just be floating around after you die having to talk to this asshole? We need to recognize this stuff for what it is: magic tricks. Because whatever is really going on in life and in death is much more amazing than this douche.

We can all learn something today from what Stan has said here. First, he realizes it's wrong to dismiss someone with unsupported beliefs as being stupid. We want answers because we need comfort. Sometimes we rely more on emotion than reason to satisfy ourselves, but that doesn't mean we lack intelligence. We poke fun, we often ridicule, but, even in *South Park*, it's always better when we try to achieve some understanding.

Second, Stan reminds us of Clifford's point that settling for easy answers not only weakens the mind, it prevents us from finding real answers. In science, philosophy, and every rational pursuit where we require answers to questions, the spirit of inquiry—combined with hard work—is what leads to progress. Settling for magical answers that make us feel good only slows us down.

And speaking of magic, Stan reminds us finally that there's real magic, wonder, and beauty in the universe. As he says, whatever is really going on in life and in death is truly amazing. We don't want to miss it, dude.

## Notes

1. See W.K. Clifford, *The Ethics of Belief and Other Essays*, ed. Timothy Madigan. (Amherst, NY: Prometheus Books, 1999). Epistemology is the area of philosophy concerned with justifying beliefs with evidence.

Good introductory epistemology texts include Robert Audi, *Epistemology: A Contemporary Introduction* (London: Routledge, 2003) and Jack Crumley, *Introduction to Epistemology* (Columbus, OH: McGraw-Hill, 1998).

2. See Blaise Pascal, *Pascal's Pensées*, trans. W.F. Trotter (New York: PF Collier, 1910). For interesting discussions of the pros and cons of Pascal's Wager, see Nicholas Rescher, *Pascal's Wager: A Study of Practical Reasoning in Philosophical Theology* (Notre Dame, IN: University of Notre Dame Press, 1985) and Alan Hájek, "Waging War on Pascal's Wager," *Philosophical Review* 112 (2003): 27–56.

# "Imaginationland," Terrorism, and the Difference Between Real and Imaginary

## Christopher C. Kirby

*Ladies and gentlemen, I have dire news. Yesterday, at approximately 18:00 hours, terrorists successfully attacked ... our imagination.*

"Imaginationland" is an Emmy winning, three-part story from *South Park*'s eleventh season that was later reissued as a movie with all of the deleted scenes included. The story begins with the boys waiting in the woods for a leprechaun that Cartman claims to have seen. Kyle, ever the skeptic, has bet ten dollars against sucking Cartman's balls that leprechauns aren't real. When the boys finally trap one, to Kyle's shock and dismay, it cryptically warns of a terrorist attack and disappears. That night at the dinner table Kyle asks his parents where leprechauns come from and why one would visit South Park to warn of a terrorist attack. They chide him for not knowing the difference between real and imaginary and he mutters, "I thought I did." What ensues is pure *South Park* genius as we discover that, in fact, *nobody* seems to know what the difference is.

As the story unfolds, it's obvious no one will be safe. The episode offers send-ups of the US "war on terror," the American legal system, Hollywood directors, the media, Christianity, the military, Kurt Russell, and Al Gore's campaign against climate change (Manbearpig is real ... I'm super cereal!) all the while reminding us that imagination is an essential feature of human life. Though much could be said about the

*The Ultimate South Park and Philosophy: Respect My Philosophah!*, First Edition.
Edited by Robert Arp and Kevin S. Decker.
© 2013 John Wiley & Sons, Inc. Published 2013 by John Wiley & Sons, Inc.

metaphysics (philosophical questions concerned with reality) at the center of "Imaginationland," this chapter looks instead at the connection between imagination and something philosophers like to call *critical thinking*—that is, being able to cut through the crap and see things clearly—something that seems to be in short supply these days, especially when it comes to thinking about terrorist threats.

Cutting through the crap is what the writers of *South Park* specialize in and this is one of the biggest reasons philosophers love the show. One of its most consistent themes is that creative imagination, even in its most outrageous and abrasive forms, is indispensable in combatting stupidity and small-mindedness. In this way, *South Park* captures a basic feature of philosophizing; thinking critically begins with thinking creatively, and that requires imagination. However, becoming a critical thinker doesn't mean just finding fault in everything. After all, there's a difference between being discerning and being a giant douche. Instead, critical thinking involves originality as well as the courage to challenge prevailing attitudes. This isn't easy, though, especially when you're surrounded by a bunch of "stupid assholes" with no imagination that seem to want "to ruin everything," in the words of Cartman in "Imaginationland Episode III."

## Critical Thinking and Theory

But that's how philosophy came into existence, because Socrates (469–399 BCE), the guy credited with starting it all, found just such a situation in ancient Athens. As it turned out, the people of Athens didn't like the way Socrates was questioning everyone and so they trumped up some criminal charges against him in an effort to make him stop. Socrates argued that he *had* to ask those questions because the gods had proclaimed him to be the wisest of all Athenians, and he didn't see how that was possible, since he felt like he didn't really know anything. Then it hit him. That's what made him wiser than everyone else … because at least he *knew* that he *didn't* know. (How's that for irony?) So, he told the Athenians he would continue asking questions until they came to the same realization about themselves. Instead of facing their own uncertainty with creativity and imagination, the Athenians turned away from it and sentenced Socrates to death. One might say that their imaginations were held hostage, not by gun-toting terrorists, but by their own fear of risking the unknown. But why does this happen? Why do only a handful of people, when faced with puzzlement or wonder, set out on the path of questioning and investigation, while most others just want to nuke the hell out of it?

Many philosophers have asked that question (or something like it) and they've come up with a whole laundry-list of answers, including: selfishness, the emotions, the desire to fit in, laziness, the standards and habits of modern living, and plain old-fashioned fear. These last two are particularly interesting when considering the lack of critical thinking that has occurred since, and about, September 11, 2001. Why have Americans acted more like the Athenians and less like Socrates since that event? After that attack, even the most mundane parts of modern living, like flying the airlines, were suddenly filled with potentially life-threatening risk. And, if there's something most philosophers can agree on, it's that we human beings are not very good at assessing risk, often sacrificing long-term values in favor of short-term ones. Ulrich Beck has devoted most of his career to working out how risks (especially global ones like terrorism, climate change, and economic crises) affect the way we think in modern society. Beck works in an area of philosophy called "critical theory," the goal of which is "the emancipation of human beings from the circumstances that enslave them."[1] He argues that with the rise of globalization and the computer age, we now live in a "world risk society," a society whose risks no longer threaten isolated groups or geographical regions, but target the entire planet. If you think we humans aren't very good at *personal* risk assessment, when it comes to assessing risk on that large of a scale, we really suck balls! But the news isn't all bad. Just like the boys in "Imaginationland," we might be able to turn it around with some imagination, critical thinking, and cooperation.

## Unimaginative Leadership?

In "Imaginationland Episode I," Stan, Kyle, Kenny, Butters, and Jimmy are all whisked away by a man looking for the leprechaun and claiming to be the Mayor of Imaginationland. Just as the boys are about to share the leprechaun's message with the citizens of Imaginationland the terrorists attack. Fortunately, the boys are able to quickly make their escape with the help of a Sean Connery-voiced dragon. In the confusion, however, Butters gets left behind. The rest of the boys awake in South Park and assume it's all been a dream until Butters' parents show up looking for their son.

The scene cuts to a debriefing room at the Pentagon where we get our first glimpse of unimaginative leadership:

SPECIALIST:    The imaginary attack appears to have been in the works for years. The effects of the attack are so far … unimaginable.

GENERAL:       We've intercepted this videotape the terrorists made for broadcast. Luckily we've kept it from being broadcast to the public. [*Clicks on a remote control, and the video appears on screen. The Fanciful Mayor is on the ground with a blindfold on. A Care Bear sits to his right with a blindfold on as well. The terrorist starts speaking then backs up to shoot a Care Bear in the head.*]

MAYOR:         No! It's just a Care Bear! [*A terrorist knocks him down with the butt of his gun. A fairy godmother walks up to check on him.*]

SPECIALIST 2:  Oh my God!

GENERAL:       [*Fast forwards the tape …*] Later in the video we can see another imaginary hostage; this one reading a forced statement.

BUTTERS:       [*Reading the statement at gunpoint …*] Praise to the mighty Allah. His divine grace a-and will have brought forth this day. [*A terrorist brings forth a severed bear head to show the viewers.*] Oh jeez! [*The terrorist withdraws.*] Uhhh, now see, your safety is at our whim. This is the price you pay, America! You have defiled Allah, and now we will turn your imagination against you! Death to the infidels! [*There's no more to read.*] Can I go now? [*Two terrorists come up and drag him away. The one wearing a vest takes the statement away from Butters.*] Stan! Kyle! Could you could you get me out of here?! [*The tape is stopped.*]

GENERAL:       Gentlemen, the terrorists appear to have complete control of our imagination. It's only a matter of time before … our imaginations start running wild ("Imaginationland, Episode I").

It seems the US leaders' imaginations are being held hostage … literally! And this mirrors the collective loss the American public felt immediately following the 9/11 attacks. As Beck wrote one year after those events,

Ever since that moment, we've been living and thinking and acting using concepts that are incapable of grasping what happened then … No one has yet offered a satisfying answer to the simple question of what really happened. The implosion of the Twin Towers has been followed by an explosion of silence. If we don't have the right concepts it might seem that silence is appropriate. But it isn't.[2]

One way to break this silence and free our imagination from its captive bonds, is to take a page out of Socrates' playbook. Whenever he spoke to the Athenians about philosophical matters, such as justice or courage, he would start by asking them to define the basic concept under discussion. When they tried to answer, he would remind them that just giving examples wouldn't suffice. Instead, he insisted they search for the common features that *any* just or courageous act would have. It might be helpful to do the same thing when thinking about terrorism.

So, what exactly *is* terrorism? We might be able to think of many instances of terrorism, but it may be more insightful, and more difficult, to identify the elements that must be present in order for *any* act to be called an act of terror. Then, once the basics have been addressed, we might be able to move on to tougher questions, like: "How do terrorist acts differ from guerilla warfare?" "From national liberation movements?" Or even: "What makes a terrorist act immoral?" "Is it possible for war to be waged on an idea ('terror')?" These are important and complex issues that we won't have time to discuss fully here, but we can't even hope to answer them unless we've first thought critically about the basics.

If we consider the origins of the word terrorism, we may start to get an idea about what it means. "Terrorism" is derived from the Latin *terrere*, which means "to frighten," and it was used initially to refer to state or government repression of its citizens. The French "Reign of Terror" of Robespierre is one example of this early usage. In more recent times, the use of the term has broadened. However, in his book, *Inside Terrorism*, Bruce Hoffman has identified several elements common among terrorist acts, as they are thought of today:

(1) *Political aims and motives.* Terrorist acts often seek to call attention to some social or political inequity, whether real or perceived. Those committing acts of terrorism intend to use terror to advance a particular cause.

(2) *Physical violence.* Terrorist acts are almost always aimed at causing or threatening physical harm or death. Often this harm involves more than just the intended target.

(3) *Psychological trauma.* Acts of terror are often designed to have sweeping psychological consequences well beyond the immediate target.

(4) *Organization.* Terrorism is perpetrated by groups with discernible chains of command or conspiratorial cell structures.

(5) *Lack of state affiliation.* Terrorist groups are typically subnational or non-state affiliated entities.[3]

Given this list, it's apparent why there would be confusion in public discussions about what qualifies as a terrorist act. The criteria are actually quite stringent. This doesn't mean that acts that don't meet those criteria are any less terrible. Many heinous acts (like Cartman feeding Scott Tenorman a bowl of chili made from his parents) might not be considered terrorism, but they're still repulsive and morally reprehensible.

## Just Because They're Imaginary Doesn't Mean They're Not Real

Now that we have an idea of how to identify terrorism, let's explore how best to deal with it. As we've seen, one of the biggest problems with the threat of terrorism is that it represents a risk that isn't tied to any particular geographical location or any particular group of people. It has become, especially since the attacks of 9/11, a pervasive problem. Beck calls this the "irony" of risk. The more we try to anticipate what cannot be anticipated … the more we are pulled into a state of anxiety that compels us to anticipate. This is worse than the Socratic irony of knowing that one doesn't know. It's more like not being able to know what it is you don't know! And that's scary! We can't use our past experiences to help us accurately predict where, when, or how the next terrorist attack will occur. In this way, Beck says, risk is sort of "omnipresent" (everywhere all at once). But, its irony goes even deeper, because risk is something that isn't real in the same sense that an attack or a natural catastrophe is real. Risk is more like a state of *becoming real.* Only when the risk is turned into a catastrophe, as when a terrorist group actually strikes, is it made real, but then, it's no longer really a risk.

These extremely frustrating qualities are part of the reason we suck at handling risk. In fact, Beck argues that there are really only three possible responses to risk—denial, apathy, and transformation.

Let's focus on the first response for a moment. The people who fall into that group, the deniers, are those who think they can manage risk or prevent it. Like the military in the Imaginationland episode, and like our own national governments, the deniers create more and more complex security measures in the false hope that they can eradicate risk.

We see several instances of this throughout "Imaginationland." As the first episode ends, Kyle and Stan are taken from Cartman's house (where Cartman is just about to collect Kyle's debt) by the General and his men. It seems the boys have information the government needs and we find out what that is in the next episode:

| | |
|---|---|
| STAN: | Look, we already told you everything we know. Some guy just showed up in a big balloon and took us into Imaginationland ... |
| GENERAL: | Do you realize what's goin' on here?! Terrorists have attacked our imagination, and now our imaginations are running wild! [*Wags his left index finger at them.*] You'd better start remembering! |
| SPECIALIST: | It was the Chinese, wasn't it? |
| KYLE: | ... What? |
| SPECIALIST: | We've suspected that the Chinese government was working on a doorway to the imagination. [*Wags his right index finger at them.*] Is that where you were?! |
| STAN: | No. |
| GENERAL: | That's it, isn't it?! Where do the Chinese keep this portal? How does it work? |
| SPECIALIST: | Is it better than ours? |
| STAN: | Your what? |
| SPECIALIST: | *Our* portal to the imagination built as a secret project back in 1962 to fight the Soviets ... |
| KYLE: | Wait. The US government has a portal to the imagination? |
| GENERAL: | Aw, see? Good job, Tom! Why don't you just tell them everything about Project X?! |
| TOM: | Yes sir. [*To the boys ...*] We built a portal to the imagination to use against the Russians during the Cold War, but we never got a ... |
| GENERAL: | THAT WAS SARCASM! I was being sarcastic, you fucking idiot! |
| TOM: | [*More chagrined ...*] Aw, jeez, I'm really sorry sir ... |

The Pentagon brass is still working with old concepts like the Cold War and state espionage—concepts that, as Beck put it, "are incapable of grasping what has happened."[4] They have no clue how to handle this new kind of threat. By the end of Episode II, after a squadron that was sent through the portal under the command of Kurt Russell (because he was "in that one movie that was kind of like this") is raped by evil Christmas critters, they decide the only solution is to send a nuclear warhead through the portal and "nuke our imagination." *South Park* has demonstrated time and time again that there's no bigger collection of unimaginative assholes than one finds in US politics, and "Imaginationland" does its best to underscore that point.

What happens when we try to eradicate risk by throwing technology and stricter security measures at it? We make the problem of not knowing even worse, because the *very idea* of prevention breaks down when faced with threats that we aren't even sure are real. "Now all possible, more or less improbable scenarios have to be taken into consideration" and "the boundary between rationality and hysteria becomes blurred."[5] When that happens, politicians are forced to promise a security they can't deliver because the political cost of failing to act, or acting too slowly, is much greater than overreacting.

The second way of dealing with risk presents us with the apathetic folks, like Cartman, who ignore what's happening around them and focus on their own individual goals and interests. Of course, this doesn't remove risk, it just covers it over and does so in a way that makes it even riskier because when something finally *does* happen, it's completely unexpected. This can give rise to a radical form of individualism as people are forced to cope with world risk by themselves (Cartman even takes on a Rambo-like role at the end of the first "Imaginationland" episode). Yet in those moments when imagined-risk becomes real-catastrophe, the individual depends on experts, "whose judgment he cannot, yet must trust" to make sense of what has happened.[6] This is one of the most pernicious ironies of world risk society.

However, if we deal with risk through transformation, we can experience what Beck calls the "enlightenment function" of world risk. Through critical reflection, we can open up new possibilities by adjusting ourselves (in part) to the circumstances, and adjusting the circumstances (in part) to ourselves. Let's take a look at what it might take to make a transformative response.

## Only You Can Help Us Win This Battle

The third and final episode of "Imaginationland" opens with an homage to the Helm's Deep scene in *Lord of the Rings: The Two Towers*. The good imaginary characters are preparing to defend Castle Sunshine against the overwhelming hordes of evil characters approaching. Their leader, Aslan of the *Narnia* series, tells Butters that he has a power in Imaginationland that he is yet to fully understand—he is a "creator."

Beck seems to suggest something similar about us when he claims that within world risk society the possibility exists of a "cosmopolitan moment" (a moment in which everyone comes together and divisions vanish). He identifies features of this moment that can get our imaginations once again working *for* us. The first, which Beck calls "involuntary enlightenment," occurs when we're forced to pay attention to aspects of our world that we otherwise typically ignore. For instance, when Hurricane Katrina struck New Orleans in 2005 or when the Indian Ocean tsunami struck parts of Southeast Asia in 2004, we were forced to see how vulnerable those living in poverty can be in the face of catastrophe, and *that* forced us to think about poverty in ways we normally might not. Japan's Fukushima nuclear disaster in 2011 and the Deepwater Horizon oil spill in 2010 led us to question the costs and dangers inherent to the way we produce energy. Likewise, the Arab Spring and Occupy movements have given us new insights about social and political inequities both at home and abroad. A constant stream of media attention surrounds events like these, and, as Beck argues, "We are children lost in a 'forest of symbols' ...we have to rely on the symbolic politics of the media."[7] However, that perpetual media blitz can also act like a mirror, reflecting the limits of our old ways of thinking and opening up new conceptual spaces for us to explore ... if we allow it.

This is the real danger of allowing our imaginations to run wild or be held hostage. We may miss the really big opportunities to learn something about ourselves, to gain a little more wisdom. Of course, this requires that we think a little outside of the box—that we think *creatively*.

This is what Butters learns to do in Imaginationland, just as the evil characters arrive at Castle Sunshine:

ASLAN:     Get everyone to the battlefield! Defend the castle walls! Quickly young boy, we need your powers now!

BUTTERS:   What powers? Ah I don't understand.

GANDALF:   You are real. You are a creator. That means you can imagine things into existence here.
BUTTERS:   I c-, I can?
ASLAN:     Santa Claus was killed in the terrorist attack. The first thing we need is for you to bring him back.
BUTTERS:   How?
GLINDA:    You just have to focus your mind. Imagine Santa and nothing else.

His first few attempts fail miserably, but after some practice, Butters starts to get the hang of it and the tide of battle begins to shift. Meanwhile, Kyle has regained consciousness in a hospital bed (after Operation Imagination Doorway has failed) only to discover that he can now hear Stan (who was sucked through the portal during the malfunction) in his imagination. Stan convinces Kyle to go back to the Pentagon and try to stop the government from nuking Imaginationland.

World risk society also provides a chance for communication across differences and borders. When we feel the *same* looming threat of risk as those we traditionally viewed as enemies, we may be more inclined to cooperate with them. This can lead to a political catharsis (a purging of harmful emotions) in which old rivalries and old battle lines are broken down. As an example, Beck quotes a Turkish reporter commenting on the unprecedented diplomacy that took place between Turkey and Greece after the earthquakes of 1999: "Who would have thought before that tears would be our common language?"[8] Likewise, who would have thought that Cartman and Kyle would ever work together, yet that's precisely what happens when they join together in trying to talk the Pentagon out of sending the warhead through the portal (although Cartman's motivation is ball-related).

The pervasive presence of world risk means that it transcends political or economic borders and forces a type of wider, cosmopolitan attitude on us in which we begin to see ourselves as citizens of the world. This might help to counteract the tendency we have to value security over liberty whenever we are faced with danger because "world risk society brings a new, historic key logic to the fore: no nation can cope with its problems alone."[9] Instead of turning inward, we should reach outward. Only critical thinking and cooperation on an international scale can counteract the uncertainty that has arisen in world risk society.

That's how the boys try to save Imaginationland, too, in Episode III. For his part, Kyle begins to see the importance of imagination and creativity and delivers a pretty philosophical speech to the Pentagon staff:

| | |
|---|---|
| KYLE: | You have to stop! |
| GENERAL: | If I'm not mistaken, you're the one who bet that leprechauns weren't real. So why do *you* care what happens? |
| KYLE: | Because I ... [*catches himself*] I ... Um ... because I think ... they *are* real. It's all real. Think about it. Haven't Luke Skywalker and Santa Claus affected your lives more than most *real* people in this room? I mean, whether Jesus is real or not, he ... he's had a bigger impact on the world than any of us have. And the same could be said of Bugs Bunny and, a-and Superman and Harry Potter. They've changed my life, changed the way I act on the Earth. Doesn't that make them kind of "real"? They might be imaginary, but, but they're more important than most of us here. And they're all gonna be around long after we're dead. So in a way, those things are more realer than any of us. [*Cartman begins a slow clap, then speeds it up. The techs in the room join in and soon everyone is applauding Kyle's speech.*] |

Of course, no sooner has the day been saved than Al Gore barges in demanding that Manbearpig be destroyed. Before anyone can stop him, he damages the portal controls, which causes it to malfunction again, pulling the warhead and everyone in the room towards it. As they fall into Imaginationland, we learn that Butters has already used his creativity to defeat the evil characters.

| | |
|---|---|
| ZEUS: | What is that? [*The missile comes down from the sky and blows up on the battlefield, killing everyone. The screen fills up with white ash. Moments later, Butters digs himself out of the ash and dusts himself off. He looks around and walks off to his left.*] |
| BUTTERS: | Huh ... [*With nothing but white around, he concentrates real hard and soon Imaginationland returns. The Barrier repairs itself, and all the imaginary characters reappear.*] |
| JESUS: | He did it! |
| FANCIFUL MAYOR: | [*Poof*] Oh look, I'm back! |
| LUKE SKYWALKER: | Nice going, kid. [*The other good imaginary characters congratulate him.*] |

| FANCIFUL MAYOR: | The evil characters! They're all behind the wall again. |
| STAN: | Dude! How did you do that, Butters? |
| BUTTERS: | Well, I just ... used my imagination. |
| ALL: | Awwww! [*Everyone has a good laugh.*] |

Of course, one philosophical question remains. If Butters imagined everyone back after the blast, are *any* of them real?

## Notes

1. Ulrich Beck, *World Risk Society* (Cambridge: Polity Press, 1998); "The Terrorist Threat: World Risk Society Revisited," *Theory, Culture, & Society* 19:4 (2002): 39–55; see also, Max Horkheimer, "Traditional and Critical Theory," in *Critical Sociology: Selected Readings*, ed. Paul Connerton. (New York: Penguin, 1976), 224.
2. Beck, "The Terrorist Threat: World Risk Society Revisited," 39.
3. Bruce Hoffman, *Inside Terrorism* (New York: Columbia University Press, 1998).
4. Beck, "Living in the World Risk Society," *Economy and Society* 35:3 (2009): 335.
5. Ibid., 335.
6. Ibid., 336.
7. Beck, *World Risk Society*, 44.
8. Beck, "Living in the World Risk Society," 340.
9. Ibid., 342.

# Dude, Listen to Reason!
## Logic Lessons Inside and Outside South Park

*Robert Arp*

The Goth kids on *South Park* crack me up because they remind me of the Gothers at the high school where I taught in the early 1990s, sitting around looking like the bastard children of Robert Smith and Tori Amos. In fact, my first reaction to seeing a group of kids dressed like that at a mall is automatically to think, "They're *all* saturnine, shady, surly, and, of course, suspect." Alliteration aside, that conclusion is unfair, isn't it? It's an example of the *fallacy of hasty generalization*. A *fallacy* is an inappropriate or incorrectly drawn conclusion from reasons that don't support the conclusion, and *hasty generalization* is a common fallacy often lampooned on *South Park*. In a hasty generalization, a person concludes something about members of a whole group based upon their observations of characteristics of a small number from the group. Most times, when we think to ourselves "they're all like that" in talking about anything—cars, movies, Goths—based on a small sample of the group we're talking about, we're guilty of hasty generalization. There's usually no way to *definitely* conclude something about the characteristics of an *entire* group since we have no knowledge of the entire group. The next member of the group we run into may turn out to be totally different from the others we've encountered thus far. In fact, many of those little Goths at the high school where I taught were not at all saturnine, shady, or surly once you chatted with them, and I was reasoning fallaciously by immediately jumping to that conclusion.

*The Ultimate South Park and Philosophy: Respect My Philosophah!*, First Edition.
Edited by Robert Arp and Kevin S. Decker.
© 2013 John Wiley & Sons, Inc. Published 2013 by John Wiley & Sons, Inc.

Any form of *stereotyping* constitutes a hasty generalization, almost by definition. Consider the way Kyle's Jewish cousin, Kyle 2, is stereotyped in "The Entity," or how Mexicans are type-cast as lazy, how gays are *all* flamboyant like Big Gay Al or Mr. Slave, and African-Americans are reverse type-cast as "richers" in "Here Comes the Neighborhood." Even Officer Barbrady commits the fallacy of hasty generalization in "Chickenlover" when, after reading a copy of Ayn Rand's *Atlas Shrugged*, he concludes that all books must be this bad, and reading "totally sucks ass." The creators of *South Park* play on people's hasty generalizations to make their points episode after episode, not only because prejudice is something that *morally* harms people, but also because it *logically* "harms" people's thinking as well.

This chapter offers a short logic lesson as an introduction to what philosophers and other critical thinkers do when they offer and criticize arguments. Logic is the study of the principles of correct reasoning associated with the formation and analysis of arguments.[1] The creators of *South Park*, for the most part, know these logical principles. They purposely violate them, though, to show the absurdities contained in certain beliefs, opinions, ideas, and arguments. In fact, much of *South Park*'s humor concerns logical violations and the absurdities, contradictions, and problems that result. The way people reason—correctly or incorrectly—has real consequences. It affects the principles they adhere to, the laws they make, the beliefs they're willing to die for, and the general way in which they live their lives.

For example, in the episode "Death," the entire community boycotts the *Terrance and Philip Show* (and sacrifices members of the community to get it taken off the air) because Mrs. Broflovski kicks off a campaign to show that it promotes immorality. Of course, this parallels reality all too often, and raises questions as to whether TV promotes immorality, as well as what people are willing to do about their perception that it does. Can we draw the general conclusion that a show like *South Park*, even if viewed by children, is bad for *all* children, from evidence that it's bad for *some* children?

Consider a parallel case. Are all Americans immoral? And if they are, should they be punished by flying planes into skyscrapers? How we live our lives, as well as how we affect others' lives, depends upon whether we reason correctly or incorrectly (you may even find what I have said to be logically questionable). In what follows, we'll consider some basics of logic using examples from *South Park* episodes, and show some differences between correct and incorrect reasoning.

## If You Do Drugs, Then You're a Hippie

*Logic* is the study of the principles behind reasoning correctly using arguments. An *argument* consists of two or more claims, one of which is called the *conclusion*. The conclusion is supposed to be supported by or demonstrated by one or more premises. A *premise* is a claim in the argument that is supposed to support or demonstrate the conclusion. The fundamental purpose of an argument is to persuade or convince someone of the truth of a conclusion. In other words, when we offer an argument, we want others to be persuaded or convinced of the conclusion we arrived at and believe to be true, and we use other claims as support for the truth of that conclusion.

My fallacious argument about Goths can be rephrased like this: "Because every Gother I've ever met and known has been saturnine, shady, surly, and, of course, suspect [the premise], therefore all Gothers I'll meet in future will be saturnine, shady, surly, and, of course, suspect [the conclusion]." A complete argument has at least one premise and only one conclusion, but arguments usually have two or more premises. So, for example, in the episode "Ike's Wee Wee," Cartman put together an argument for why we should be convinced drugs are bad that sounded like this: "If you do drugs, then you're a hippie; if you're a hippie, then you suck; if you suck, then that's bad [premises]; So, if you do drugs, then that's bad [conclusion]."

Both the conclusion and the premises in an argument are claims. A *claim* is a statement or judgment that puts into words a person's beliefs or opinions. Meaningful claims tell us that something is or is not the case about reality. Claims can be either true or false (not both). For example, the claims "I am typing this chapter on a laptop" and "Chewbacca is a Wookiee" are true, whereas the claims "Rob Arp was the 40th President of the United States" and "The sun revolves around the earth" are false. A claim is found true or false through *evidence*, which includes sense experience, explanations and theories, the testimony of other people, and appeal to appropriate authority. "I am typing this chapter a laptop" is true because of the evidence of my own senses; "Chewbacca is a Wookiee" is true by the definition of

"Chewbacca"; "Rob Arp was the 40th President of the United States" is false because of the testimony of the senses of others and authorities; and "The sun revolves around the earth" is false because of indirect sensory evidence and the well-established heliocentric theory that shows the planets orbit the sun. It's difficult or even impossible to show that some claims are true or false with evidence. Claims like "God exists," "Abortion is always immoral," and "I have an immortal soul" fall into this ambiguous category. That is probably why ideas, issues, and arguments surrounding these claims are considered to be *philosophical*.

As rational critical thinkers, we have beliefs we think are true about reality, and we express those beliefs or opinions in written or spoken claims. But we can't stop there. We often have to convince others why we hold these beliefs, and when we do this, we must give a reason or set of reasons (the premises of our argument) for why we hold to a particular belief (the conclusion). So, for example, in "The Passion of the Jew," Kyle believes strongly that the Jewish community in his hometown should apologize for Jesus's death. If asked why the Jewish community in his hometown, or anyone, should be convinced or persuaded to apologize, Kyle might offer the following:

| | |
|---|---|
| *Premise 1:* | Jews are known to have been partly responsible for the death of Jesus |
| *Premise 2:* | And, since an action like this requires that one should apologize |
| *Premise 3:* | And, since the Jews in South Park are part of the Jewish community |
| *Conclusion:* | Therefore, the Jewish community in South Park should apologize for Jesus's death. |

Let's note a few things about this argument: first, it's written in *standard form*. Putting an argument in standard form means placing the premises of the argument first, the conclusion last, and clearly dividing the premises and conclusion like I've done above. This is a handy tool because it keeps the logical form and the parts of the argument clear. As we'll see later, standard form makes the argument easier to analyze when we're trying to see if the conclusion follows from the premises, as well as seeing whether all the premises are true.

Notice the word *since* at the beginning of the premises and the word *therefore* at the beginning of the conclusion. The word *since* is an example of a premise indicator word, like *because, for, for the reason that*, and *as*, among others. The word *therefore* is an example of a conclusion indicator word, along with words like *hence, so, thus, this shows us that, we can conclude that*, and *we can reason/deduce/infer that*, among others. Premise-indicating and conclusion-indicating words are important because they help us find the premises and conclusion in an argument. At times, it can be difficult to tell if someone is putting forward an argument or not. It's therefore helpful to look for these indicator words to see if there's an argument in front of you and, if so, then you can identify what the conclusion and the premises of the argument are. Unfortunately, indicating words aren't always present, and people sometimes place the conclusion in different places in their argument (sometimes it will be the first claim, sometimes the second, sometimes the last). In such cases you'll have to infer and supply these words to make the structure and parts of the argument apparent.

## Deductions and Inductions

There are two main kinds of argument, *deductive* arguments and *inductive* arguments. In deductive arguments, the arguer intends her conclusion to follow from the premises with *absolute certainty*. This means that if all her premises are true, then the conclusion must be true without a doubt. To say that a conclusion *follows* from a premise means that we've reasoned appropriately from one claim (the premise) to another claim (the conclusion). Cartman puts forward a deductive argument in "The Tooth Fairy Tats 2000" episode that goes something like this:

| | |
|---|---|
| *Premise 1*: | If the boys combine their lost teeth, then they'll get money from the Tooth Fairy |
| *Premise 2*: | If they get money from the Tooth Fairy, then they can buy a Sega Dreamcast |
| *Conclusion*: | Hence, if the boys combine their lost teeth, then they can buy a Sega Dreamcast. |

If the two premises are true, the conclusion must absolutely be true. We can also see that there's no other conclusion that could correctly follow from these premises. In fact, from looking at the premises alone you know the conclusion before even seeing it. The previous argument about Jews apologizing for Jesus's death is also a deductive argument. Just like with the Tooth Fairy argument, if all the premises are true then the conclusion must be true; there's no other conclusion that possibly could be drawn from the premises, and you know exactly what the conclusion is without even seeing it.

In inductive arguments, the arguer intends his conclusion to follow from the premises with a *degree of probability*. Here, if all of the premises are true, then the conclusion probably or likely is true, but it could be false. In the "Towelie" episode, the boys notice that when they speak about anything having to do with towels, Towelie shows up, and so they reason like this:

| | |
|---|---|
| *Premise 1*: | In the past, when we mentioned towel-related things, Towelie showed up |
| *Premise 2*: | And, because we will mention something towel-related now |
| *Conclusion*: | We can conclude that Towelie will show up. |

Provided these premises are true, the conclusion is probably or likely true, but not definitely so. It's what we call an "educated guess" that Towelie will show up, given past experience. But because Towelie has regularly appeared in the past doesn't *guarantee* that he *will* show up now.

Consider Stan's reasoning at the end of the episode "Scott Tenorman Must Die" after it's revealed that Cartman orchestrated the death of Scott's parents and added their bodies to the chili, while the band Radiohead witnessed the entire thing so they could make fun of Scott for being a wussy:

| | |
|---|---|
| *Premise 1*: | Since Cartman does horrible things to people for even minor offenses (like being cheated out of $16.12) |
| *Premise 2*: | And since we (the boys) commit offenses against Cartman, and he may retaliate like he did with Scott |
| *Conclusion*: | Therefore, we'd better not piss Cartman off in the future, for fear of retaliation. |

Again, even if both of the premises are true, it doesn't follow with absolute certainty that the boys had better not anger Cartman in the future; they may be willing to take the risk. As it turns out, the boys piss off Cartman many times without the kind of retaliation inflicted on poor Scott Tenorman. So, the conclusion is at worst false, and at best, not well supported.

## The Good, the Bad, and ... Well, That's It Really

But our goal isn't just to slap together arguments. We need to form *good arguments*, and we need to evaluate the arguments of others. There are good arguments and there are bad arguments in both the deductive and inductive realms. A good argument, in either realm, is one in which the conclusion logically follows from the premises and the premises of which are all true. If either one of these conditions is absent, then the argument "sucks" and should be rejected.

When the conclusion of a deductive argument follows from premises, we call this argument *valid* (it's *invalid* if the conclusion doesn't follow with certainty). When an argument is *valid* and *all* the premises are true, such a good argument is said to be *sound*. The conclusion absolutely, positively, without a doubt, is true, and this is a good thing! In the case of an inductive argument, if its conclusion is *very likely* to follow from its premises, this means that the argument is *strong* (or *weak* if the conclusion very likely doesn't follow). When an inductive argument is *strong* and *all* the premises are true, such a good argument is said to be *cogent*. The conclusion most likely or probably is true, and this is a good thing too!

So, as rational critical thinkers, we always have to go through this two-step procedure of checking our own arguments and the arguments of others to see if (1) the conclusion follows from the premises (is the argument deductively valid or inductively strong?) and (2) all of the premises are true. If the argument fails the (1) or (2) test (or both), then we should reject it. This also means we're rejecting the argument's conclusion as either absolutely false or probably false. For example, Cartman's argument for pooling together the boys' teeth probably is a bad one because Premise 2 ("If they get money from the Tooth Fairy, then they can buy a Sega Dreamcast") seems false. Even if they get money from the Tooth Fairy, they won't be able to buy a

Sega Dreamcast, because the Tooth Fairy only gave Cartman two dollars. Two dollars times four boys is only eight dollars and, even if we're talking about a used Dreamcast, that's not enough. So, in the case of this particular deductive argument, the conclusion "If the boys combine their teeth, then they can get a Sega Dreamcast" is false. On the other hand, the Towelie argument was a good one. It was true that the few times they mentioned towel-related things, Towelie showed up. Given this, they had a strong case for the conclusion that he'd show up again, asking, of course, "Wanna get high?"

## "If Chewbacca Lives on Endor, You Must Acquit"

At times, checking to see if conclusions follow from premises and if premises are true can be difficult. Some words are ambiguous, having multiple meanings. And some people try to get us to believe the truth of claims in order to deceive us, sell us something, get us to vote for them, or share their ideology. People will even try to convince us a conclusion follows from a premise or premises when it really doesn't. Just think about what the cartoon Johnny Cochran does with the Chewbacca Defense (a satire of the real-life Cochran's closing arguments in the O.J. Simpson case) in the episode "Chef Aid."

In the episode, Alanis Morissette comes out with a hit song "Stinky Britches" that Chef had written some 20 years ago. Chef produces a tape of him performing the song and takes the record company to court, asking only that he be credited for writing the hit. The record company executives then hire Cochran. In his defense of the record company, Cochran shows the jury a picture of Chewbacca and claims that, because Chewbacca is from Kashyyyk and lives on Endor with the Ewoks, "It does not make sense." Cochran continues: "Why would a Wookiee, an eight-foot tall Wookiee, want to live on Endor with a bunch of two-foot tall Ewoks? That does not make sense ... If Chewbacca lives on Endor, you must acquit! The defense rests." The jury is so convinced by Cochran's "argument," that they deny Chef's request to give him credit, but they also find Chef guilty of harassing a major record label, fining him two million dollars to be paid within 24 hours. Friends of Chef then organize "Chef Aid" to pay his fine.

We laugh at Cochran's defense because it has absolutely nothing to do with the actual case. It's even more absurd when the Chewbacca

Defense is also used to "prove" Chef is guilty of harassing the very record company that had produced his stolen song. The issue of Chewbacca living on Endor is completely irrelevant to whether Chef should receive credit for the song, or whether he's actually harassed the record company. As rational thinkers, we recognize this, laugh at the absurdities, and wonder why anyone in their right mind would connect the Chewbacca Defense with these other issues.

As we saw earlier in this chapter, logicians have a special term (a *fallacy*) for these bad arguments in which the conclusion doesn't follow from premises. Fallacies are so common that logicians have names for different types of fallacies. The Chewbacca Defense, for example, is an instance of the *red herring* fallacy, which gets its name from a police dog exercise in which policemen used strong-smelling red herring fish in an attempt to throw dogs off the trail of a scent. In a red herring fallacy, claims and arguments that have nothing to do with the issue at hand are offered in order to point to the truth of a conclusion that the arguer wants us to accept. In the episode "Weight Gain 4000," Wendy has a legitimate complaint against Cartman for cheating to win the essay contest, but people refuse to accept her conclusion because they're distracted by the excitement of Kathy Lee Gifford coming to town. Even after Wendy shows the damning evidence that Cartman had just handed in a copy of Thoreau's *Walden* as his essay, they simply don't care about whether Cartman cheated or not. This happens in a lot of *South Park* episodes; it's a humorous way for Trey and Matt to make their points about people's faulty and crazy reasoning.

## Slippery Slopes

The *slippery slope* is another fallacy often lampooned on *South Park*. A person commits this fallacy when she claims that some initial occurrence or belief will inevitably lead to a further chain of events that we want to avoid, and so we should avoid the initial occurrence or reject the belief. It's as if there's an unavoidable "slippery" slope with no way to avoid sliding down it. Mrs. Broflovski's reasoning about the banning the *Terrance and Phillip Show*, mentioned earlier, might go something like this: "If we allow something like the *Terrance and Phillip Show* on the air, then it will corrupt all of our kids, then shows like this one will crop up all over the TV, then more and more kids will be corrupted, then all of TV will be corrupted, then the corrupt TV producers will corrupt other areas of our life, etc., etc. So, we must take the *Terrance and Phillip Show* off the air; otherwise, it will lead to all this bad stuff!" We can clearly see the slippery slope. It isn't necessarily true that the corrupt TV producers will corrupt other areas of our life, but all of a sudden we're at the bottom of the slope! What just happened?

In "Clubhouses," Mrs. Marsh uses a kind of slippery slope fallacy combined with a hasty generalization to respond to Stan grabbing a cookie. The humor comes from the fact that she's going through a rough separation with her husband: "You men are all alike. First you get a cookie and then you criticize the way I dress, and then it's the way I cook! Next you'll be telling me that you need your space, and that I'm sabotaging your creativity! Go ahead Stanley, get your damn cookie!" Her conclusion is that Stan shouldn't grab a cookie because, otherwise, all of these other things will happen. The hasty generalization comes from the "you men are all alike" comment.

A *false dilemma* fallacy draws a conclusion from only *two* options, when there are three or more actual options. People are inclined to an "all or nothing" approach to winning their arguments, and this tempts them think in terms of false dilemmas. In some situation, couldn't it be that we have a little bit of both, so that we get a "both/and," not an "either/or," as our conclusion? In "Mr. Hankey, The Christmas Poo," the people of *South Park* give into all-or-nothing kind of thinking when they conclude that the only way not to offend anyone is to rid the school's Holiday Show of any and all religious references. This kind of logic has disastrous consequences: the show is ruined and people wind up fighting over it. Could they have *included* a few other religious traditions, instead of *excluding* all of them? But the "both/and" strategy, which can often avoid a false dilemma, might not always have the best consequences. Consider "Chef Goes Nanners": even though a "both/and" solution is reached and some "ethnic diversity" is added to the South Park flag, it's doubtful whether this is good, let alone right, for the townsfolk.

A fallacious *argument from inappropriate authority* sounds like what it is: it's incorrectly drawing a conclusion from premises that come from an untrustworthy, non-qualified, or illegitimate source posing as an authority. The best way to avoid this fallacy altogether is to *become* an authority, at least to some extent, by getting all the relevant facts, understanding issues, doing research, checking and double-checking your sources, dialoguing with people, having your ideas challenged, defending your position, and being open to revising your position. But we can't become authorities on everything, so we need to rely on others. In "Do the Handicapped Go to Hell?" Father Maxi claims that Kyle (who's Jewish) and Timmy (who can only communicate his own name: "Timm-aah!") will both go to hell if they don't confess their sins and accept Christ as their savior. At first glance, the conclusion that Kyle and Timmy will go to hell doesn't *seem* to be a fallacy of appeal to inappropriate authority. After all, Father Maxi is an authority of the Church. However, after investigating Church doctrine, you'll see that no human being—pope, priest, or layperson—can make pronouncements about who'll burn and who won't.

An *ad hominem* fallacy occurs when we dismiss a person's arguments because of their actions, background, personality, or ideology. In other words, instead of focusing on the person's argument, the person herself is attacked (*ad hominem* is Latin for *to the man*). This strategy of discrediting a person's argument by discrediting the person is common. But a person and their argument are two distinct things. For example, in "Butt Out," a cartoon Rob Reiner argues that kids in South Park shouldn't smoke, and he campaigns for a law to ban smoking in the town. Not only is Reiner portrayed as having his own junk food vice, but he deceptively uses the boys to get the law passed. Now, even if Reiner does have a junk food problem, and even if he does something immoral in trying to get the boys to help him, what does this have to do with the truth of the argument about whether kids should smoke, or whether laws against smoking should be passed in South Park? The answer is, absolutely nothing! Yet, we might be duped into opposing such a law against smoking if Reiner's apparent hypocrisy and deviance were pointed out. But that would be misguided since cartoon Reiner's hypocrisy and deviance have nothing to do with the arguments for or against smoking.

## The Defense Rests

Part of the appeal of *South Park* is how it points out the flaws in our thinking. We all sometimes forget to check if our premises are true, or we believe that a conclusion follows from premises when it doesn't.

But the biggest logical problem we all have stems from our staunchly held emotional beliefs, the ones that we just can't let go of no matter what evidence and arguments are presented to us. Some people are almost *phobic* in their fear of letting go of some key belief.

In "All About the Mormons," Stan yells at the Mormons for believing in their religion without any proof, and they smile and explain that it is a matter of faith. Without insulting the Mormons, or any religion for that matter, in that moment Stan was hinting at exactly what every rational critical thinker should do. As you read the chapters in this book, be mindful of claims, arguments, deductive arguments and inductive arguments, good and bad arguments, and fallacies pointed out by the authors. Hopefully, the authors have avoided fallacies and bad arguments in putting forward their own positions! But with this logic lesson in mind, you can be the judge of that for yourself.

# Note

1. For more extensive discussions of logic, see Gregory Bassham, William Irwin, Henry Nardone, and James M. Wallace, *Critical Thinking: A Student's Introduction* (New York: McGraw-Hill, 2004); Jamie Carlin Watson and Robert Arp, *Critical Thinking: An Introduction to Reasoning Well* (London: Continuum, 2011); Patrick Hurley, *A Concise Introduction to Logic* (Belmont, CA: Wadsworth Publishing, 2006); Anthony Weston, *A Rulebook for Arguments* (Indianapolis, IN: Hackett Publishing, 2000).

# Part II

# SOUTH PARK AND ... RELIGION

# Science, Religion, South Park, and God

### David Kyle Johnson

*Perhaps the great Dawkins wasn't so wise. He was intelligent, but some of the most intelligent otters I've ever known were completely lacking in common sense.*

—The Wise One

*Science is simply common sense at its best; that is, rigidly accurate in observation, and merciless to fallacy in logic.*

—Thomas Henry Huxley

In the two-part episode "Go God Go" and "Go God Go XII," Cartman accidentally travels to the year 2546 after trying to freeze himself so he doesn't have to wait three more weeks for the release of the Nintendo Wii. In the future, belief in traditional religions has been eradicated by a belief in science, and atheism seems to be its own brand of religion. "Science" has replaced "God" in many common phrases ("Oh my Science!") and opposing atheistic factions wage war over the great question of what atheists should call themselves (personally, I favor Allied Atheist Allegiance—that way it has three As).

A world in which atheism has replaced religion is the dream of Oxford evolutionary biologist and "New Atheist" activist, Richard Dawkins. He thinks that religious belief is irrational superstition that leads to violence (like the inquisition), intolerance (like homophobia), ignorance (like creationism), and corruption (like red hot Catholic love). In fact, in "Go God Go," it is the cartoon version of Dawkins

*The Ultimate South Park and Philosophy: Respect My Philosophah!*, First Edition.
Edited by Robert Arp and Kevin S. Decker.
© 2013 John Wiley & Sons, Inc. Published 2013 by John Wiley & Sons, Inc.

himself who pioneered the efforts culminating in religion's demise. Encouraged by his lover Mr(s). Garrison, who converts to atheism after s/he realizes that God is a Spaghetti Monster, Dawkins campaigns against religion, which is eventually eradicated.

The "Go God Go" saga raises some very important questions. In the episode, the scientific worldview stamps out religion. But are science and religion really in such irreconcilable conflict? Would the supremacy of a scientific worldview really lead to atheism? In the future of 2546, Dawkins' atheism becomes its own religion. But is the New Atheism really just a new religion? And would the elimination of religion and the triumph of science really diminish the amount of violence in the world, or will people always just find something else to wage war over?

## Hail Science! Hail Science!

First, we have to understand what science is. Contrary to how the race of otters in 2546 treat it, science is not a set of doctrines. Science is a method for discovering the truth about the world. Scientists today accept many things as true—Einstein's theory of relativity, for example. But relativity is not a *doctrine* of science. Scientists today accept it because our best evidence suggests that it is true, but if another competing theory were shown to be worthier via the scientific method, they would change their minds. This, in fact, has happened numerous times. Thomas Kuhn (1922–1996) called such events "paradigm shifts."

So what *is* the scientific method? It's a system of routines for discovering the most adequate theory—the theory that is most fruitful, simple, and conservative, and that has the widest scope. A theory is *fruitful* when it makes successful predictions; is *simpler* when it makes fewer assumptions; is *conservative* when it doesn't contradict itself or common knowledge; and has *wide scope* when it can explain a number of different things. Relativity, for example, beat out Newton's seventeenth-century physical laws by successfully predicting that light bends around massive objects (like our sun), by explaining Mercury's irregular orbit, and by not referencing gravity as a fundamental force.[1] To use the scientific method, scientists propose numerous alternate theories, compare them according these four "criteria of adequacy," and then accept the best one.

This kind of reasoning is called abduction or "inference to the best explanation." In "Mystery of the Urinal Deuce," Stan and Kyle use abduction to discover that the government wasn't responsible for 9/11. Which theory is simpler, raises fewer questions, explains more, and coheres with what we already know? That a few pissed off Muslims flew planes into buildings? Or that an "all-knowing and all-powerful" Bush administration executed "the world's most intricate and flawlessly executed plan ever, ever" by having "explosives planted in the base of the towers, then on 9/11 [they] pretended like four planes were being hijacked when really [they] just re-routed them to Pennsylvania and then flew two military jets into the World Trade Center filled with more explosives and shot down all the witnesses in flight 93 with an F-15 after blowing up the pentagon with a cruise missile." Obviously, it was "a bunch of pissed off Muslims. What are you, retarded?"[2] A theory's adequacy, we might say, is a "raging clue."

Science also tries to avoid logically fallacious reasoning. Mr(s). Garrison suggests to Dawkins that s/he believes in God because "you can't disprove God." As a good scientist, Dawkins points out the fallacy in Garrison's reasoning: "Well, what if I told you there was a Flying Spaghetti Monster? Would you believe it simply because it can't be disproven?" Dawkins is invoking a common, rather silly example that actually makes a serious point.[3] You're committing a logical fallacy if you think the fact that something hasn't been proven false is good reason to believe it's true. That particular fallacy is called an "appeal to ignorance." Of course, very little can be proven with complete certainty. In fact, nothing in science is certain—not even that the world is round. It's possible that future discoveries will overturn the current consensus. And as Pierre Duhem (1861–1916) and W.V. Quine (1909–2000) taught us, you can always save a hypothesis by changing your background theory.[4] But that's not good enough reason to believe that the world is flat or that there is a Flying Spaghetti Monster. Rational people proportion their belief to the evidence; they don't believe whatever the hell they want just because it can't be authoritatively proven or disproven.

This point seems to be lost on Matt and Trey, however, as they mock Dawkins' point vicariously through Mr(s). Garrison's response. "You're right. It's so simple. God is a Spaghetti Monster ... I totally get it now. Evolution explains everything. There's no great mystery to life—just evolution and God's a Spaghetti Monster. Thank you

Richard." Like Mr(s). Garrison, they're offering an appeal to ignorance.[5] Through sarcasm they may be suggesting that because science can't explain everything, there's still reason to believe in God. I like to call this the "mystery therefore magic" fallacy. The fact that something remains a mystery isn't reason to believe that the supernatural—in this case, God—explains it. Believing in "mystery therefore magic" would lead me to conclude that Penn & Teller really have supernatural magical powers since I can't figure out most of their tricks.

A good scientist also knows personal experience alone can't establish the truth of a theory. Much more than we realize, our senses are easily fooled. As a result, really good evidence has to come from carefully controlled experiments. In "Bloody Mary," Stan's dad Randy stopped being an alcoholic after the statue of the Virgin Mary sprayed ass blood all over his face, but that isn't evidence that the blood cured his alcoholism. Instead, what was at work was probably the placebo effect—when someone's belief that a treatment works makes it seem to them that it actually worked.

When we think of science, we usually think of biology, chemistry, and physics. But scientifically minded people don't stop there. They apply the scientific method to everything it can be applied to. We might say that the only doctrine of science is that you should always, when possible, proportion your belief to the evidence—you should always accept the most adequate theory. Not doing so is unscientific and irrational.

## Being Too Soft?

Many philosophers argue that science and religion are perfectly compatible. Stephen Jay Gould (1941–2002), for example, argued they can't conflict because they are about two totally different things. Religion is about ethics and meaning, but science is about explaining the way the world works.[6] The problem is, religion doesn't just restrict itself to ethics and meaning.[7] Religion also makes statements about the way the world is: souls exist; God exists and controls the world; Jesus healed the sick, walked on water, and rose from the dead; Muhammad rode to Mecca on a super fast horse named Buraq and then ascended into heaven to talk Allah down from requiring prayer 200 times a day (they settled on five).[8] Since these are factual claims, and science is a method for discovering factual truths about the world, these claims are open to scientific scrutiny. As you might have guessed, they do not fare well.

Take, for example, the claims about Jesus. Sure, it's possible that he was a god/man who healed the sick, walked on water, and rose from the dead. But it's also possible that he was merely a charismatic human about whom stories were adapted and exaggerated. Which is the better theory? The latter is certainly more conservative; everything we know suggests that the dead stay dead, that humans can't walk on water, and that you can't heal diseases without medical treatment. It is also simpler; it doesn't require supernatural entities and forces reaching out from beyond the world. The latter theory also explains a lot, like why Jesus's story was embellished over time. The earliest Christian writings don't include his miracles or much of his life, and each succeeding Gospel is more elaborate than the last.[9] It also fits with the fact that Jesus's life story wasn't written by eyewitnesses; biblical scholars agree the Gospels were written by literate, Greek-speaking Christians decades after Jesus's life, not Jesus's illiterate Aramaic speaking disciples.[10] And it explains why Jesus's story shares so many elements with stories of other god/men that came before him. In the stories of Perseus, Attis, Mithras, and Dionysus, you can find virgin births, miraculous healings, water walking, and even executions that turn into resurrections.[11] The theory that stories of Jesus are embellished is even fruitful. If the Gospel writers were willing to embellish and add to Jesus's story, we should expect to find others willing to do the same thing. And we've found exactly that! Ancient Gnostic gospels like those of Thomas and Pseudo-Matthew, which fictitiously exaggerate the life of Jesus, were discovered just last century. Apparently, Jesus didn't have to sing the "imagination song" to get to live and serve on the Council of Nine in Imagination Land with Aslan, Zeus, Morpheus, Wonder Woman, Luke Skywalker, Popeye, Gandalf, and Glinda the Good Witch of the North. As Butters might put it, in a Jewpacabra mating call, "I don't think Christ has much basis in reality."

If you're a Christian, this may all be hard to swallow, but try applying the same logic to claims outside your religion. Take Sathya Sai Baba, for example, a modern day Indian with millions of followers who has claimed to have healed the sick, made objects appear out of nowhere, turned water into oil, been in two places at once, and even raised the dead.[12] What do you think is more likely: that he really was a reincarnation of Shiva performing miraculous feats as he claimed; or that gullible, uneducated people mistook magic tricks for miracles and that the stories about him are exaggerated? What's more likely: that he really raised the dead; or that people living in third-world conditions without hospitals are apt to sometimes mistake sickness for death and thus mistake a natural a recovery for a resurrection?[13]

Before you answer, keep in mind that the *first* world only properly developed the ability to confirm death in the past century. Recall also the episode "Super Best Friends," in which Stan found out how Jesus changed water into wine.

JESUS:  Behold, ordinary water; clear, clean. Okay, now turn around. [*Stan hesitates* ...]
JESUS:  Turn ... turn around. [*Stan turns around. Jesus puts the water behind the table and pulls out a pitcher of wine.*]
JESUS:  Okay, now turn back. [*Stan turns* ...]
JESUS:  It is now wine!
STAN:   That's it. That's how you did that trick? ... That trick sucks, Jesus.
JESUS:  Oh, I guess it worked a little better on people 2000 years ago.

People are pretty easy to fool—especially when they want to believe.

The idea that Sathya Sai Baba is a miracle-working god/man probably seems as silly to you as Mormonism did the first time you watched "All About Mormons" and Scientology did the first time you watched "Trapped in the Closet." You were just instinctively applying the scientific criteria of adequacy. The theory that Joseph Smith and L. Ron Hubbard made it all up is much more adequate than convoluted stories about reading gold plates out of a hat and intergalactic lords named Xenu. But you can't *rationally* apply these criticisms to other religions and then refuse to apply them to your own. After all, there are living eyewitnesses and YouTube videos of Sai Baba's miracles, yet it still makes sense to deny their reality. How much more should you doubt the story of Jesus, which has been passed down from non-eyewitnesses over two thousand years and through multiple languages? The same applies to other articles of faith, like the doctrine of souls, faith healings, divine intervention, answered prayers, religious experiences—I could go on. Although certain beliefs based in religion like claims of ethics and the meaning of life aren't incompatible with scientific thinking, some of the most important beliefs are.

Many religious academics realize this and doubt such doctrines; they just believe in God. After all, as Stan points out to Mr(s). Garrison, even if evolution is true, there could still be a God. Evolution could just be "the answer to how and not the answer to why." He's right. There is nothing about evolution specifically that is incompatible with belief in God.[14] But is science itself incompatible with belief in God?

## Ha, Ha, Ha. You Believe in a Supernatural Being

Cartman witnesses heads exploding when the United Atheist Alliance attacks the Unified Atheist League, and he exclaims "Jesus Christ!" Spheck mocks him: "Ha, ha, ha. You believe in a supernatural being." By 2546, science has replaced traditional religions and everyone is an atheist. But does being scientific necessarily entail atheism?

Not necessarily. About 51% of scientists today say they believe in a "universal spirit or higher power." However, 41% of scientists say they don't, and that's far more than in the general population, where only 4% don't believe. If you get more specific and ask just about God, only 33% of scientists believe, compared with 83% of the general population.[15] Although science doesn't necessarily entail atheism, they're clearly correlated. This is because most scientists understand that the kind of evidence for God based on "scientific reasoning" is faulty. God isn't needed to explain the origin of the universe, its design, or human origins, either. Quantum mechanics, the conservation of energy, and evolution provide much better explanations.[16] Science simply doesn't need God.

That's not to say science has explained everything, but good scientists know that the fact we haven't explained something isn't a good reason to stick God in as the explanation. To do so would be to commit the "mystery therefore magic" fallacy, and to actually hold back scientific research and progress. For example, if we had been satisfied with explaining diseases by demon possession, we would have never discovered the germ theory of disease. Besides, any theory that appeals to God will always be *less simple* than a scientific competitor because it will always require at least one more huge assumption: God's existence.[17] (But, of course, if God looks like he did in "Are You There God? It's Me, Jesus," that assumption is not so big.)

Can a scientist simply choose to believe in God anyway, by faith alone? If you're dedicated to the scientific method, you can't believe something despite evidence to the contrary. That's the only dogma of science: you should proportion your belief to the evidence. But it's debatable whether there actually is evidence against God's existence. So what if there isn't evidence either way?[18] When a scientifically minded person is presented with the option of deciding whether something is true or false without evidence either way, can they rationally choose to go either way?

William James (1842–1910) thought so. He argued that when a person is forced to make an important decision about what to believe without evidence either way, she has the right to choose to believe what she wishes. There's some precedent for this. There's no evidence in the scientific sense, for example, to support the belief that freedom is a fundamental human right or that happiness is fundamentally good. Yet most of us wouldn't think you're *irrational* for believing such things. It's not scientific, sure. But it's not *contrary* to science.[19]

The problem is, belief in God is a belief about what exists, and when it comes to beliefs about existence, the burden of proof falls on the believer. For example, if I want to rationally believe that there's a killer whale named Willzyx on the moon, even though I have no evidence either way, I can't. To believe rationally, I need to have evidence in favor of Willzyx's existence.[20] When it comes whether something exists or not, and there's no evidence, preference should be given to disbelief. Even if we lack conclusive evidence, preference should be given to atheism.[21]

## Maybe Just Believing in God Makes God Exist

So, it's going to be difficult to retain a literal belief in God if you want to be scientifically minded. It could set off a "Retard Alert" and you may end up in the corner with a dunce's hat that reads "I have faith." But what about a non-literal belief? As The Wise One pointed out to his fellow otters, "Maybe some otters do need to believe in something. Who knows, maybe just believing in God makes God exist." Of course, this can't *literally* be true, since believing something doesn't make it true. The world was round even when everyone believed it was flat.

But perhaps there's a way to believe in something without "actually" believing it. As the mayor of Imaginationland said about leprechauns in the Imaginationland trilogy, "Just because they're imaginary doesn't mean they aren't real."

Some scientifically minded theologians and philosophers acknowledge the conflict between science and religion but maintain that religious beliefs are still true—just not literally true. They are more like "the truth" of a good book. *The Lord of the Rings* contains truth, even though the events it depicts never occurred and its characters don't really exist. Some view religion in this way, as mythically true: God doesn't literally exist, Jesus didn't really resurrect, but the stories about God, Jesus, and his followers contain mythical truths that are worth (non-literally) believing.[22] This might even be the way little Mormon Gary approaches Mormonism. At the end of "All About Mormons," he tells Stan:

> Maybe us Mormons do believe in crazy stories that make absolutely no sense. And maybe Joseph Smith did make it all up. But I have a great life, and a great family, and I have *The book of Mormon* to thank for that. The truth is, I don't care if Joseph Smith made it all up, because what the church teaches now is loving your family, being nice, and helping people. And even though people in this town might think that's stupid, I still choose to believe in it.

This makes you wonder about the 33% of scientists who continue to believe in God. Are they ignorant of the problems we've been considering? Do they turn a blind eye to them to protect their social connections and cherished beliefs? Or might they say they believe that God exists, but merely think it is mythically true?

## Oh My Science!

The atheists of the future seem to worship science as if it were a god. "Science be praised!" "Science help us!" "Oh my Science!" "Science H. Logic" has even replaced "Jesus H. Christ." Matt and Trey seem to be implying that Dawkins' brand of New Atheism is *itself* a religion that worships science. Is this fair or accurate?

"Religion" is notoriously difficult to define. Some say the only difference between a religion and a cult like Blainetology is its popularity. Roughly, however, we might say a religion is a set of doctrines regarding the universe and supernatural forces that includes rituals and moral laws. Is the New Atheism a religion by this definition?

In some ways, maybe it is. "God doesn't exist" is a doctrine about supernatural forces. Although it doesn't have rituals, it does have a law: "You should, when possible, proportion your belief to the evidence." But this isn't a moral law—it's just what you have to do if you want to be rational. And, although science is concerned with describing the universe, it's not a set of doctrines about the universe, but merely a method for gaining knowledge about it. So I don't think it is fair or accurate to call the New Atheism a religion.

Of course, some New Atheists tend to be a bit evangelical; they redirect every conversation to religion, forcibly engage in religious debate with the uninterested, and try to convert everyone they know. But these are signs that someone is interested and passionate about something, not that something is a religion. True, some religions try to gain converts, but some religions don't (like most forms of Judaism and Buddhism) and some non-religions do (like political ideologies). As a teenager, I used to relate everything to *The Simpsons* because, as we all know, "*The Simpsons* have done everything, already." But that doesn't make *Simpson*-watching a religion. Sure, evangelism is annoying, but promoting something doesn't make it a religion.

Even if the New Atheism was a religion, it isn't guilty of one of religion's main vices. Religion is both notoriously intolerant of challenges to its dogmas and extremely resistant to change. If you say the church is wrong about something—for example, that St. Peter was really a rabbit—you'll be labeled a heretic, excommunicated, ostracized, burned at the stake,[23] or even boiled in a rabbit stew. The Catholic Church didn't even officially admit that Galileo was right about the Earth revolving around the sun until 1992—a full 350 years after he died.[24] The New Atheism, on the other hand, invites counterargument; Dawkins gets upset when he isn't invited to debates. And science is set up to determine which challenges have merit, and which ones don't. That is how scientific progress is made. If you fail to admit when you have been proven wrong, then you might be ostracized—like Andrew Wakefield, who still pushes his theory that vaccines cause autism despite the fact that many independent, large, well-controlled studies have proven him wrong.[25] But no scientists have ever cooked someone in a rabbit stew for not proportioning their belief to the evidence.[26]

Do New Atheists worship science? Not in any conventional sense. Science has proven to be our most effective method for determining the truth about the world, and the New Atheists respect it for that. But if another more effective method came along, they wouldn't think twice about abandoning science. The Great Otter seems to think that atheists believe that reason and logic is "all there is." But that's a mischaracterization. There are a lot of things about which science is silent—meaning, ethics, value—and most atheists know this.[27] When science can speak, you should listen to it, but few atheists think that science is the only thing speaking.

## Getting Rid of All of the Isms

"Go God Go" depicts atheistic factions at war over what atheists should call themselves. At the end of the episode, by calling Dawkins on his Crank Prank Time Phone and revealing to him that Mr(s). Garrison had a sex change, Cartman changes the past and prevents Dawkins from having such an influence. As a result, the future changes. The factions are no longer at war because they've learned to get rid of all the "isms." "Long ago we realized, 'isms' are great for those who are rational, but in the hands of irrational people, 'isms' always lead to violence."

Dawkins famously condemns religion because of all the violence for which it has been responsible. As he says to Mr(s). Garrision before he ... uh ... let's just call it "the motorboat": "Can you imagine a world without religion? No Muslims killing Jews. No Christians bombing abortion clinics. The world would be a wonderful place without God." But by having atheists fight over what to call themselves, Matt and Trey suggest that it doesn't matter. Even if we rid ourselves of religion and replace it with atheism, we'll just find something *else* to fight about.

Religion *has* led to a lot of violence—the Crusades, the Spanish Inquisition, witch trials, 9/11, and more. And it's certain that the end of religion wouldn't eliminate all violence. People will always find something to fight about, whether there are "isms" or not—like those "stupid French Chinese [who] think they have a right to Hawaii." But it's much easier to justify horrendous evils in the name of protecting an infinite good, like God. What's a few thousand innocent women and children killed in a Crusade compared to the glory of the infinite creator of all? Without religion, it would be much harder to find justification for killing someone because they disagree with you. "Kill the table eaters in the name of almighty science," isn't really going to fly. Sure, eliminating religion wouldn't end violence, but wouldn't it at least reduce violence? After all, in "*The Simpsons* Already Did It," the tiny Sea People didn't wage war on each other until they started worshiping Cartman and Tweek. How would they have found an excuse to annihilate themselves if not for religion?

Perhaps one could find some excuse for killing in atheism, but I'm not sure what that excuse would be. The fact that Matt and Trey had to appeal to such ridiculous plot devices is telling, because no atheist is really going to think reason can settle a value question like what atheists should call themselves. Even if they did, why would they care enough to kill each other over it? No atheist has ever threatened to kill a creationist for teaching pseudoscience in a public school science class. If they're not willing to kill *others* in the name of protecting rationality and science, what would atheists kill *each other* over? Even if atheists worship science as a god, science only has one rule—and, as far as I know, no one has ever killed anyone because they didn't proportion their belief to the evidence.[28]

To justify their war, the atheists of 2546 "quote" Dawkins: "The Great Dawkins said we cannot tolerate those who don't use reason ... Using logic and reason isn't enough. You have to be a dick to everyone who doesn't think like you." I love Matt and Trey, but they're just not being fair to Dawkins here. Dawkins is, quite notoriously, intellectually vicious to his opponents. He will degrade their intelligence, say they are deluded, and call them idiots. He can be a bit of a dick. But this is certainly no different than what Matt and Trey have done to Tom Cruise, Rob Reiner, Paris Hilton, Matt Damon, Ben Affleck, Jennifer Lopez, John Edward (the biggest douche in the Universe), Al Gore, Michael Jackson, Mel Gibson, Saddam Hussein, Mormons, Scientologists, and a host of other people who sued South Park in their 200th episode. And that's great. Matt and Trey aren't obligated to agree with anyone or respect their intelligence. But neither is Dawkins. And they can't fairly criticize Dawkins for doing the very thing that they do—at least, not without being hypocrites.

As Cartman disappears into the past, his friends from the future ask him to tell everyone in the past, "No one single answer is ever the answer." But that's silly; that's naive relativism.[29] Even when the answer to a scientific question eludes us, there's still an answer. We just don't know what it is. Some answers we do know, and when intelligent people see stupid people defending stupid answers, they should call them out. That's what Dawkins does, and that's what Matt and Trey do. (Though there's no reason to be a dick about it.) That's what freedom of speech is for.[30]

# Notes

1. At the time, Newton's laws would have been more conservative only because they were the prevailing view—it was "common knowledge." But conservatism is only one of the four criteria listed here, and you can't let it trump the others; progress would never get made.
2. In case you have wondered about 9/11 conspiracy theories, see www.debunking911.com, accessed Feb. 10 2013. It's a nice catalogue that debunks the usual claims of 9/11 conspiracy theorists. More highly, I recommend Theodore Schick and Lewis Vaughn's *How to Think about Weird Things* 6th edn. (New York: McGraw-Hill, 2010), which not only debunks 9/11 conspiracy theories (pp. 281–286), but—by teaching you the method of abduction—will show why all conspiracy theories are irrational, as are a host of other beliefs, such as belief in UFOs and ghosts.
3. It's a real example, one that was made up to prove exactly this point. Many atheists belong to The Church of the Flying Spaghetti Monster (FSM) ironically. You can the FSM's website at, www.venganza.org/, accessed Feb. 10, 2013.
4. The Duhem–Quine thesis tells us that no hypothesis can be tested in isolation; the predictions a hypothesis makes depend on the background assumptions it is built upon. A damning faulty prediction can be excused away if one is willing to change the background assumptions. For example, different assumptions about how light operates could "explain" how the earth could look round from space even though it is flat.
5. They have also committed another logical fallacy: straw man. They have misrepresented Dawkins' position to make it easier to attack. He did not suggest that God is a Spaghetti monster, that evolution explains everything, or that there is no mystery to life. He was simply pointing out a logical fallacy.
6. Stephen Jay Gould, "Nonoverlapping Magisteria," *Natural History* 106 (1997): 16–22.
7. Most philosophers suggest that what religion says about ethics and meaning, science can say little about. Sam Harris, however, would disagree. In *The Moral Landscape: How Science can Determine Human*

*Values* (Free Press, 2010), Harris argues that science can inform moral evaluation by helping us determine what actions lead to pain and suffering and which ones lead to happiness and human flourishing. He admits, however, that philosophical argument is needed to establish that such things determine the moral rightness and wrongness of actions.

8. Will Matt and Trey ever retell this story and put a "This is what Muslims actually believe" scroll at the bottom?

9. The earliest documents of the New Testament belong to St. Paul, and he mentions very little about Jesus's life.

10. See Bart Ehrman's *Forged: Writing in the Name of God—Why the Bible's Authors Are Not Who We Think They Are* (New York: Harper One, 2011).

11. Religious critics often exaggerate the similarities between Jesus and specific gods, but it is undeniable that nearly every element (if not all) of Jesus's story can be found attributed to at least one god/man that came before him. For a nice rundown of some of the major similarities, see chapter 5 in Tom Flynn's book *The Trouble with Christmas* (Amherst, NY: Prometheus Books, 1993).

12. He died in 2011.

13. Not all Indians live in such conditions, but the people who claim that Sai Baba raised someone from the dead do. Certainly, no one has ever seen Sai Baba strolling through the morgue of a hospital, touching corpses, and helping them walk out.

14. It's only incompatible with certain extreme literalist interpretations of scripture that where drummed up in the late nineteenth century after evolution had already received mainstream acceptance. See Karen Armstrong's *The Bible: A Biography* (New York: Atlantic Books, 2007).

15. Science is particularly incompatible with evangelical Christianity. Evangelical Protestantism is the highest among the general population (28%), but the lowest among scientists (4%). See "Scientists and Belief," a poll conducted by the Pew Forum on Religion and Public Life on Nov. 5, 2009, http://www.pewforum.org/Science-and-Bioethics/Scientists-and-Belief.aspx, accessed Feb. 10, 2013.

16. Quantum mechanics can account for the Big Bang as an uncaused quantum event, the conservation of energy explains why the universe's basic forces balance out in a way that allows life to appear and evolve, and evolution itself explains our apparent design.

17. That's not to say that a hypothesis that includes God could never be the most adequate one. Although it likely won't be simpler, it's possible for it to be more conservative, explanatory or fruitful than other theories.

18. For more on whether or not there is evidence against God's existence, see my other chapter in this volume, "Cartmanland and the Problem of Evil."

SCIENCE, RELIGION, SOUTH PARK, AND GOD
69

19. Alex Rosenberg might disagree, however. See chapter 5, "Morality: The Bad News," in *The Atheist's Guide to Reality: Enjoying Life without Illusions* (New York: W.W. Norton & Company, 2011).
20. Here I am borrowing from Bertrand Russell's (1872–1970) celestial teapot example.
21. For more on when faith is nor is not rational, see my chapter, "Taking a Leap of Faith: A How-to Guide," in *Inception and Philosophy: Because It's Never Just a Dream* (Malden, MA: Wiley-Blackwell, 2011).
22. Biblical scholar Bart Ehrman defends this thesis in the eighth chapter of his book *Jesus, Interrupted: Revealing the Hidden Contradictions in the Bible (And Why We Don't Know About Them)* (New York: Harper One, 2010). Ludwig F. Schlecht does a wonderful job arguing that William James and John J. Caputo also held this view in "William James and the Post Modern Religion of John J. Caputo" (*Streams of William James* 6:1, 2004). (You can find it here: http://williamjamesstudies.org/newsletter/Streams_6.1.pdf, accessed Feb. 10, 2013.) In my experience, this view, or something very similar, is common among theologians. Unfortunately, if they ever said this in straightforward terms from a pulpit, they would be run out of town on a rail.
23. That actually still happens in some places in the world. See Manesh Shrestha, "Nepalese woman accused of witchcraft and burned alive" (CNN, Feb. 18, 2012), found at, http://articles.cnn.com/2012-02-18/asia/world_asia_nepal-witchcraft-burning_1_shamans-nepalese-capital-local-police-report?_s=PM:ASIA, accessed Feb. 10, 2013.
24. The official ban of Galileo's works was lifted in 1758, but the church was still refusing to publish anything that treated his heliocentric theory as truth as late as 1820. Although the theory just naturally gained consensus (as the church just didn't talk about it and lost its authority on scientific matters), the church still didn't admit that it was wrong, and had treated Galileo unjustly, until 1992 when Pope John Paul II said that, "Thanks to his intuition as a brilliant physicist and by relying on different arguments, Galileo, who practically invented the experimental method, understood why only the sun could function as the centre of the world, as it was then known, that is to say, as a planetary system. The error of the theologians of the time, when they maintained the centrality of the Earth, was to think that our understanding of the physical world's structure was, in some way, imposed by the literal sense of Sacred Scripture ..." (from *Human Nature in Its Wholeness: A Roman Catholic Perspective*, ed. Daniel Robinson, Gladys Sweeny, and Richard Gill (Washington, DC: Catholic University of America Press, 2006), 169). In fact, as late as 1990, Cardinal Ratzinger (who became Pope Benedict XVI in 2005) was still insisting The Catholic Church had done nothing

wrong. "The Church at the time of Galileo kept much more closely to reason than did Galileo himself, and she took into consideration the ethical and social consequences of Galileo's teaching too. Her verdict against Galileo was rational and just, and the revision of this verdict can be justified only on the grounds of what is politically opportune." (See Ratzinger's 1994 *Turning point for Europe? The Church in the Modern World—Assessment and Forecast,* translated from the 1991 German edition by Brian McNeil (San Francisco, CA: Ignatius Press), 98. Pope John Paul officially apologized for its treatment of Galileo in 2000 when he officially recognized and apologized for a large number of the Church's wrongdoings over the previous 2000 years, including the trial of Galileo.

25. For a through debunking of Wakefield's claims, see Paul Offit's *Autism's False Prophets: Bad Science, Risky Medicine, and the Search for a Cure* (New York: Columbia University Press, 2008). Not only was Wakefield's original study too small, badly done, and later contradicted by numerous larger well-conducted studies, but it also turns out that he lied about the data. See "Wakefield's article linking MMR vaccine and autism was fraudulent," *BMJ* 2011; 342:c7452.

26. Although, to be fair, it can sometimes get heated. Scientists have lied about and slandered one another on occasion when they disagree.

27. It's worth noting, however, that some philosophers would suggest that science may also be incompatible with ethics and meaning in the same way it is incompatible with belief in God. They suggest that *objective values* and *ethical truths* are unnecessary entities, and don't do any explanatory work, just like God. This is a more controversial thesis than the one I present here. Once again, see Rosenburg's *Atheist's Guide to Reality*, specifically chapter 2.

28. That's not to say that all atheists have been a barrel of laughs. Pol Pot and Stalin were atheists and they killed millions. But they didn't find their excuse for doing so in atheism itself. They had established what were basically non-theistic state religions, and were executing people to protect them. Anyone not loyal to the state was put to death.

29. Relativism is often what people hide behind when they can't defend their belief from criticism but want to continue to believe. For a refutation of relativism, see my article "Wikiality, Truthiness, and Gut Thinking: Doing Philosophy Colbert-Style" in William Irwin and Kyle Johnson's *Introducing Philosophy Through Pop Culture: From Socrates to South Park, Hume to House* (Malden, MA: Wiley-Blackwell, 2010).

30. For the quintessential defense of the freedom of speech, see chapter 2 of John Stuart Mill's *On Liberty* (New York: Dover Publications, 2002).

# "Your Magic Is No Match for Our Powers Combined!"
## Religious Pluralism and the Search for Truth

### *Jeffrey Dueck*

Religion is a persistent cultural and philosophical issue in *South Park*. From the animated shorts *Jesus vs. Frosty* and *The Spirit of Christmas*, to recent episodes such as "Go God Go," "Fantastic Easter Special," "Cartoon Wars Part I," and "Cartoon Wars Part II," Parker and Stone provide biting commentary on religious belief. Along with these episodes, in this chapter we'll talk about "Super Best Friends," where the kids are seduced by illusionist David Blaine and his growing cult, and Jesus and the Super Best Friends must come to the rescue. We'll look at important philosophical questions the episode raises, including miracles and the difference between the natural and supernatural. More generally, we'll also talk about the nature of religious *pluralism*—the co-existence of many different claims to religious authority—and how faith relates to reason in a world of diverse beliefs.

## Let's Meet the Super Best Friends

In "Super Best Friends," David Blaine comes to town and wows the crowds with his masterful illusions. Afterward, the South Park boys decide to participate in one of the "camps" offered by the "Blainetologists." Of course, the group turns out to be a cult, which

*The Ultimate South Park and Philosophy: Respect My Philosophah!*, First Edition.
Edited by Robert Arp and Kevin S. Decker.
© 2013 John Wiley & Sons, Inc. Published 2013 by John Wiley & Sons, Inc.

exalts Blaine as a powerful messianic figure and preaches allegiance to him. Stan is uncomfortable with all of this and after struggling with whether to leave his friends behind, seeks out the help of Jesus (who, if you'll remember, resides in a modest dwelling in South Park where he hosts a public access TV show). Jesus challenges David Blaine at a Denver rally, but Christ's first-century-style miracles come across as simple party tricks compared to Blaine's illusions. Jesus calls in a Justice League-like committee comprised of figures of some of the world's major religions—the Super Best Friends—for help. Each hero brings a special power to the table: Muhammad with the power of fire, Krishna with shape-shifting powers, and Joseph Smith with ice powers. When the Blainetologists advocate a mass-suicide in an attempt to gain tax-exempt status from the US Government (by having all their members drown in the one-foot-deep Reflecting Pool on the Mall in Washington, DC), Jesus and the Super Best Friends show up to put a stop to Blaine's evil—except for Buddha, who doesn't believe in evil. Blaine animates a giant statue of Abraham Lincoln to thwart the Super Best Friends, who use their combined powers to create a mammoth John Wilkes Booth to bring an end to the great emancipator's destructive force. Meanwhile, Stan rescues the other boys from the Blainetologists and concludes the episode by decrying money-hungry, controlling cults and supporting the harmony and necessity of all the world's religions.

## Pick Any Religion, and Picture It in Your Mind

While we laugh at Parker and Stone's portrayal of the major religions and their prophets, we also might feel uncomfortable or uncertain about the episode. For example, what are we to think about the conclusion Stan reaches at the end of the show? Should we agree with his idea that all religions are equally viable and should co-exist in harmony? This seems appealing in some ways, but we might also wonder how feasible it would be to hold all religions to be equally true. After all, different religions make different claims about what is true or best, and "Super Best Friends" seems to show that, while some religions should be recognized as equally significant, not *every* approach to religion is equally good. David Blaine's religion is criticized as being like a cult, and most people find the deceptively controlling and brainwashing practices of cults to be both immoral and definitely *not* in line with the will of a god. Philosophers have offered three different theories to deal with the diversity of religions: religious pluralism, religious exclusivism, and religious inclusivism.

Many people believe that the best way to deal with the diversity of religions is to treat all religious beliefs—as far as possible—as relatively equal. The viewpoint that all religions should be considered equal in terms of their truth and effectiveness is called *religious pluralism*. The "fact of pluralism," is merely the observation that there are many world religions that have a large number of adherents and have stood the test of time. But the *philosophical* position known as pluralism goes beyond this obvious empirical fact. It says that because there are so many religions around the world and because many of them produce religious experiences for religiously minded people, we should consider these religions to be roughly "on par" with one another in terms of their truth. In other words, we shouldn't claim that one religion is better than another, as long as everyone gets along (like members of the Super Best Friends), allowing each religion to foster the greater good of humankind.

One such pluralist is John Hick (1922–2012), who argued that central to any religion is the idea of "salvation." For Hick, salvation is always as a transformation from self-centeredness to divine-reality-centeredness. Religion is all about appreciating a higher power and the compelling message of looking beyond ourselves to help others. For Hick, this personal transformation occurs through love and compassion. And since all religions do about as well at producing devout, loving, and compassionate people, we should conclude that all are about on par with respect to their power to "save" people. Other differences about specific doctrines, history, and ideas about the divine reality should be de-emphasized and we should focus on the truth expressed in all religions.[1]

It seems that, despite their implied religious affiliations, most of the boys support this viewpoint (though Cartman regularly voices condescending remarks about many religions, including Kyle's Judaism). And the fact that the combined powers of the Super Best Friends proves to be stronger than just one prophet on his own seems to further indicate the truth of pluralism. Other moments on *South Park* embrace pluralistic ideas, too. To cite one example, at the end of "All About Mormons," the Mormon kid Gary implies a belief in religious pluralism when he notes that "loving your family, being nice, and helping people" are the real essentials of any religion.

## Go God Go

But responding to the fact of religious diversity with pluralism isn't the only option. Indeed, it's poor reasoning to infer all religions are equally true from the observation that there are many successful religions. By comparison, if there's diversity of opinion about the human rights that people have based on their race, then are we justified in saying that each viewpoint equally expresses the truth on the matter? Do we have to say that the racist, bigot, and supremacist are as correct as someone who believes in racial equality? Or, how about Cartman's ongoing response to the hippie lifestyle? Does being rational mandate that any sincerely held view should be respected as even *partially* true? What about when Cartman tries to clear out hippies in South Park with a giant "Hippie Digger" drill? Is this okay simply because he's sincere? In general, the mere fact that people disagree about their beliefs doesn't mean that everyone is equally correct.

To the contrary, certain belief systems stake "exclusive" claims to clear, uncompromising conditions for the truth of their own doctrines. They exclude any incompatible beliefs, claiming that they're untrue. For example, Islam claims that there is no God but Allah, and that Muhammad is his prophet. Doesn't this imply that other ideas about god(s) are mistaken, and that Muhammad must be seen as preeminent among other prophets? Or take Christianity, which certainly has exclusivist elements: Jesus claims to be the *only* way to God (John 14:6), for instance. If this were true, wouldn't every other path to salvation be a false one?

Perhaps the most familiar response to the diversity of world religions is *religious exclusivism*. It says that the claims of one religion are true, and that anything incompatible with the tenets of this one religion must be false. For most beliefs, this approach makes perfect sense. If I think South Park is located in Colorado, and you think it's located in Alaska, can both of us be right (both of us could be *wrong*, of course)? This same perspective even applies to many moral questions. In viewing "Cartman Joins NAMBLA," we seem justified in thinking the members of the North American Man/Boy Love

Association are wrong in their treatment of children, despite their leader's requests for us to tolerate them. But when it comes to religion, something causes many of us to hesitate from being so exclusivist. So many people feel so passionately about their religious beliefs that we feel it's wrong to say someone is right and another who disagrees is wrong. Or maybe we truly feel that there is no way to evaluate the truth of religious doctrines, and so we can't comment on whether or not any one particular religion is true. Better to hold all religions equal if none can give clear reasons for why they are more valid. While exclusivism permeates many of our beliefs about facts and morals, many people feel that exclusivism about *religion* is somehow disingenuous or arrogant.[2]

Of course, it is hard to avoid thinking we're right about our own beliefs—why else would we believe them? In "Go God Go," the creators of *South Park* train their sights on these questions from the atheist perspective. Famed atheist Richard Dawkins convinces Mr(s). Garrison that evolution and a viewpoint based on strictly natural reasons are the right sort of beliefs. But Cartman (hoping to avoid a three-week wait for the forthcoming release of the Nintendo Wii) accidentally time-travels into the future and arrives in the year 2546, in a world where religion has been discarded and various atheist factions are fighting over a new "Great Question"—how to best frame atheism! Each group is convinced they're right about their brand of atheism, and so again it seems impossible to avoid a commitment to exclusive beliefs. After changing the past (including the break-up of Dawkins' and Garrison's romantic relationship), Cartman witnesses a peaceful future where religious perspectives co-exist again. And so we return to the pluralistic position: freedom to pursue one's beliefs is presented as preferable to heavy-handed constraint, whether religious or atheistic. The story also shows that a healthy society cannot—and should not—give up tolerating varying viewpoints. In a properly functioning world, pluralism is inevitable and should be celebrated. And yet the inevitable differences between the deeply held beliefs existing within a pluralistic society do nothing to remove the tensions that come from exclusivity.

And so we come to a third approach to religious diversity, called *religious inclusivism*. This view says that one religion is superior to others with respect to truth, but includes other religions and their followers under the grace and salvation of that one true religion. Karl

Rahner (1904–1984), a Catholic theologian and inclusivist, states that non-Christian people around the world who have honest faith in their religion should be considered "anonymous Christians." That is, they'll receive the grace and salvation of Christianity (the only *true* religion) in the midst of their religious lives without even knowing it. For Rahner, Christian salvation is the only genuine way to be saved, but God is gracious enough to extend that salvation to honest adherents of other faiths. Inclusivism seems therefore to represent a "middle-of-the-road" approach.

## 2 + 2 = 5

All this is fine and good, but we don't just want to list the possible responses to the fact that religious diversity exists; we also want to understand and evaluate the reasons why a person could believe in pluralism, exclusivism, or inclusivism. The branch of philosophy that examines how beliefs can be justified by reasons is called *epistemology*, and the phrase *epistemic parity* refers to the appearance of equal validity that different reasons for believing often seem to have.

For example, the circumstances of our childhood have a deep impact on our beliefs as well as on the reasons available to us for *why* we believe them. The *South Park* boys learned this early on in their adventures with Starvin' Marvin, and we have a lot of fun watching them interact with people of different cultures and religions throughout the series. If culture and upbringing provided *all* of the reasons for why someone holds the religious beliefs they do, then we should be pluralists about religion. After all, our learning experiences as children impact us *all* deeply. But, as we saw earlier, culture and upbringing can't be the only kinds of valid reasons for belief; otherwise, everyone would be justified in any of her beliefs just because she was raised to have them. Mr. Mackey's believing that $2 + 2 = 5$ (while smoking mar-e-joo-on-e, m'kay?) or Cartman thinking that a certain race of humans is inferior may be *explained* based on upbringing, but it isn't *justified*. And even if I *was* justified in holding a belief because of how I was brought up, this certainly does not imply that the belief must be *true*.

We can also look for good reasons by investigating the internal consistency of a set of beliefs. For instance, we might reject a religion because it makes claims that are self-defeating, or it has some doctrines that clearly contradict other doctrines it maintains. For example, if someone claimed to be a Christian Muslim, then that person would be saying that they believed Jesus was God (a Christian belief) and a mere human (an Islamic belief) *at the same time.* While there are incoherencies and contradictions to be found in the world's religions, people either ignore them, rationalize them through a leap of faith, or use philosophy to show how these incoherencies and inconsistencies aren't genuine. Since it would be difficult to understand the persistence of most world religions over time if they advocated blatant contradictions, it seems likely that they don't suffer from *radical* inconsistencies.

The final type of reasons we could look to is *empirical* evidence. In other words, what do our five senses reveal to us about the diversity of religions and an appropriate response? As we saw, John Hick thought we should judge all religions to be on par with each other because we can observe a kind of equality in the *results* of religious life (selfless, loving, compassionate people). Yet it's hard to imagine how a clear empirical test could measure how loving and compassionate all the various adherents of religions are. So we might also look at the history of a religion, judging whether it advanced by suspicious developments; or we could examine the lives of the great prophets of religions, aiming to see whether or not there was consistency and plausibility in their teachings. A further kind of empirical evidence might be the testaments of believers in the past. While this couldn't *prove* that a religion is true, there might be evidence for this if vast numbers of people testified that a set of religious beliefs and practices was life-changing, compelling, and purpose-giving. But are these kinds of evidence the *only* empirical standards for the truth of a religion?

## "David Blaine Will Now Eat His Own Head"

"Super Best Friends" focuses on another kind of evidence, namely, miracles. David Blaine is portrayed as a magician who's also a powerful miracle-worker, while Jesus's "tricks" depend far more on the audience's gullibility than on authentic power. Miracles are mocked throughout the episode and, yet, in the end we see each of the Super

Best Friends demonstrating fantastic abilities. And this leads us to consider one of the most important underlying questions about the justification of religious belief: is there a way of understanding and evaluating reasons for belief that takes into account the central role of *supernatural* elements of religion? Or can we only take into account evidence from the *natural* world?

David Hume (1711–1776) asked this question with respect to miracles. His argument against reasoned belief in miracles runs something like this: a miracle is a violation of laws of nature, which have been established by past human experience. The only kind of evidence for miracles is the testimony of witnesses. But testimonial evidence for supernatural events is almost always of a limited amount and dubious quality. Hume thinks that this kind of evidence could *never* outweigh the overwhelming experience that validates laws of nature. So, rational belief in a miracle could never be justified.[3]

While this argument focuses on miracles (as does the battle between David Blaine and the Super Best Friends), the underlying issue is the conflict between natural and supernatural evidence. Since our standards of rationality are very much based based on common, day-to-day experiences of "natural" life, it seems difficult to fit supernatural kinds of experience into this framework. Even John Hick frames pluralism in terms of experience of the natural world: specifically, the empirically verifiable actions of people. It might appear that evaluating the reasons for religious belief has to involve a *reduction* of supernatural evidence into terms familiar from the natural realm of day-to-day life. But then, why are the supernatural elements of religion needed at all? If, as Hick says, the only thing that matters is moving from self-centeredness to divine-reality-centeredness, resulting in love and compassion, then why not get rid of the supernatural, "divine reality" altogether and just focus on encouraging loving and compassionate behavior? Why get hung up on divine incarnation and virgin birth when the same amount of Christmas spirit can be promoted by Mr. Hankey, the Christmas Poo? Why, from the pluralist perspective, is Kyle's Judaism or Stan's Christianity any different from honest, compassionate atheism?

The answer is that the *content* of their beliefs is different, even if the actions those beliefs lead to *appear* to be the same. And this has parallels with both miracles and the issue of pluralism. When a religious person and a non-religious person confront a supposed miracle, there is a common observable event but a difference in explanation—the religious person sees a supernatural cause, while the non-religious person sees a merely yet-to-be-known natural cause. In the case of pluralism, different religious practices may result in the same helpful actions and moral character, but there are very different claims about *reality* serving as the motivating force in each case.

The danger of ignoring the content of beliefs while also advocating for pluralism is that religious viewpoints will get watered down. Philosopher of science Karl Popper's (1902–1994) notion of "falsification" does just this. Popper said that the more a theory presents us its conclusions in terms of what should happen if it's true, the better we're able to evaluate it.[4] For Popper, what makes a theory "scientific" is not just that it can be confirmed, but that its claims about reality are testable in such a way that failure to falsify it counts as credit toward its truth. If we dilute the content of incompatible belief systems in a manner like this, then we get pluralism, but the cost is that we're really unable to put viewpoints to good tests. In "Fantastic Easter Special," this problem appears in the *Da Vinci Code*-esque battle over the supposed secret history of Christianity between William Anthony Donahue (and his ninjas) and the Hare Club for Men. The Hare Club protects the secret that St. Peter was really a rabbit, and that the intention of Christ was for rabbits in the line of Peter to head the Church. After Jesus saves the day, Snowball the rabbit is elected pope, driving home the point that good religious leaders should humbly and tolerantly lead, but shouldn't tell people what to do—in this case because they literally can't speak! As ridiculous and comical as the episode is, it reinforces the challenge of maintaining authentic religious positions, true to their origins and belief content while still fostering pluralism. The question remains: if all religions seem to be practically the same in terms of observable results, how should we deal with their unobservable spiritual claims?

## You Gotta Have Faith

Even David Hume agrees that the answer to this last question is *faith*. Seeing an event as a miracle instead of as a strange natural event depends on faith. What separates religion from science and other methods for empirical explanation is that it requires a kind of belief that transcends the limits of reason. This might seem like a cop-out to some, a crutch for people who can't deal with life in terms of the natural world. But, leaving behind such condescending remarks, there is an important philosophical point here. The way reason functions in our dealings with the natural world doesn't operate according to cold, hard rules and facts. Life doesn't always fit into our preconceived notions. It's possible that risk-taking, transcendent faith might be required to discover some kinds of truth. William James (1842–1910), an American pragmatist, argues this point in his essay "The Will to Believe."[5] Establishing a friendship, for example, requires us to take risks that don't have clearly predictable results. But we're justified in taking those risks because of the good that can be achieved as a result. Or imagine a situation where you are lost while hiking and you have to choose which way you'll proceed to find the way home. Is it rational to just stay put, to avoid making *any* decision because the evidence isn't clear? Shouldn't you make your best educated guess, commit to your plan and hope for the best?

Parker and Stone want to maintain the importance of religious belief in people's lives even as they mock some of what religious faith is about in episodes like the ones we've discussed. Their mockery urges us to separate closed-minded fervor from genuine religious expressions. While, as we saw, practices of love and compassion can be developed without religious faith, it may be justifiable to honestly follow such a faith in dealing with experiences that are genuinely, religiously compelling. When it comes to our sense of the divine—whether we have none, whether it's ingrained from childhood or discovered in a heightened moment of illumination— faith is a justifiable response, given the limits of logical, empirical reasoning.

This is to say that while standards of empirical evidence should be maintained in our search for religious truth, they might not be our only concerns. Stan has every right to be suspicious of South Park Jesus telling him to look away while he turns water into wine. But questions about the miracles of the historical Jesus can't be confronted so directly. And for most religiously minded people, belief in miracles doesn't "appear from nowhere." Rather, a whole religious way of life is usually in place for them. Interactions with God, with other people in communities of faith, and other life experiences shape and confirm their beliefs about doctrines, historical events, and miracles.

None of this says we should reject rational or empirical standards, but instead it presents an enlarged scope within which a person's beliefs can operate. Under certain rationally and socially justifiable conditions, we should advocate for the right of people to find meaning and purpose in religious ways of life.

## Waiting for God (Oh!)

All this brings us full circle. If it is possible that God exists, and if faith enables a person to experience such a supernatural force, then perhaps that person is rationally justified in moving past merely empirical evidence in hopes of finding supernatural confirmation. And if this is true for religious belief in general, then why can't a person who's attached to a particular religion be within their rights to believe their religion's exclusive claim to truth? Certainly tolerance should be advocated, to the extent that anyone who lives by general ethical and social standards in practicing their beliefs should be allowed to do so. But as Mr. Garrison found out in "The Death Camp of Tolerance," there are limits to what should be tolerated. As we saw earlier, it may be impossible to avoid committing to exclusivist positions (as the camp master says, "Intolerance will not be tolerated"). Even religious pluralists must hold that some views about religion are better than others—namely, that pluralistic views are better than exclusivist or inclusivist views. As contemporary philosopher Alvin Plantinga has argued, the person who holds their beliefs to be exclusively correct is not necessarily guilty of any wrongdoing.[6] If we're compelled by evidence, doctrines, and by experiences outside the natural while acting morally and rationally considerate of others, we're within our rights to believe as we will.[7] It's good to beware the Blainetologists of our world, but we should also be careful about surrendering rationally justifiable ways of life that may help to define us.

## Notes

1. See John Hick, *God Has Many Names* (Louisville, KY: Westminster John Knox Press, 1982); *An Interpretation of Religion: Human Responses to the Present* (London: The Macmillan Press, 1989);

82 JEFFREY DUECK

*A Christian Theology of Religion: A Rainbow of Faiths* (Louisville, KY: Westminster John Knox Press, 1995).

2. For more on this issue, see Alvin Plantinga, "Pluralism: A Defense of Religious Exclusivism," in *The Philosophical Challenge of Religious Diversity*, ed. Kevin Meeker and Philip Quinn (New York: Oxford University Press, 2000), 172–192; also Philip Quinn, "Toward Thinner Theologies: Hick and Alston on Religious Diversity," in *The Philosophical Challenge of Religious Diversity*, 226–243.

3. See David Hume, *An Enquiry Concerning Human Understanding*, ed. Tom Beauchamp (Oxford: Oxford University Press, 2006), 83–99; also, *The Natural History of Religion*, ed. H.E. Root (Stanford: Stanford University Press, 1967).

4. Among his many works, see *Conjectures and Refutations: The Growth of Scientific Knowledge* (New York: Routledge, 2002).

5. William James, *The Will to Believe and Other Essays in Popular Philosophy* (New York: Dover Publications, 1956).

6. See Alvin Plantinga, *Warranted Christian Belief* (Oxford: Oxford University Press, 2000).

7. Besides Alvin Plantinga, other thinkers have advocated this position. See, for example, Robert Merrihew Adams, *The Virtue of Faith and Other Essays in Philosophical Theology* (Oxford: Oxford University Press, 1987).

# Cartmanland and the Problem of Evil

## David Kyle Johnson

Cartman is an ass. More precisely, Cartman is a manipulative, self-centered bastard whose every action is directed either toward increasing his own happiness or decreasing the happiness of others. He deserves to be miserable. When misfortune befalls Cartman, we think it good. When fortune smiles on him, we think something evil has happened—he doesn't deserve it. This is exactly the conclusion Kyle draws when Cartman gets his own amusement park. In the episode "Cartmanland," Cartman learns that he's the heir to his grandmother's estate—just after he objects to being required to attend her funeral because it is "taking up [his] whole Saturday." He inherits one million dollars, and uses the money to purchase the local amusement park, renaming it "Cartmanland," and buying television commercial time to declare that the best thing about Cartmanland is, "You can't come ... especially Stan and Kyle." For a time, Cartman is completely happy, spending all day, every day, riding any ride he wants without waiting in line.

Understandably, Kyle views Cartman's happiness as an evil. Cartman doesn't deserve happiness and his attaining it just isn't right. But according to Kyle, the problem is much deeper. Kyle observes that the course of events isn't just unbelievable. Given his worldview—which includes a belief in God—these events are impossible. God, if he exists, is all-good and all-powerful, and so he would surely prevent all evil. If we assume, like Kyle, that such a God exists, it would be impossible for Cartman to attain such happiness. But, since Cartman's

*The Ultimate South Park and Philosophy: Respect My Philosophah!*, First Edition.
Edited by Robert Arp and Kevin S. Decker.
© 2013 John Wiley & Sons, Inc. Published 2013 by John Wiley & Sons, Inc.

happiness is undeniable, Kyle is forced to revise his worldview and conclude that God doesn't exist.

Kyle's argument is a form of the "problem of evil"—more specifically, it is an example of the *logical problem* of moral evil. The problem centers on the fact that the existence of moral evil—that is, evil caused by human action—seems incompatible with God's existence. If Kyle had a Ph.D. in philosophy, he likely would have expressed the problem like this:

*Premise 1*:    If God exists (and he's all-good and all-powerful), he would not allow Cartman to be completely happy (for that's a great evil).

*Premise 2*:    But now that Cartman, thanks to his grandmother, has his own amusement park, Cartman is completely happy (again, a great evil).

*Conclusion*:   Therefore, God does not exist.[1]

This argument is valid; that is, if its premises are true, its conclusion is true. If you object to the argument, you have to show that one of its premises is false. That's exactly what many philosophers have tried to do. As we look at some solutions to this problem that have been proposed by the citizens of South Park, we'll see how close they are to solutions proposed by philosophers, both old and new. Some solutions clearly fail, others might not—but they'll raise others problems. In the end we'll see just how serious a threat the problem of evil is to belief in God.

## "And That's It?" The Story of Job

In "Cartmanland" when Kyle's parents discover he no longer believes in God, they take it upon themselves to restore his faith by telling him the Old Testament story of Job, about a righteous man who suffers horrendous evils and yet retains his belief in God. As Kyle's parents tell the story, God allows Satan to inflict suffering upon Job in order to prove that Job would remain faithful in any circumstances. Satan destroys all his property, kills his family, and infects Job with disease. Yet, despite all of the horrible things that happen to him and his family, Job still praises God.

Kyle's response to the story is quite telling: "And that's it? That's the end? That's the most horrible story I have ever heard. Why would God do such horrible things to a good person just to prove a point to Satan? ... I was right. Job has all his children killed and Michael Bay gets to keep making movies. There isn't a God." Kyle has some very good points. Not only do most of Michael Bay's movies (like *Pearl Harbor*) suck, but the actions of God in the Job story don't jive with how we view God today. Most people would not think it morally justified to cause that kind of suffering to *prove a point* to anyone, much less Satan. More importantly for us, the story of Job doesn't even address the problem of evil. Yes, Job continues to believe in God despite suffering horrendous evil, but that isn't enough reason to conclude that doing so is rational. People do irrational things. (The jury in the episode "Chef Aid" found Johnny Cochran's Chewbacca defense persuasive, after all, but that doesn't mean it was a good argument.) The story Kyle's parents tell doesn't really challenge one of the premises in the argument, and so seems to be inadequate as a response to it.

If we look deeper at Job's story, however, we can at least find an argument. At the end of the story God speaks to Job, basically saying, "You can't question me; my ways are beyond your understanding." This notion is echoed today by "skeptical theists" who argue that, since God may have reasons beyond our comprehension for allowing evil, evil that seems unjustified isn't evidence against God's existence. For all we know, such evils are actually good.

Skeptical theism, however, has its problems. First of all, it's mathematically unsound. Even though God may have reasons beyond our comprehension, when you simply crunch the numbers with probability calculus, evil that seems unjustified still reduces the probability of God's existence.[2] Secondly, it's a bit hypocritical. Theists claim, on the one hand, a wealth of knowledge about God: he's the omnipotent, omniscient, omni-benevolent, omnipresent, three-in-one creator of the universe who hates some things (abortion and hippies), loves others (Republicans and Cheesy Poofs), and sent his son to die on the cross for our sins. To turn around and demand that his reasons for allowing evil are, on the other hand, beyond our grasp is just too convenient. Lastly, skeptical theism leads to moral agnosticism. For all I know, God has some reason to allow Cartman's happiness; but for all I know the Holocaust prevented some even greater future evil. If I have to take into account all future possible good consequences in my moral deliberations, I can't know whether anything is objectively right or wrong.

Biblical scholars know that the story of Job is an inadequate response to the problem of evil. Atheism was not even an option when the book of Job was written, and the belief that God was "all good" and would never cause suffering didn't become prevalent until after Plato's (429–347 BC) philosophical influence had worked its way through Christianity—long after Job was written. Job probably wouldn't have viewed his suffering as any kind of evidence against God's existence. At best the author of Job was trying to persuade readers to remain devoted to God during difficult times. In the story, Job's friends offer up theodicies (reasons why God allows evil), yet the author of Job has God condemn these friends for their words. If the author of Job was trying to answer the problem of evil, he would likely have been doing the very thing he thought God would condemn.

## The Sweet Milk of Our Tears

The fact that God condemned Job's friends for offering excuses on his behalf hasn't stopped philosophers and theologians from doing so, and nor did it stop Chef. In "Kenny Dies"—the only episode in which Kenny dies and "stays dead" for a while—Stan wrestles with the problem of evil, asking Chef how God could let Kenny die. Chef tells him that God "gives us life and love and health, just so that he can tear it all away and make us cry, so he can drink the sweet milk of our tears. You see, it's our tears, Stan, that give God his great power." Although this answer seems cruel, and clearly wrong, it mirrors a certain type of answer to the problem of evil. Like Jonathan Edwards (1703–1758) and John Calvin (1509–1564), Chef suggests that God allows evil to occur for his own benefit.[3] Edwards and Calvin suggest that God allows evil because he wishes to punish evildoers, and this benefits God himself. As Edwards suggests, punishing evildoers is the most perfect way for God to demonstrate his holiness (his hatred of sin) and thus bring glory to himself.[4] The idea is that a benefit to God outweighs any evil done to humans.

Not many philosophers find this solution satisfactory. God demonstrating his holiness at our expense—making some do evil, which others suffer, and punishing the evildoers for it—doesn't seem to be better than Chef's explanation. We just don't think God is that cruel.

In fact, this would be a bit like Cartman inventing the Jewpacabra—a creature that "drinks blood, hides in the night, and has absolutely no belief in the divinity of Christ"—so that he can look good protecting everyone from it (and be the only one at the Easter egg hunt). Further, it's not clear why God would have to punish evildoers to demonstrate his holiness. Isn't God all-powerful? Couldn't he have established this fact with equal effectiveness in some other (non-evil) way? It certainly seems so. Chef, Edwards, and Calvin clearly aren't on the right track.

## "You *Are* Up There!"

After Stan and Kyle try to sneak into Cartmanland, Cartman decides he needs a security guard. Since the security guard won't accept rides on the attractions as payment, Cartman's forced to let two people a day into his park to pay the security guard's salary. Cartman's problems escalate when he discovers that he needs ride maintenance, food, drink, cotton candy, video surveillance, a box office, and janitors. Soon, Cartman has a fully functioning and successful amusement park. But since he now has to wait in line to ride his rides, he doesn't want it anymore and sells it back to the owner for the original million. Most of his money is immediately seized by the IRS (since he didn't pay any taxes when he owned the park) and the rest goes to Kenny's family (since Kenny died on the Mine Shaft ride). Now, Cartman is miserable. He stands outside the park, throwing rocks at it, and the security guard who once worked for him sprays mace in his face.

Stan brings Kyle outside to witness these events, saying, "Look Kyle, Cartman is totally miserable ... even more miserable than he was before because he had his dream and lost it." Stan's observation restores Kyle's belief in God. Clearly, according to Stan and Kyle, Cartman's suffering has somehow relieved the tension between the existence of God and the evil of Cartman's happiness. Their answer is this: God, being all-good, wanted to accomplish a great good—the *perfect suffering* of Cartman. But the only way to accomplish this great good was to give Cartman perfect happiness (a temporary evil) and then rip it away. Since the good of Cartman's suffering outweighs the evil of his brief happiness, an overall greater good was achieved, justifying the evil of his happiness.

This answer mirrors a common way in which theists—believers in God—answer the problem of evil. They challenge one premise in the argument, the suggestion that God would prevent evil if he wanted to and could, suggesting he might have other desires that trumped the desire to eliminate evil. In other words, they suggest that God might not guarantee the absence of evil because there might be something he desires more than the absence of evil, something that *requires* the existence of evil. What might that be? The answer: the presence of good. Although it's true that God doesn't like evil, it's also true that God loves (and wants to accomplish) good. If certain goods can only be achieved by allowing certain evils—as long as the good outweighs the evil allowed—then allowing that evil is justified. In fact, since the world is a better place if those evils are allowed and outweighed, you would expect God to allow them because he wants the world to be *as good as possible*. The argument says that the existence of evil doesn't contradict God's existence, because it's not true that God would necessarily prevent all evil. God would—and should—allow evil that accomplishes a greater good, and so the presence of evil isn't conclusive evidence against God's existence. According to this "greater goods" response to the problem of evil, the mutual existence of both God and evil is logically possible.

But questions remain. What kind of goods can only be accomplished by allowing evil? Stan and Kyle see Cartman's suffering as a good that could only be accomplished at the expense of Cartman's brief happiness. The theist philosopher Richard Swinburne suggests that God allows evil in order to create goods like compassion, generosity, and courage.[5] You can't compassionately heal the sick unless there is sickness. You don't need to generously offer to find a place like the planet Marclar for Starvin' Marvin to live, unless Marvin is indeed starvin'. Mysterion can't courageously save the world from Cthulhu unless BP releases the Elder God to wreak havoc on the world by accidentally tearing open a portal to another dimension by drilling for oil. These good acts are made possible only because they are responses to evil.

But there are a couple of problems here. First, not all evils have goods flow out of them in this way; the evil of the history channel's Thanksgiving special comes to mind. Also, remember that in order to justify the evil done in service of good, the evil has to be *necessary* to bring about the goods and these goods have to outweigh the evil. But, as wonderfully compassionate as most doctors are, none think their compassion justifies or outweighs the suffering of their patients. As generous as the boys are to help Marvin, they'd much rather he was never starvin' in the first place. Mysterion's courage doesn't outweigh the havoc that Cthulhu wreaked. So, what good might both outweigh and only be possible because of certain evils?

## Free Hat, Free Willzyx, Free Will

Most often, theists propose that the greater good that justifies God's allowing evil is *human free will*. As Augustine (354–430) put this argument, only free acts have the possibility to be good acts; if we don't have free will to choose between good and evil, nothing we do is truly good.[6] Unless we have the option of *choosing* evil, we can't be given moral credit for choosing good, and if we cannot be given moral credit for an action, it can't be truly good. So without free will, there can be no good. But if we are to have free will—if we are to truly have the option of doing evil—we must remain unhindered. God can't stop Cartman from selling ass burgers to his fellow classmates if Cartman is going to have the freedom to not do so. Likewise, God can't force Cartman to set up Token with Nicole (in "Cartman Finds Love") if his action is be to be truly morally good (which, arguably, it is not anyway given Cartman's motivations). The "risk of evil" is necessary if there is to be any good in the world. Since God loves good—and presumably wants to accomplish good more than he wants to avoid evil—the risk of evil is one that he is willing to take (even though he hates evil). If so, the existence of evil is compatible with the existence of God.

Why, though, is free will a greater good? If God would have interfered with Hitler's free will and made him decide to like the Jews, instead of exterminating them, wouldn't that have been worth it? Is the preservation of Hitler's free will really more important than the lives of 6 million Jews? Those who defend the free will solution answer this objection by suggesting that the greater good is found in preserving human free will in general. Hindering free will in one instance might lead to a greater good, sure, but if God does that once, he would have to do it every time. And if God always steps in to prevent us from making evil decisions, how are our decisions to do right truly free and thus morally good? To preserve the greater good of free will in general, God has to maintain a policy of never interfering with our decisions. He has to let us choose what we will and live with the consequences, even if that risks genocide.

But there are still a couple of problems here. First, the free will solution is contrary to the way most people conceive of God. Most people think that God is in control of everything—who will be elected president, who they will marry, whether or not they will get that job they applied for, whether Cartman's Christian rock band "Faith + 1" will go double myrrh, and so on. This is presumably why people pray to God, to make such things happen. But God can control elections only if he controls how people *choose* to vote; he can choose who you marry only if he controls whether your spouse *chooses* to marry you; he can get you that job only if he controls the decisions of your potential boss; he can make Faith + 1 go double myrrh only if he controls what people decide to buy. So, you can accept the free will solution only if you accept that God really *isn't* in control of such things. Rejecting the idea that God controls human decisions might get you out of the problem of evil, but it entails that God isn't really in control of the world. The free will defense comes at a high price.

A second problem is that the free will defense only addresses half of the problem. Sure, it might explain evils resulting from human decisions, but not all evil is caused by humans. After all, in the "Cartmanland" episode, part of the reason that Kyle lost his faith was because he developed a hemorrhoid. And we can't explain that true, anal evil by pointing to human free will. Such evils are called "natural evils," and they also include earthquakes, tsunamis, hurricanes, tornados, diseases, and Mecha-Streisand—all events that cause suffering but are not caused by humans.[7] Ultimately, one wonders, if God is the designer of our universe but is also supposed to be all-good, why did he design a natural order that makes such evils inevitable? If I built a house with puppy-killing machines (that randomly strike out and kill any puppy within reach) embedded into the walls and then made my puppies live in my house, I could hardly be said to be a loving master of my puppies. Yet our world is designed with human-killing machines like earthquakes and diseases built right in. If the world has a designer, how could we think the designer is morally perfect? The free will solution doesn't even address this problem.[8]

## "Are You There God? It's Me, Jesus"

Perhaps the best attempt at a solution to both the moral and natural problem of evil is John Hick's "soul making" theodicy. In his book *Evil and the God of Love*, Hick suggests that evil—both moral and natural—occurs in the world so that we, individually and as a species, can develop our character.[9] Even if God ensured that we always acted in good ways—perhaps by bestowing upon us perfect characters—those actions wouldn't be as good as actions that come from characters that we develop *ourselves*. To ensure that the world contains the best kind of actions, God allows evil to exist so that we can respond to it, developing and perhaps even perfecting our characters. So, even though specific evils may go unanswered, the world as a whole is better if we develop our characters, something we can only do by responding to evil. Hick says the presence of evil, both moral and natural, is justified.

Hick's reasoning mirrors that of cartoon Jesus in "Are You There God? It's Me, Jesus." In this episode, the South Park masses are ready to crucify Jesus because he promised that God would appear at the millennium, and he hasn't. Stan and Jesus have a conversation in which Jesus claims that "life is about problems, and overcoming those problems, and growing and learning from obstacles. If God just fixed everything for us, then there would be no point in our existence." Even though Jesus is talking about why God doesn't always answer prayers, the point seems to be the same. The reason that God doesn't "fix everything for us" is because, if he did, we wouldn't be able to learn and grow from facing obstacles. And, after all, our learning and growing is important (even more important than the elimination of evil).

Many philosophers are not satisfied with Hick's answer, however. First, it's not clear that all evil actually does contribute to "soul making." How might an innocent fawn burning to death in a forest fire, or the rape and murder of a small child develop our character? And how exactly did the Haitian earthquake of 2010 or the Indian Ocean tsunami of 2004 develop the characters of the hundreds of thousands they killed? Perhaps it strengthened the character of the few who responded to the crises, but some philosophers argue that unless an evil's greater good actually benefits the one who suffers from the evil, that good cannot justify the evil. Besides, I doubt any member of Doctors Without Borders thinks the development of their character justifies the disasters they respond to. Their character is certainly laudable, but I can guarantee that each one of them wishes each disaster never happened, no matter how much it provides them an opportunity to develop their individual souls. Besides, there seems to be far more evil than we need for character development. (Can't the boys learn their lessons at the end of each episode without Kenny dying so often?) And don't we create enough evil on our own? Do we need God to help out by adding natural evil on top of it all?

## "Go God Go"

Let's get one thing clear: the validity of the problem of evil doesn't disprove God's existence. But that doesn't mean belief in God is rational. Very few things can be proven or disproven conclusively, but the rational person *proportions belief to the evidence*. And the existence of seemingly unjustified evil seems to be pretty good evidence that God doesn't exist.

Of course, that doesn't keep people from believing. Some people claim to have evidence God exists that outweighs the evidence against him—like arguments that make God the first cause, or designer of everything. Yet even most theistic philosophers agree that these kind of arguments fail.[10] Some others may claim evidence in the form of a mystical or religious experience. Mystical experiences are a dime a dozen, however, and lead to a whole range of contradictory beliefs. Few philosophers think such experiences provide any kind of justification for religious belief. Still others, like theistic thinker Alvin Plantinga, claim that God has revealed himself to them through a divine sense, like a tree reveals itself to you through your sense of sight. But our ordinary perceptions are not always trustworthy and should be doubted in the face of contrary evidence. How much more should we doubt a divine sense, which may or may not even exist, in light of contrary evidence like seemingly unjustified evil?

Others might justify their belief in God with something like "Pascal's Wager," which runs: "I'll believe in God anyway. I have nothing to lose and everything to gain." But, again, most philosophers agree that this reasoning is faulty. Belief in God does come with risks; you *could* waste the only life you have on religious pursuits. And confidence in the benefits of theistic belief requires a lot of assumptions: how do you know that God wouldn't rather spend eternity with intellectually honest people who don't believe things without evidence for personal gain, instead of with people who are willing to ignore evidence and believe whatever they think is most beneficial?

Of course, you can choose to take that leap of blind faith anyway. Belief despite evidence to the contrary isn't rational, though. Is it noble? Is faith really a virtue? It's often said that it is, but do you really respect someone who believes something despite evidence to the contrary—like Cartman believing in Jewpacabra despite the fact that he knows he just made it up? And might you be harming others with your belief? Many people think religious belief is personal, that it only affects you. But think about that. The Salem witch trials, 9/11, the Inquisition, the Crusades—they were all fueled by religious belief. And I'm sure you can think of a few more evils in this world today that are, too. Even if you aren't responsible for these particular evils, might your religious belief add legitimacy to religious institutions and structures that are? Are you doing anything to combat the evils your religion licenses?[11]

This isn't a blanket condemnation of everyone who believes in God. But, just as Butters should think about all the times Cartman has gotten him into trouble the next time Cartman appears asking for help, so you should consider the problem of evil as you evaluate your own belief in God.

## Notes

1. It is important to note that one could substitute any evil for "Cartman's complete happiness" and the conclusion would still follow. Often, when the argument is made, the phrase "evil exists" is substituted for "Cartman's complete happiness."

2. See David Kyle Johnson, "A Refutation of Skeptical Theism" in *Sophia* (first published online, Nov. 10, 2012, by Springer Publishing: http://link.springer.com/article/10.1007/s11841-012-0326-0, accessed Feb. 11, 2013).

3. See John Calvin, *Institutes of the Christian Religion*, trans. Henry Beveridge. (Grand Rapids, MI: William B. Eerdmans Publishing Company, 1957), book 1, chapters 16–18; book 3, chapter 23. Also see

Jonathan Edwards, "Wicked Men Useful in Their Destruction Only," in *The Works of President Edwards*, vol. 6, ed. Edward Parsons and Edward Williams. (New York: B. Franklin, 1968). Edwards is mainly addressing the doctrine of hell, but clearly realizes that the existence of evil is necessary for God to demonstrate his holiness.

4. For a wonderful rendition of Edwards argument, see William J Wainwright, "Jonathan Edwards and the Doctrine of Hell," in *Jonathan Edwards: Philosophical Theologian*, ed. Paul Helm and Oliver Crisp. (London: Ashgate Publishing, 2004).

5. See chapters 9 and 10 in Richard Swinburne's *Providence and the Problem of Evil* (Oxford: Oxford University Press, 1998).

6. See "On Free Will," in *Augustine: Earlier Writings*, trans. John Burleigh. (Philadelphia: Westminster Press, 1953).

7. Given that Streisand chose to turn herself into Mecha-Streisand, Mecha-Streisand would not be a natural evil if you counted Barbra Streisand as a human. But this is something I am sure Matt and Trey are not willing to do; thus they probably view Mecha-Streisand as a natural evil.

8. A solution some suggest is this: "Natural evil is a result of Adam and Eve's sin which corrupted and imperfected the world." No professional philosopher or theologian would ever take such an answer seriously, however. First, the Adam and Eve story isn't literally true. Second, it provides no explanation for how the sin causes natural disasters. How exactly does eating a piece of fruit change the laws of physics? And as divine punishment for the sins of our forefathers (or even our own), the suffering natural disasters inflict on us is far out of proportion to the severity of our sins. "Adam ate an apple so I'm going to kill hundreds of thousands, including children, in a Tsunami?" God can't be that cruel. For more on this, and the severity of the problem of natural evil and what it entails, see my article "Natural Evil and the Simulation Hypothesis," *Philo* 14:2 (Fall/Winter 2011).

9. See John Hick, *Evil and the God of Love* (San Francisco: Harper, 1978).

10. For more on these arguments, see my forthcoming course with The Great Courses on Metaphysics. http://www.thegreatcourses.com/.

11. For more on the virtue and rationality of faith, including when it may be rational or virtuous to believe something by faith, see my chapter, "Taking a Leap of Faith: A How-to Guide," in *Inception and Philosophy: Because It's Never Just a Dream* (Wiley-Blackwell, 2011).

# Part III

# SOUTH PARK VERSUS ... RELIGION

# "Respect My Religiositah!"
## South Park and Blasphemy

### David Koepsell

Since the publication of *South Park and Philosophy* in 2007, Parker and Stone have made some additional forays into religious satire, poking fun at staunch supporters of the Catholic Church (via the Easter Bunny) and "militant agnostics" among others. Most importantly for this chapter, in episodes 200 and 201 (with the inspired titles "200" and "201") the "Cartoon Wars" controversy resurfaced, inspiring real-life death threats aimed at Parker and Stone. Additionally, *The Book of Mormon* opened on Broadway. This musical comedy extends the obsession with Mormonism in several *South Park* episodes, featuring a playful, biting, yet loving portrayal of its adherents.

### Don't Make Fun of My Faith!

*South Park* is a show born in blasphemy. Its very first, unaired, episode from 1995 was entitled "Jesus vs. Santa: The Spirit of Christmas" and involves a fight scene in which Jesus employs judo and hurls profanities at jolly old Saint Nick. Since this auspicious start, *South Park*'s creators have spared no major religion in their taunts and mockery. Targets of the *South Park* kids' mockery have included Judaism, Mormonism, Buddhism, Hinduism, Catholicism, and Islam. Today, when there are riots inspired by cartoons and terror bombings fueled by religious rage and sectarian hatred, how can we justify what some consider fuel

*The Ultimate South Park and Philosophy: Respect My Philosophah!*, First Edition.
Edited by Robert Arp and Kevin S. Decker.
© 2013 John Wiley & Sons, Inc. Published 2013 by John Wiley & Sons, Inc.

for the flames? Is there a role for mockery in public discourse of even the most cherished beliefs of billions of believers, or does *South Park* go too far? Answering these questions involves discussing whether there are topics that are off limits for public dialogue or satire, as well as whether and to what degree there is an individual duty to self-censor certain forms of speech concerning "offensive" topics.

No one has ever accused *South Park* of being the pinnacle of good taste. In fact, the filth and offense that Cartman, Stan, Kyle, and Kenny (however muffled) spew are an essential part of its spectacle, if not its charm. In the past decade, affronts to religious belief have abounded, but a few particularly offensive ones now command our attention, thanks to some recent events also involving cartoons. In 2006, Isaac Hayes, the voice of Chef, left due to "religious intolerance" toward his own religion, Scientology. Comedy Central censored episodes depicting the Prophet Muhammad, including a brilliant bit of double satire in which Muhammad delivers a helmet to Peter in a mock episode of *Family Guy*. This censorship is odd, given the show's long history of religious mockery, none of which had garnered nearly as much attention prior to 2006's "Cartoon Wars" episodes.

Has the public climate changed so radically that, all of a sudden, religious mockery is off-limits, or did *South Park* cross some line? It seems as though the former is true, and we are experiencing a cyclical up-tick in tension among religious groups as well as a renewed sensitivity. Historically, religion has been fair game for mockery, satire, and ridicule. In fact, *South Park* has done a brilliant—and offensive—job of mocking, satirizing, and ridiculing religion with little-to-no controversy for 16 years. Let's look at the history of its blasphemy.

In the episode "Jewbilee," Kenny poses as a Jew to join Kyle at "Jew Scouts" where the young Jewish "squirts" make macaroni pictures and soap sculptures for a delighted Moses. In the same episode, Kyle admonishes Kenny: "It's not stupid, Kenny! This is my faith, and you shouldn't make fun of it!" Nonetheless, the entire episode proceeds to do just that.

In "Are You There God? It's Me, Jesus," Jesus is initially treated like the millennial version of Punxsutawney Phil as a predictor of the apocalypse. When Jesus realizes that people are waiting for a sign from him, he goes to his "dad" saying that, if he could help Jesus, this would help with his "one big shot at a comeback." When God refuses,

Jesus arranges a concert with Rod Stewart in Las Vegas, of course. When God himself fails to appear readily at the big event, people become angry enough to try to crucify Jesus *again*. In a touching finale God *does* appear, only to explain to the boys that they will never have menstrual cycles.

Parker and Stone spare no major faith, or lack thereof, as in "Go God Go," where "militant atheist" Richard Dawkins is mocked, and "The Poor Kid," in which "militant agnostics" are amusingly portrayed. In "Super Best Friends," they skewer several at once. When Jesus attempts, and fails, to break the cult-like spell cast by magician David Blaine, he turns to the Super Best Friends, a sort of ecumenical Justice League that includes Lao Tse, Muhammad, Krishna, Joseph Smith, and "Sea Man." Among the jolly blasphemy bandied about in this episode, Muhammad is given the power to shoot fire from his hands, Joseph Smith has magical ice-breath, and Lao Tse can "link mentally with fish." Finally, despite their superpowers, the Super Best Friends are advised by Moses on the best way to defeat a Blaine-animated Lincoln monument. It involves Lao Tse using his powers of Taoism to animate a giant stone John Wilkes Booth. Interestingly, Muhammad's depiction in this episode was not censored by Comedy Central. And as far as we know, no riots ensued.

In August 2002, while sexual abuse scandals peaked in the daily news, "Red Hot Catholic Love" aired. Besides portraying pederasty as an expected and normal portion of the priesthood, the episode reveals that a giant Queen Spider runs the Vatican and interprets Catholic law. Offenses against Judaism and Christianity abound in "A Ladder to Heaven," "Christian Hard Rock," and "The Passion of the Jew." There's more Jesus/Santa hilarity in "Red Sleigh Down," and Catholics got slapped again—this time through a mocking reference to a miraculous icon of Mary that bleeds from its ass—in "Bloody Mary." Bill Donahue, who leads a Catholic anti-defamation group and who protested episodes of *South Park*, is made pope briefly in "Fantastic Easter Special" from 2007, in which he attempts to squelch the "blasphemy" of the "Easter Bunny" (who was allegedly the real St. Peter in a *Da Vinci Code* twist suppressed by the church for millennia). In the episode, in order for Jesus to save Kyle, Stan, and Stan's father from Donahue, Kyle has to kill Jesus so he can regain his superpowers. Of course, the Jew has to do it. Kyle agrees only if Cartman never finds out. Turns out, Peter's rabbit form was intentional, because rabbits can't speak, and no bunny is going to lecture church members on how to live.

Finally, Joseph Smith makes another appearance in "All About Mormons," where Stan and his family learn all about Mormonism after Stan befriends a young Mormon kid named Gary. The history of Mormonism is not-so-subtly critiqued by a chorus that sings, "dumb, dumb, dumb, dumb" with each episode in the tale. When Stan finally decides the story is unbelievable, Gary tells him to believe whatever he wants, but not to denounce him. Stan has a nice family, Gary explains, and he was only trying to be nice, not to convert Stan and his family. Then, in a rare moment of Mormon obscenity, Gary tells them to "suck my balls."

And so, as we see, *South Park* has been littered, not with just offense and mere critique, but also with what, in earlier times, would have been considered punishable blasphemy. Thank the Super Best Friends for free speech!

## Suck My Balls: Is Nothing Sacred?

Frankly, nothing is sacred on *South Park*. But in the first half of the twentieth century, long before the show bravely shattered all pretense of taste, blasphemy could get you thrown in jail, even in the United States with its groundbreaking First Amendment.

The First Amendment protects speech, but not absolutely. Despite the plain guarantee of "freedom of speech," courts, legislatures, and custom have long prohibited certain forms of speech. Notably, and of no comfort to Parker and Stone, obscenity is not protected, and most of us are familiar with the community standards test for obscenity. Besides obscenity, blasphemy has been punished for some time. As late as 1867 in the United States, it was illegal to contract to lease rooms as a forum for lectures concerning the potential truth of Christ's teachings. In 1870, a Pennsylvania court held that the "Infidel Society of Philadelphia" was not entitled to receive a bequest because it was illegal, despite the facts that the society was legally incorporated and the bequest's language and execution were technically correct.[1] Prosecutions for blasphemy were for some time supplanted by prosecutions for "obscenity." Charles C. Moore of Lexington, Kentucky edited the free-thought journal *Blue Grass Blade* and was prosecuted under the state's obscenity laws, serving jail time in 1899. His crime was publishing speculations about the divine nature of Jesus. In 1891, Moses Harman, the editor of an anarchist publication named *Lucifer the Light Bearer* out of Topeka, Kansas, also served jail time for publishing obscene materials speculating about established religious dogmas.[2] If you ask me, that dude was just asking for trouble.

In 1940, the Supreme Court finally extended the protections of the First Amendment to religious criticism and religious argument. In *Cantwell v. Connecticut*, the Supreme Court held:

> In the realm of religious faith, and in that of political belief, sharp differences arise. In both fields the tenets of one man may seem the rankest error to his neighbor. To persuade others to his own point of view, the pleader, as we know, at times, resorts to exaggeration, to vilification of men who have been, or are, prominent in church or state. [patriotic appeal to foundation of US liberties omitted] ... The essential characteristic of these liberties is, that under their shield many types of life, character, opinion and belief can develop unmolested and unobstructed.

This essentially nullified state and local blasphemy ordinances that had been in effect, and enforced so as to bring people to jail for public challenges to the dominant religion—Christianity. The court's ruling echoes the reasoning of the philosopher John Stuart Mill (1806–1873). In his *On Liberty*, Mill makes a compelling case for free and open dialogue on every topic, including those held most sacred by church and state. He argues that only free and open discussion can shake out the truth of any matter. But then Mill made himself liable to prosecution for his own lectures, calling into question the divine authority of the Bible in 1851.[3]

Despite the 1940 ruling in *Cantwell*, two years later, the same court refused to extend their reasoning to "profanity," whatever the fuck that is. In *Chaplinsky v. New Hampshire*, Justice Frank Murphy ruled that profanity enjoyed no First Amendment protection in a case in which a Jehovah's witness—clearly tired of knocking on doors—proclaimed publicly that all religion was a "racket" and then, while being arrested, called the cop a "God damned racketeer" and a "damned fascist." The court reasoned that these exclamations were not a part of the "exposition of ideas," and that the social interest in order and morality clearly outweighed any potential benefit from those words. As Leonard Levy points out, the *Chaplinsky* decision "violates the establishment clause of [the First] amendment by favoring religious beliefs over nonreligious beliefs."[4] This is because "profanity," unlike mere "obscenity," invokes the name of God.

Now, in these enlightened times, neither profanity nor blasphemy is routinely punished, and freedom of speech is extended to the likes of *South Park*, as long as no breast nipples make an appearance. But, despite the legal protection now seemingly afforded the rampant profanity and blasphemy of *South Park*, we should ask whether there's any virtue in self-censorship, tolerance, kindness, and humility, before considering Comedy Central's outright and unprecedented censorship of the show.

## Can't We All Just Get Along?

Nah, not really. That is, we can't unless we all agree not to take affronts to our cherished beliefs personally and, oh, not to kill each other over them, too. Now, with no First Amendment of its own, the European Union's Convention on Human Rights has demonstrated a renewed effort to revive old notions of human rights so as to punish those who denigrate any religion. Recently, there was a failed effort to expand Britain's blasphemy statute in response to the Danish cartoon controversy and other recent disputes, in order to protect religions other than the official state religion (Anglicanism). These efforts seem to follow a line of reasoning that holds certain beliefs are beyond mockery, beyond criticism, and beyond question. But is there a human right to have our beliefs so valued by others?

While the Human Rights Commission in Europe believes so, it is difficult to make an honest philosophical argument for that point of view. Nonetheless, in 1983, the Commission held as much, basing its decision obliquely on the Convention on Human Rights, Article 10. The case involved one Professor James Kirkup, who had published a poem entitled "The Love That Dares to Speak Its Name" that was treated as blasphemous by the Crown and censored. Kirkup took his case to the European Human Rights Commission, alleging that the censorship violated his rights of free expression under that the EU Charter, Article 10. The Commission found the British blasphemy law too vague for Kirkup to conclude his poem was proscribed by it, and that the law may have been too restrictive for a "democratic society."

However, the Commission found that the law did protect the rights of others and was necessary in a democratic society. The Commission held that there was a civil right "not to be offended in [one's] religious feelings by publications." So the law itself did not violate Kirkup's human rights, although its use in his case was unwarranted.[5]

Under the US Constitution, blasphemy can't be legitimately prosecuted, at least for now. Instead, speech may be restricted for other more secular purposes. This is so because elevating *any particular* faith's belief-set above others and beyond criticism, or even ridicule, would violate the establishment clause of the First Amendment, while elevating *every* faith's belief-sets to that level would elevate religion over other sorts of belief and severely cut back free speech. You could claim absolute protection from criticism simply by declaring your set of beliefs "religious," seeking tax-exempt status, and suing those who dare question you … just like Scientologists. Oops! Did I say that? Let's *pretend* I did, and look closely at Comedy Central's reactions to the Islam/*Family Guy* and the Tom Cruise "Trapped in the Closet" episodes, both of which aired in 2005–2006, and both of which were censored by the network.

## Comedy Central Caves In

*South Park* laid a double-whammy on Comedy Central, Scientology, *Family Guy*, and Tom Cruise in these two episodes, which aired within a few months of each other. "Trapped in the Closet" finds Stan attracted to Scientology to heal his alleged depression. Stan learns Scientology dogma while being made into a sort of messiah for the religion/cult. In a none-too-subtle and basically unrelated aside, Tom Cruise gets trapped in a closet, and refuses to come out … of the closet. After this episode aired, Isaac Hayes quit the show, citing the show's "intolerance" of religious beliefs (like this was a new thing). In the episode, Stan learns the actual dogma of Scientology in brief. The "President" of Scientology tells Stan a short version of the story of Xenu, based directly on the actual Scientology OT III document, and this is accompanied by an on-screen caption reading, "THIS IS WHAT SCIENTOLOGISTS ACTUALLY BELIEVE."

Recall that the same device was used in the "All About Mormons" episode that detailed the actual beliefs held sacred by the Church of

Jesus Christ of Latter-Day Saints. But recall also the "dumb, dumb, dumb, dumb" chant. The harshest critique of Scientology comes from Stan's honest desire to transform the church from a profit-making venture into a force for good in people's lives. By a long shot, this show was more kind to Scientology than was "All About Mormons" to Mormonism. Yet, Comedy Central did not re-air the episode after its November 16, 2006, debut, and it's suggested it never will.

In "Cartoon Wars Part II," which aired in April 2006, levels of parody intertwine. Combining the revelation that *Family Guy* is really created by manatees with the appearance of a Bart Simpson-like character who shares Cartman's loathing for *Family Guy*, this episode skewers Comedy Central itself by comparing it to a fictional Fox network that is allegedly censoring the appearance of the Prophet Muhammad in a fictional episode of *Family Guy*. In turn, this episode was itself censored, and a clip featuring the Prophet (as seen in "Super Best Friends") delivering a "salmon helmet" to Peter was replaced by a black screen with text: "Mohammed hands Peter a football helmet." Then another caption follows marked by the distinctly sour tone "Comedy Central refuses to broadcast an image of Mohammed on their network." It cuts back to the citizens of South Park saying how this wasn't bad at all, not offensive or degrading. The show then cuts to a shot of terrorist leader Al-Zawahari, vowing revenge. The revenge takes the form of an Al-Qaeda cartoon featuring various Americans, President George W. Bush, and Jesus all pooping on one another. Of course, the fact that Comedy Central chose not to censor that scene, which was objectively much more objectionable than Muhammad delivering a football helmet to Peter from *Family Guy*, has never been explained. Moreover, Parker and Stone have depicted Muhammad on *South Park* for years, as he makes an appearance, along with many other characters, in the rapid-fire musical montage opening.

## 200–201: The Cartoon Wars Escalate and Guess Who Caves Again?

Episodes "200" and "201" from 2010 saw the return of various targets of Parker's and Stone's wrath, including Tom Cruise. The Super Best Friends make an appearance, as does the Prophet Muhammad, yet again. And, once again, Tom Cruise becomes the butt of homosexual innuendo, depicted as holding a job packing fudge in a fudge factory. Naturally, Stan (who had previously forced Cruise into a closet by denigrating his acting) calls the actor a "fudge packer" because this is literally what Cruise is found to be doing. Cruise sues Stan, and Stan's father forces him back to the factory to apologize, which Cruise agrees to do if Stan and the boys will help Cruise find Muhammad (since the Prophet supposedly has powers that make him immune to ridicule). Apparently, he possesses some form of magical "goo." Kyle and Stan enlist the help of the Super Best Friends to help find Muhammad. Meanwhile, the Ginger Separatist Movement threatens South Park with violence if Muhammad is not turned over to them. They're sick of all the "ginger" jokes and want his goo, too. In episode "201," the boys take Muhammad to Dr. Mephesto's lab for analysis (in the aired episode, Muhammad is blocked out by a black box marked "Censored," and all references to him are "bleeped"). He is then abducted by the Gingers, who begin negotiating for his release to 200 interested celebrities (who want his immunity) if the Gingers can get access to the celebrities' "goo transfer machine." Tom Cruise successfully uses the machine, rating a black box over his own image. Meanwhile, the Super Best Friends arrive to liberate Muhammad. A fight ensues, "Seaman" leaps on Cruise's back, and a series of predictable jokes ensue. Cruise wonders how it's possible that he's being ridiculed, when Kyle explains: "There is no goo, you see. I learned something today ..." Then the rest of his monologue along with Jesus's and Santa Claus' lines are all bleeped. Before "201" aired, the group "Revolution Muslim" posted a warning that Parker and Stone could be harmed or killed if the episode aired. Comedy Central censored the image and audio references to Muhammad. This censorship was loudly and vehemently lambasted, even more so than that for the "Cartoon Wars" episodes, but to this day Comedy Central will not re-air "201," nor is it available on the network's websites. Thankfully, it is available on DVD in its entirety, however.

As a result of the censorship, comedians Bill Maher and Jon Stewart both made public statements against censorship on their shows, and now a new annual "Everyone Draw Muhammad Day" has begun. The irony and shameful hypocrisy is that that the episode contains blasphemy and near-libel of every other sort, yet only Muhammad is spared—clearly his "goo" is powerful stuff.

## Is South Park Responsible for the Decline of Western Civilization?

Every generation has its *South Park*. It was *The Simpsons* more than a decade ago and before that, explicit lyrics à la 2 Live Crew and, before that, punk. And before that, it was rock 'n' roll, drugs, hoop skirts, two-piece bathing suits, chewing gum, sarsaparilla—you get the picture. There's always a scapegoat. Civilization isn't declining. The fact that there were no cartoon riots in the US—nor have there been *South Park* riots—indicates that freedom of speech is working. Tolerance does not require silence, nor does it require an absence of criticism, mockery, or even ridicule.

In fact, many of the blasphemous episodes of *South Park* make just this point. In "The Passion of the Jew," Stan lectures Mel Gibson, who insists that being a good Christian requires enjoying Gibson's "The Passion." "No, dude, if you wanna be Christian, that's cool, but, you should follow what Jesus taught instead of how he got killed. Focusing on how he got killed is what people did in the Dark Ages and it ends up with really bad results." In "Red Hot Catholic Love," Randy, having once again learned a lesson from his son, reclaims his faith, observing: "[Father Maxi's] right, Sharon. We don't have to believe every word of the Bible. They're just stories to help us to live by. We shouldn't toss away the lessons of the Bible just because some assholes in Italy screwed it up." In "Do the Handicapped Go To Hell?" Timmy's inability to give confession or complete his first communion doom him to hell according to Father Maxi, even while some nuns suggest that because he is good, he shouldn't go to hell. Finally, in "All About Mormons," Gary, the little Mormon kid, voices the lesson that Parker and Stone frequently teach in their messed-up way:

> Look, maybe us Mormons do believe in crazy stories that make absolutely no sense, and maybe Joseph Smith did make it all up, but I have a great life, and a great family, and I have *The Book of Mormon* to thank for that. The truth is, I don't care if Joseph Smith made it up, because what the church teaches now is loving your family, being nice, and helping people. And even though people in *this* town might think that's stupid, I still choose to believe in it. All I ever did was try to be your friend, Stan, but you're so high and mighty you couldn't look past my religion and just be my friend back. You've got a lot of growing up to do buddy.

This same loving yet mocking attitude is displayed in spades in Parker's and Stone's hit musical *The Book of Mormon*, illustrating even more clearly their love of Mormons while ridiculing their religion. In a radio interview I did when the show opened, the Mormon counterpoint to my point of view was in near complete agreement with me. They're really nice people, and no death threats have ensued over the musical either.

*South Park*'s ultimately pragmatic view of religion is just this: they mock not the belief, but the believer, and credit the believer where their lives reflect good, ethical practice. They also point out hypocrisy wherever possible. Because the show treats nothing as sacred, this lesson comes across as genuine rather than as preachy. By mocking everything, the show's lessons have a deeper meaning. So, what good did Comedy Central do by censoring a depiction of Muhammad giving someone a helmet? What positive impact is there from refusing to re-air an episode that explains the actual tenets of Scientology? In fact, *South Park*'s continual quest for reason and its mockery of irrationality is legitimate cultural criticism. The mockery of religion is subordinate to mockery of society, a society that overreacts to perceived affronts. There's plenty to be offended by in *South Park*, and it's all treated on an equal basis. Nothing is sacred, and that's what comedy is about. To quote Gary, from the end of the soliloquy above, if you don't like it, Comedy Central, "suck my balls!"

## Notes

1. *Zeisweiss v. James*, 63, Pa. 465.
2. See Fred Whitehead and Verle Muhrer, *Free Thought on the American Frontier* (Amherst, NY: Prometheus Press, 1992).
3. John Stuart Mill, *On Liberty* (New York: Penguin Book, 1975). See *The Infidel Tradition: From Paine to Bradlaugh*, ed. Edward Royle. (New York: Macmillan Publishers, 1976), 206.
4. Leonard Levy, *Blasphemy: Verbal Offense Against the Sacred, from Moses to Salman Rushdie* (Chapel Hill, NC: University of North Carolina Press, 1993).
5. *Lemon v. U.K.*, Decision of the Commission, May 7, 1982. 5 E.H.R.R 123, para. 11. Also see Sheldon Leader, "Blasphemy and Human Rights," *The Modern Law Review* 46 (1983): 338–345.

# Mary's Menses and Morality
## Blasphemy in South Park

*Kevin J. Murtagh*

In "Bloody Mary," a statue of the Virgin Mary is depicted as bleeding, apparently "out its ass." People come from all over to witness this supposed miracle, and a cardinal is sent by the Vatican to inspect the statue. He looks closely at the blood mark, and the statue seemingly farts and sprays blood all over his face. "It's a miracle!" he decrees. Shortly thereafter, Pope Benedict XVI shows up to inspect the statue himself. After the statue "farts" blood into his face, he declares that the statue is not bleeding out its ass, but out its vagina, and that a "chick bleeding out her vagina is no miracle. Chicks bleed out their vaginas all the time."

A statue of the Virgin Mary *bleeding out its ass*? The thought alone is disgusting, and finding out later that the statue was just having its period does nothing to lessen the disgust. And menstrual blood being sprayed *on the pope's face*? This all struck me as over the line, and something about it seemed *wrong*. Have I "gone soft" as I've gotten older? Perhaps I've become a bit of a prude, the kind of person that younger people like to mock for being too stuffy and serious. But I doubt that. After all, "Bloody Mary" made me laugh, even as I cringed.

Are Parker and Stone doing something morally wrong by using blasphemy for comic effect? There seemed to me something morally wrong about the "Bloody Mary" episode. I had, you might say, an *intuition* that some moral boundary was crossed. But, though moral philosophy (the branch of philosophy that's about what we ought to

*The Ultimate South Park and Philosophy: Respect My Philosophah!*, First Edition.
Edited by Robert Arp and Kevin S. Decker.
© 2013 John Wiley & Sons, Inc. Published 2013 by John Wiley & Sons, Inc.

do and how we ought to live) can sometimes begin with intuitions, it can't end with them. A philosophy that proclaims an action moral or immoral has to be grounded in good reasons and solid evidence along with intuitions. Perhaps examining this question through the lens of *utilitarianism*—a very influential moral theory popularized by John Stuart Mill (1806–1873)—will help us to answer it. Utilitarians attempt to calculate the potential positive and negative consequences of acting in a situation. They believe that the morally right decision is the one that promotes the greatest balance of positive over negative consequences, taking everyone who's affected by the decision into consideration.[1] So, from a utilitarian perspective, it may be that blasphemous humor is morally acceptable on grounds that it makes a lot of people happy; or, it may be immoral on grounds that it causes a lot of shock, anger, and displeasure. But before we discuss this ethical issue, it will be helpful to get a better idea of what blasphemy is.

## What in God's Name Is Blasphemy?

"Blasphemy" is difficult to define. Like many words, we have a general idea of what it means, but giving a precise definition of it proves to be difficult. Blasphemy is characterized by irreverence or disrespect for something deemed sacred, such as a god, gods, or "people of God" like the pope, priests, and nuns. Often in *South Park*, a sacred figure is depicted as performing actions that are at odds with his supposed character. The episode "201" provides lots of examples of this sort of blasphemy, including the exchange between Jesus and Buddha after Buddha snorts cocaine:

> JESUS: Buddha, will you lay off that stuff already? It's getting to be a problem.
> BUDDHA: Oh, and you're one to talk, with all of your Internet porn.
> JESUS: Watching porn isn't like doing coke, fag.

In addition to this kind of irreverence, blasphemy often involves showing contempt for or hatred of God.[2] Consider the Mole in the *South Park* movie, who calls God many names, including "cocksucking asshole," "bitch," "faggot," and "fucking rat." If there are any clear instances of blasphemy, these certainly are.

Playing on or making statements that contain religious stereotypes isn't necessarily blasphemy, though. In the episode "Jewpacabra," Cartman claims that "a bloodsucking creature called the Jewpacabra" is in South Park, and he describes it as being "like a Sasquatch, only more elusive, more ferocious, and a little more greedy." This statement, of course, plays on the stereotype that Jews are greedy. As such, it may involve prejudice, but not blasphemy. It's important to point this out, since *South Park* is full of humor that trades on religious stereotypes. This sort of humor, provided it does not also show disrespect for the sacred, is not blasphemous. Of course, that doesn't mean that it's morally acceptable. It just means that it's not blasphemous.

It may also be helpful to offer a definition of blasphemous humor. This is difficult for the same reason that defining blasphemy is difficult: we have a general idea of what *humor* means, but how to formulate a precise definition? Whatever humor is, it seems to have something to do with amusement or funniness.[3] So, for our purposes, we can define *blasphemous humor* as some presentation that's intended to be amusing or funny, in which something deemed sacred is portrayed in a disrespectful or irreverent manner. This definition is far from perfect, but it will suit us just fine. Given this definition, it's clear that *South Park* contains a great deal of blasphemous humor.

## Do You Care at All About People's Feelings? A Utilitarian Perspective

Now that we've clarified some concepts, we can return to our question. Are Parker and Stone doing something morally wrong by using blasphemous humor? Let's attempt to answer this question with utilitarian ethics.

In Chapter 2 of his book *Utilitarianism*, Mill explains his theory in the following way: "The creed which accepts as the foundation of morals 'utility' or the 'greatest happiness principle' holds that actions are right in proportion as they tend to promote happiness; wrong as they tend to produce the reverse of happiness. By happiness is intended pleasure and the absence of pain; by unhappiness, pain and the privation of pleasure."[4] Mill believes there's a single basic moral principle, which he refers to as the "principle of utility" or the "greatest happiness principle." This principle demands that we focus on the consequences of our actions and, in particular, on the happiness and unhappiness produced by them. The moral action will be the one that produces the greatest balance of happiness over unhappiness, everyone considered.

Now, we can't just take into consideration the happiness and unhappiness of those we care about, or those in our community; we have to account for *everyone* who's affected, directly or indirectly, by the action. Beyond this, we must weigh the happiness and unhappiness of each individual equally. Mill is very clear that I can't treat my own happiness as more important than yours, and I cannot take the happiness of my friends to be more important than the happiness of strangers just because I happen to have a close bond with my friends. The happiness of every individual affected by the action must be given equal weight.

A utilitarian needs to consider alternative courses of action and, for each course, must attempt to determine the balance of happiness over unhappiness that would be likely to come about as a result. Here are two alternatives: (1) Parker and Stone making *South Park* with the blasphemous humor, the way they do in fact make it, or (2) Parker and Stone making it without the blasphemous humor. Which course of action would have better consequences? Or, to pose the question in a way that's closer to the language of Mill's theory, which course of action would produce the greater balance of happiness over unhappiness? To answer this question, we need to look at the ways in which the blasphemous humor in *South Park* leads to happiness and the ways in which it leads to unhappiness.

First, let's look at the negative consequences. Quite obviously, blasphemous humor is offensive to many people, and offending people tends to promote unhappiness. Returning to "Bloody Mary," it's clear why Christians were offended by that episode. According to Christian teachings, Mary was the mother of Jesus Christ, the son of God. As the mother of Jesus, Mary is considered to be a sacred figure in the Christian faith. Many Christians pray to Mary, and Catholics especially view her as an individual of immense spiritual importance. So, it's not terribly surprising that many Christians were offended by an episode that depicted a statue of Mary spraying blood out of a bodily orifice onto people's faces (whether it's her "ass" or her vagina seems to matter little). This offense was presumably compounded by the fact that she sprayed blood onto the face of a cardinal and, later, the pope.

In "Cartoon Wars Part I," we actually find Cartman (of all characters!) objecting to blasphemous humor. A little set-up is required here. In this episode, the adults in South Park are terrified because an episode of *Family Guy* that will be aired shortly is supposed to contain a depiction of Muhammad, the Islamic prophet and a sacred figure in the Muslim faith. Muslims consider any sort of depiction of their prophet to be blasphemous, and the adults in South Park are worried that Muslims will be upset by the *Family Guy* episode and will react violently.[5] The episode airs, with the image of Muhammad blacked-out, and Cartman, Stan, and Kyle discuss whether or not it was wrong for the people behind *Family Guy* to attempt to show an image of Muhammad:

| | |
|---|---|
| STAN: | What? What's the big deal? |
| CARTMAN: | What's the big deal? You guys, they just made fun of the religion of an entire group of people. What, you guys think that's okay? Do you care at all about people's feelings? |
| KYLE: | Since when do you care about being sensitive to people's religion, Cartman? |
| STAN: | Yeah, you rip on people's religion all the time! |
| CARTMAN: | That's different! I'm just a little boy! That's a cartoon! Millions of people watch it! How would you feel, Kyle, if there was a cartoon on television that made fun of Jews all the time? Huh? |
| KYLE: | Uhhh … |
| CARTMAN: | I'm telling you guys, it's wrong! |

According to Cartman, it's wrong for the creators of *Family Guy* to use blasphemous humor in this instance because it will offend many people and, thereby, hurt their feelings. What compounds the wrong is that "millions of people watch it," so the offended Muslims will know that millions of people are seeing this depiction of their prophet. The fact that the show is so popular intensifies the insult and increases the unhappiness of the Muslims. Here, Cartman is arguing like a utilitarian, or at least he's backing up his view with reasons that a utilitarian would recognize as relevant. (Of course, Cartman doesn't really care about Muslims. He just hates *Family Guy* and wants it off the air, but that doesn't change the argument.)

The unhappiness that results from offending people is a direct consequence of blasphemous humor, but there may also be some bad *indirect* consequences as well. Utilitarianism demands that we take all consequences (those that are reasonably foreseeable, at least) into account, both direct and indirect. So, what negative consequences might indirectly result from blasphemous humor? In her article "'Just Joking!' The Ethics of Humor," Robin Tapley writes that joking is "another way of putting a belief out into the community. Whether one personally holds a belief to be true is really not the point. It is that beliefs put out into the community, especially in the disarming guise of humor, have the power to challenge, desensitize, confirm, or reinforce our own beliefs and the beliefs that are prevalent in the society."[6] Here, Tapley is writing specifically about jokes, but what she says would hold true for humor in general.

If Tapley is right, the importance for our discussion is clear. Blasphemous humor could lead people to be less tolerant and sensitive in their dealings with certain religious groups, or religious people in general. More people might be tempted to respond to religious claims like a member of the Unified Atheist League in "Go God Go": "Ha, ha, ha. You believe in a supernatural being." Of course, I can't *prove* that the blasphemous episodes have any lasting desensitizing effects, and I don't know of any research that specifically investigates the relationship between exposure to blasphemy and religious sensitivity and tolerance. But there is good reason to believe that what people watch on television and in the movies can have an effect on their attitudes and emotions. Consider the research that supports the claim that exposure to media violence often has the effect of desensitizing people to violence and increasing violent and aggressive behavior.[7] Of course, exposure to violence and exposure to blasphemy are different, but it seems reasonable to suppose that exposure to blasphemous humor could have a desensitizing effect. It's clear how all of this relates to happiness and unhappiness. A lack of sensitivity and tolerance leads to ridicule, conflict, and a lack of respect for others, and, thereby, unhappiness.

## South Park Has the Potential to Make People Think

So far, we've focused on the negative consequences of Parker and Stone's blasphemous humor, looking at ways that it leads, or could lead, to unhappiness. But there are positive consequences as well, and no utilitarian evaluation is complete without looking at both sides of the coin. Again, we need to look at both direct and indirect consequences. Quite clearly, there is at least one positive direct consequence: many people find the blasphemous humor funny. They are entertained by it, and when people are entertained, they tend to be happier. There's really no need to offer extensive support for that.

What good *indirect* consequences result from the blasphemous humor in *South Park*? Let's return to "Bloody Mary." There was much more going on in that episode than the images of a statue of Mary spraying—well, you know. Here's a bit more about the plot. Stan's dad, Randy, is convinced that he is an alcoholic and that he is power-less to control his addiction. When Randy finds out about the bleeding statue, he believes that if he is touched by Mary's "divine ass blood" he will be cured, so he goes to visit the statue, gets sprayed by the blood, and believes that he is cured by this "miracle." He's sober for five days, but then finds out that the bleeding statue is not a miracle (recall the pope's words: "A chick bleeding out her vagina is no miracle"), so he decides that he has not been cured and begins drinking heavily. Stan is upset and they have the following exchange:

> STAN:     Dad, you don't have to do this! You have the power. You haven't drank since seeing the statue.
> RANDY:   But the statue wasn't a miracle!
> STAN:     Yeah. The statue wasn't a miracle, Dad. So that means you did it. That means you didn't have a drink for five days all on your own.

The message here is clear. According to what Stan says, rather than looking to a divine power for help with our problems, we should recognize that we have plenty of willpower and that we can help ourselves.

Now, we're not concerned here with examining the value of this particular message, and Alcoholics Anonymous—which is being sati-rized in this episode—has helped a great many people. What we're concerned with (and this won't come as a surprise to *South Park* fans) is showing that this episode has a message. It has content and presents ideas and, in its own way, makes an argument. Sometimes the message is good, and other times it's bad. But, because there is a message, *South Park* has the potential to make people think. It can, and often does, promote reflection and discussion about important issues. The other chapters in this book are testament to that.

## You Have to Hit Them With a Sledgehammer

But why the blasphemy? Is it really necessary for the good consequences? Yes. People are too complacent. Unless they are somehow
shocked, many people neglect discussing important moral and social
issues. To quote the character John Doe from the movie *Seven*,
"Wanting people to listen, you can't just tap them on the shoulder
anymore. You have to hit them with a sledgehammer. And then you'll
notice you have their strict attention."[8] (I'm aware that the character
is a serial killer, but I like the quotation.) It would be wonderful if
people were more inclined to engage in reflection and discussion
about important issues; however, for whatever reason, they seem not
to be so inclined. Blasphemous humor can shock, unsettle, prod, and
provoke people into thinking and talking.

And to make the tie into utilitarianism explicit, reflection and
discussion are beneficial to individuals and society as a whole. A
society in which there is more discourse and greater exchange of ideas
is, on balance, happier than a society with less social dialogue.[9] In
another book, *On Liberty*, Mill details the benefits of open dialogue.
Discussing ideas, he says, can help to bring us closer to the truth, and
even when it doesn't, discussion of someone's false opinion can help
to prevent the contrary true opinion from becoming "a dead dogma,"
as opposed to "a living truth."[10]

So, we've explored the negative and positive consequences, both
direct and indirect, of blasphemous humor in *South Park*. Now we need
to consider the two main alternatives and their consequences. The first
alternative is *South Park* as is, with the blasphemous humor. The second
alternative is *South Park* without the blasphemous humor. If Parker and
Stone took this second alternative, many of the negative consequences
would be avoided, but many of the positive consequences would be
lost. Sure, the people who were offended would be spared the offense,
and the risk of desensitization and promotion of intolerance would be
avoided. But the show wouldn't have been as funny or as shocking and
controversial and, probably, it would have a much smaller audience.
And if watching *South Park* can be a valuable experience, as I have been
arguing, then many people would have gone without that experience.

Comparing these two alternatives through a utilitarian lens
involves attempting to figure out which course of action would

produce a greater balance of happiness over unhappiness. Figuring this out is, predictably, difficult. First of all, we aren't even close to having all of the relevant information about the actual consequences of the blasphemous humor in *South Park*. Throughout this discussion, I've been using generalizations, analogies, and intuitions. This is often unavoidable when examining a moral issue through a utilitarian lens. Secondly, there is no precise way to measure happiness and unhappiness, so our judgments are imprecise and, to a large extent, intuitive.

All that said, it seems that a greater balance of happiness over unhappiness is brought about by making *South Park* with the blasphemous humor. Of course, people are offended by it, and this fact can't be ignored. But I wonder how many people are actually directly caused significant pain by the blasphemy in *South Park*. Certain media watchdog groups have spoken out against the show, and the Catholic League for Religious and Civil Rights kicked up a lot of dust over "Bloody Mary." But most people who find the blasphemous humor offensive probably don't watch the show in the first place. If they hear about the blasphemous episodes, they may be somewhat distressed, but they probably don't get too terribly upset about the latest *South Park* episode. In short, we need to remember that interest groups aren't necessarily expressing the widespread outrage of the sectors of the population they claim to represent.

Regarding the potential for negative indirect consequences, I'm skeptical as to the extent to which the blasphemous humor in the context of most *South Park* episodes promotes insensitivity and intolerance, especially given that there are aspects of the show that may counteract whatever negative influences there are. Consider the fact that Uncle Jimbo, an intolerant, closed-minded character, is often portrayed as a complete idiot. Also, many of the episodes contain messages of tolerance. In "Go, God, Go," atheist Richard Dawkins is mocked for his supposedly intolerant attitude toward religious people. He is ridiculed for apparently teaching "that using logic and reason isn't enough. You have to be a dick to everyone who doesn't think like you." That episode ends with a character from the future stating one of the lessons: "Tell everyone in the past for us that no one single answer is ever the answer." In another episode, "Super Best Friends," Stan gives voice to the following lesson: "See, all religions have something valuable to teach, but, just like the Super Best Friends learned, it requires a little bit of them all." Whether or not that statement is true, it is certainly an expression of tolerance.

*South Park's* blasphemy operates within the context of an episode and a series of episodes, making the evaluation of its use a complex matter. But all in all, the blasphemy draws a lot of attention to a show that can be very rewarding. *South Park* is indeed a rare show. It is massively successful *and* it tackles important issues, often very explicitly. The characters make arguments all the time. They state their views clearly, and you don't have to be a careful viewer constantly searching for subtext to get the message and the food for thought.

## Just Pissing People Off

I've argued that a public presentation containing blasphemous humor can have negative consequences that are undeniably morally relevant and that it is morally justifiable to use blasphemous humor *if it is an important part of a presentation that has significant social value.* In other words, there must be positive consequences to offset the negative ones. This view has the implication that blasphemous humor "just to piss people off" is morally wrong. If there are no, or minimal, foreseeable positive consequences to offset the negative ones, the blasphemous humor is morally unjustifiable. This implication seems right. Whatever else morality is about, an important part of morality involves being concerned with the consequences of actions and refraining from hurting others pointlessly or merely for profit. So, when people use blasphemous humor gratuitously or merely for financial gain, they are indeed acting wrongly and deserve our moral condemnation, God damn it.

## Notes

1. See John Stuart Mill, *Utilitarianism* (Indianapolis: Hackett Publishing, 2003).
2. See, for example, the entry for "blasphemy" in *Shorter Oxford English Dictionary*, ed. William Trumble and Lesley Brown (Oxford: Oxford University Press, 2002).
3. See, for example, the entry for "humour" in *Shorter Oxford English Dictionary*.

4. Mill, *Utilitarianism*, 7.
5. In case you spent a portion of 2006 under a rock, after the republication in European newspapers of Danish cartoons that depicted Muhammad as a terrorist, violence erupted in, among other places, Afghanistan.
6. Robin Tapley, "'Just Joking!' The Ethics of Humor," *Yeditepe'de Felsefe* 4 (2005): 175.
7. For a discussion of this claim, see the research and discussion in Steven Kirsh, *Children, Adolescents, and Media Violence: A Critical Look at the Research* (Thousand Oaks, CA: Sage Publications, 2006). See also: Dave Grossman and Gloria DeGaetano, *Stop Teaching Our Kids to Kill: A Call to Action Against TV, Movie, and Video Game Violence* (New York: Crown Books, 1999); the papers in Ulla Carlsson (ed.), *Children and Media Violence* (Philadelphia: Coronet Books, 1998); and Henry Nardone and Gregory Bassham, "Pissin' Metal: Columbine, Malvo, and the Matrix of Violence," in William Irwin (ed.), *More Matrix and Philosophy: Revolutions and Reloaded Decoded* (Chicago: Open Court, 2005), 187–190.
8. *Seven*, dir. David Fincher, 127 min., New Line Cinema, 1995, DVD.
9. Consider the general misery and injustices of various kinds of totalitarian regimes, both past and present, where there is limited freedom of speech and expression. See, for example, Michael Halberstam, *Totalitarianism and the Modern Conception of Politics* (New Haven, CT: Yale University Press, 2000).
10. J.S. Mill, *On Liberty* (London: Penguin Books, 1974), 97.

# 10

# *South Park, The Book of Mormon*, and How Religious Fundamentalists Always Find a Way to Be Naive and Arrogant at the Same Time

*Roberto Sirvent and Neil Baker*

A sacred religious text turning into rectal blockage? Mormon angels descending from the starship *Enterprise*? Sounds like blasphemy to most people, but for Trey Parker and Matt Stone, it's business as usual. When we heard the news that the creators of *South Park* were bringing their take on religion to Broadway, it was music to our ears.

*The Book of Mormon* begins as missionaries Kevin Price and Arnold Cunningham eagerly await a location assignment for their two-year mission. The wide-eyed and ambitious Elder Price just knows that he's destined to do something incredible, and his partner, rotund and a bit gauche, is thrilled to be have been paired with him. Now Elder Price has been praying to go to his favorite place in the whole world, Orlando, Florida, but "Heavenly Father" seems to have other plans. Instead, Elders Price and Cunningham are charged with bringing the good book (of Mormon) to poverty-stricken Uganda. Still, they're consoled by the thought that if Africa is anything like what they remember from *The Lion King*, it can't be all bad.

As you can probably guess, the situation in Uganda isn't like *The Lion King* at all. Nevertheless we get the feeling that no amount of evidence to the contrary will be enough to convince these Mormons that

*The Ultimate South Park and Philosophy: Respect My Philosophah!*, First Edition.
Edited by Robert Arp and Kevin S. Decker.
© 2013 John Wiley & Sons, Inc. Published 2013 by John Wiley & Sons, Inc.

there's something fundamentally wrong with their Disney-drenched worldview. Even as Elder Price prepares to confront a hardened Ugandan warlord, we find him belting out:

> I believe—
> That the Lord God created
>         the universe
> I believe—
> That he sent his only son
>         to die for my sins
> And I believe—
> That ancient Jews built boats
>         and sailed to America
> I am a Mormon, and a Mormon just believes!

## A Mormon Just Believes

So why pick on Mormons? The temptation is to take *The Book of Mormon* as a blanket criticism of the Mormon Church, or even of religion in general. But while Elder Price's conviction that the Garden of Eden was in Jackson County, Missouri, may strike us as odd, it doesn't seem to be his belief *itself* that rubs us the wrong way so much as the *way* that he holds it. What is at once amusing and concerning about the "courage" that Elder Price musters in his anthem "I Believe" is that it's defined by an absolute unwillingness to question what clearly seems questionable. This sort of unabashed dogmatism is often associated with *religious fundamentalism*, and in this chapter we'll be giving it some thought. Here's where philosophy can help us. Unlike fundamentalists, philosophers love to ask the difficult questions, and in the pages that follow we'll be letting *The Book of Mormon* and *South Park* get us started asking a few good philosophical questions of our own.

Religious fundamentalism is the real problem that *The Book of Mormon* and *South Park* usually have in mind when they tackle the topic of religion. When we use the word "fundamentalism" we're referring to a certain style of thinking, and so by "religious fundamentalism" we mean only to talk about this intellectual style within a religious context. We're not holding any particular religious movement in mind. The American philosopher Charles Sanders Peirce (1839–1914) famously coined the phrase "the fixation of belief" to describe a phenomenon familiar to anyone who's ever been in a heated discussion on religion or politics: people don't seem to change their minds all that often.[1] This is what happens whenever someone tries to remain so absolutely certain about something she entirely refuses to admit that her beliefs could be wrong. Throughout this chapter we'll see *The Book of Mormon* and *South Park* expose this way of believing for what it really is: a naive and arrogant approach to God, the world, and what it means to be human.

## You're Making Things Up Again

Abandoned by his mission companion, Elder Cunningham has no choice but to convert the Ugandan village on his own. But there's a problem. He's never actually read *The Book of Mormon*. In fact, it isn't uncommon for adherents of the religions "of the book" not to have read the book. (In a society with compulsory primary education we easily forget that throughout history, illiteracy has been the rule.) Nonetheless, given his upbringing, Elder Cunningham does know a thing or two about the story of Joseph Smith. His most difficult project then becomes finding some way to make a story about nineteenth-century America relevant for an audience in twenty-first century Africa. Waltzing into your back yard to dig up golden plates left behind by ancient New England Jews might make for a great American success story, but in an African culture that has to deal with the horrors of AIDS and female circumcision, it's really not all that interesting. As one villager puts it, "Christ never said nothin' about no clitoris!"

In the song "Making Things Up Again," Elder Cunningham's solution is to "fill in the gaps" of the Mormon story using details from the culture in Uganda and his own experience. He's convinced that even though he can't recall anything about female mutilation in the story of Joseph Smith, the practice goes against the will of Christ. Thinking quickly, he "reads" that just before a group of men in ancient New York were about to perform circumcision on a Mormon woman, Jesus teamed up with Boba Fett to stop them (and, naturally, turn them into frogs). In response, his father and Joseph Smith come together to scold him for "making things up again." He was doing far too much "interpreting." But what's ironic about Elder Cunningham's way of bridging the culture gap is that it offers a surprisingly accurate analogy for what almost always happens when religious traditions are transposed into new and different contexts.

Fundamentalist groups tend to understand the world entirely in terms of their "fundamental" or unquestionable beliefs. Now, as the super-intelligent sea otters of the future make clear in the *South Park* episode "Go God Go XII," there are many fundamentalist groups out there that have no particular religious affiliation at all. (In this episode, an atheist leader is quoted as saying, "Our answer to the question is *the only* logical answer"—a telltale sign of fundamentalist thinking.) Where religious fundamentalism is concerned, however, fundamental beliefs will usually originate in sacred texts. But a fundamental can't be a fundamental if it's open to multiple interpretations. For this reason, fundamentalists will insist that there is *only one legitimate way to interpret their scripture*. This one "correct" reading might be dictated by a prominent religious leader, or the group may claim to have determined the author's original meaning in an objective sense. In any case, fundamentalist groups use their sacred texts to pin their faith down into a neat set of dogmas. This kind of thinking lies behind the accusation leveled against Elder Cunningham that in trying to make his Mormon faith understandable and applicable in a new setting, he's "taking the holy word and adding fiction."

This kind of thinking is also what makes the fundamentalist's strategy for interpreting texts both naive and arrogant. First, let's look at the naivety of the religious fundamentalist. In essence, if I believe that I possess the "true" meaning of a certain passage of scripture, what I'm saying is that every alternative interpretation is just that, an interpretation. The word "interpretation" is a red flag to many fundamentalist groups because it seems to imply that the reader has neglected to simply read what is there. In fact, philosophers who study hermeneutics, or the theory of interpretation, refer to this mindset as "naive realism." A big problem with this approach is that the naive realist has fooled herself into thinking that she can somehow rid herself of all her cultural preconceptions and prejudices and just "see" the objective meaning of the text. Philosopher Hans-Georg Gadamer (1900–2002) is famous for arguing that our particular place in history and the world will not just *sometimes* but *always* direct our interpretation.[2] This isn't to say that some interpretations aren't better than others; we're probably right to ask just how Boba Fett made his way into Elder Cunningham's story. We can, however, recognize the naivety of the fundamentalist's assumption that there is some objective "essence" behind the text that's the same for everyone, regardless of their cultural background and life experience.

Already we can begin to see the arrogance of fundamentalist interpretation wrapped up in its naivety. Joseph Smith is convinced that the truth of God has been corrupted by Elder Cunningham's extra cultural "baggage," and so he doesn't hesitate to condemn the elder. But what exactly might the "pure" gospel look like? The answer is simple enough for Elder Price, and we find it in the song "All-American Prophet." There Price informs his potential converts that God's favorite prophet "didn't come from the Middle East like those other holy men." In fact, it just so happens that God's truest voice in history was a white American—just like Elder Price! And if Africans want to reach God, they'll have to start looking more like Elder Price, too.

Here of course Parker and Stone are poking fun at how the pictures of God that religious fundamentalists pull from their scriptures almost always end up turning into self-portraits. Elder Cunningham's sin helps us see that the naive conviction that there's only one right way to interpret a sacred text leads to the arrogant assumption that God shares all of our particular interests and goals. This sort of attitude once brought the renowned German theologian Friedrich Schleiermacher (1768–1834) to quip that "religion never appears in a pure state."[3] By taking *their* truth as *the* truth, religious fundamentalists arrogantly ignore the fact that their interpretations, like everyone else's, are driven by their own presuppositions and values.

## Boys Should Be With Girls, That's Heavenly Father's Plan

Elder Price is struggling with doubt. Why would God choose to send him to Africa when clearly a missionary of his caliber belongs somewhere else? Orlando, Florida, comes to mind. Luckily, Elder McKinley has plenty of experience battling doubt, and he's more than happy to give his fellow elder some advice. You see, throughout Elder McKinley's life he's struggled with difficult feelings of his own—difficult *homosexual* feelings. But these kinds of feelings go against what all Mormons know to be God's design, and Elder McKinley has discovered the secret to beating them:

> When you're feeling certain feelings
> That just don't seem right
> Treat those pesky feelings
> Like a reading light
> And turn 'em off!

Simple enough, right?

The playful tone here belies the frightening reality that Elder McKinley's absurd suggestion is actually a very common "remedy" in religious communities around the world. Most Christian churches teach their members that it's a good thing to respect God's "original design" for the creation, but exactly what this "design" might look like is another issue entirely. Only in communities characterized by religious fundamentalism do people claim to have direct access to the *precise content* of God's plan for the way people ought to live their lives. Let's call this kind of thinking *moral fundamentalism.* The moral "fundamentals" that these religious groups impose on themselves and others most often originate in their sacred scriptures. And while fundamentalist groups occasionally admit that their rules are difficult to apply in some specific cases, they'll insist that, where the big moral questions are concerned, what they preach is God's timeless and unchanging will, the "gospel truth."

It's not hard to see the naivety and arrogance involved with moral fundamentalism, but Parker and Stone make it impossible to miss. Keith Ward, a contemporary philosopher of religion, has suggested that when it comes to the relationship of scripture to moral reasoning, what's more important than blind and dogmatic obedience to an ancient text is the difficult work of interpreting and applying the moral principles of scripture that aren't always clearly stated. Many times a certain principle will need to be reformulated or rethought in order to make sense in a new situation. In other cases we might even need to reconsider the moral quality of a particular text in light of new perspectives on human nature and the natural world.[4] For these reasons it's important to recognize that appealing to scripture when discussing morality in a contemporary context involves a complex process of interpretation. Some of the funniest and most profound moments from *South Park* and

*The Book of Mormon* comment on the insanity that results when religious communities try to skip over this tough process.

Elder McKinley's ridiculous idea that he can simply "turn off" his sexual orientation has already introduced us to the naivety of moral fundamentalism. Does he *really* think that this will work? Parker and Stone ask us the same question in the *South Park* episode "Cartman Sucks," where Butters is sent to Christian conversion therapy because his father suspects he may be "bi-curious" and "confused." There, an ex-gay (but distinctly flamboyant) speaker announces, "With Jesus I can just say no, and not be confused anymore." Of course, Butters is much too young to understand the controversies surrounding sexuality, and if he's confused it's because he doesn't know exactly what it is that he's supposed to be confused about. The real irony, however, lies in the fact that despite his age and innocence, Butters is probably one of the least naive characters in the episode. Like Elder McKinley, the adults of *South Park* cling to the childish notion that determining the moral choice in life's difficult questions is a simple matter of asking what the Bible says.

The eminent Christian theologian Reinhold Niebuhr (1892–1971) warned us that when any institution claims "unconditioned truth for its doctrines and unconditioned moral authority for its standards," it can't help but develop into "just another tool of human pride."[5] Returning to "Cartman Sucks," we see Parker and Stone picking up on Niebuhr's critique. When Butters' young friend Bradley finally exclaims in agony and self-hatred that his homosexuality has made him an abomination of God, his counselor responds, "No, no, we're *fixing* you." Not for a second does the counselor enter into a process of real moral reflection, for this would introduce the risk that it may be his own moral code that needs fixing. A textbook case of arrogance, and, unfortunately, not an uncommon one.

But the arrogance that inevitably follows a lack of appreciation for the complexity of moral problems isn't restricted to right-wing groups. In fact *The Book of Mormon* saves some of its harshest criticism for a moral conviction that shows up across the political spectrum. In "I Am Africa," the missionaries triumphantly proclaim, "Africans are African, but we are Africa!" Taking a direct shot at Bono (Elder Cunningham exclaims that he's become just like the shades-sporting musician and activist), the musical asks us to question the idea that's wheedled its way into mainstream morality that third world nations are incapable of escaping poverty without our help. It's by no means clear what the role of the West should be in the moral issue of poverty, but what is certain is that benefit concerts and bracelets tend to swell more American egos than African economies.

## God Has a Plan for All of Us (That Plan Involves Me Getting My Own Planet)

In a heroic (and hilarious) turn, Elder Price manages to overcome all doubt about his providential calling and decides to take up his mission in Uganda once more. As a Mormon, he has a special knowledge of God's will for history and of his own place within the divine plan. His only task, then, is to continue believing precisely what he's always believed. There's no reason for him to wonder whether or not the things he feels his faith calling him to do are sensible things, or whether they're at all likely to work. He's on the side of the good, the side of God, and he knows with certainty that his Lord will see him through.

So he tries to convert a warlord.

> A warlord who shoots people
> In the face
> What's so scary about that?
> I must trust that my Lord
> Is mightier
> And always has my back.

The Enlightenment philosopher John Locke (1632–1704) once puzzled over this sort of certainty in groups that promote what he called a religious "enthusiasm" among their membership. He found it particularly strange that "whatsoever odd action they find in themselves a strong inclination to do, that impulse is concluded to be a call or direction from heaven, and must be obeyed: it is a commission from above, and they cannot err in executing it."[6] Locke's subject is very familiar to us by now, even if his flowery language seems a little dated (his *Essay Concerning Human Understanding* is more than a century older than the holy scriptures that Joseph Smith published). Locke's commentary applies to a belief that Elder Price shares with nearly all religious fundamentalists, that God reveals his will to select people in special and direct ways. Not coincidentally, these "revelations" almost always mirror the agendas and values of the group in question. As we know, Parker and Stone love to poke fun at this kind of thinking.

The belief that there is a God who acts in order to direct the course of history is not necessarily a bad belief simply because most religious fundamentalists happen to hold it.[7] We haven't been trying to call into question any particular belief so much as a particular *way* of holding beliefs. We would argue, though, that the more dogmatic a believer is, the more likely she will be to confuse her own will for God's will. And this is never a good thing.

Take one of Elder Price's beliefs as an example. For the greater part of the musical, he's convinced that God's mission would be better served if he were carrying out his work in Orlando rather than Uganda. Call me cynical, but I'd be willing to bet that if he were a bit more open to having his beliefs questioned, he might realize that his own desires had just as much to do with his holding this belief as any divine revelation he may have received. At this point Elder Price might have a thing or two to learn from Stan in *South Park*. In the episode "The Biggest Douche in the Universe," Stan exposes the self-proclaimed psychic John Edward, who alleges that he hears mysterious "voices" in his head. Just like Elder Price, Edward believes he has somehow tapped into a reality higher than human reason and that his "feelings" can therefore be trusted as infallible guides. But Stan won't have any of it. When Edward tells him about the voices, Stan quickly replies, "We all hear voices in our head. It's called intuition." Indeed we all have feelings that come from some other place than reason—only, by adulthood most of us have learned that these feelings shouldn't always be acted upon.

Naivete and arrogance inevitably go hand in hand when this kind of thinking crops up. In the episode "Probably," Cartman receives a divine revelation informing him that God wants everyone to give him a dollar. Of course, in this case Cartman is fully aware of his own manipulative schemes, but what's worse than this is when a religious leader utters similar things actually *believing* that his message comes directly from God. The fundamentalist's remarkably naive certainty that his own human desires play no role in his perception of God's will also has the convenient implication that his words carry the unconditioned force of divine authority. This is the worst sort of naivety and arrogance, for by refusing to recognize that he is still human, the religious fundamentalist effectively names himself God. The famous philosopher and theologian Blaise Pascal (1623–1662) had this kind of narcissism in mind when he remarked, "Men never do evil so completely and cheerfully as when they do it from religious conviction."[8]

## I Am a Latter-Day Saint!

Elder Price has been blessed with a new revelation. Sure, upon his visit to Uganda the Mission President had been horrified by Elder Cunningham's "additions" to the scriptures, and for this reason he refused to name even a single member of the new African church a bona fide Latter-day Saint. And, yes, Elder Price's valiant attempt to convert a warlord resulted only in a hospital visit and a permanently shaken faith. Nevertheless, his experience as an African missionary has taught Elder Price something new about his faith, something very important. As he explains, "We are still Latter-day Saints, all of us. Even if we change some things, or break the rules, or have complete doubt that God exists. We can still work together to make *this* our paradise planet."

As paradoxical as it may sound, a genuine, fruitful faith isn't possible until we start learning how to *doubt*. In fact, religious conviction misses its mark whenever it refuses to open itself in humility to the questions of those who hold opposing perspectives. Like Elder Price before his "conversion," religious fundamentalists cling to a tenuous faith that requires certainty, simplicity, and security in order to sustain itself. By contrast, the French philosopher Jacques Ellul (1912–1994) suggested that the "movement of faith is unceasing, because no explanation it offers is ever finished."[9] This, I believe, is the lesson that Elder Price has learned.

Fundamentalist thinkers have the luxury of living in a black and white world of cold absolutes. The rest of us, fortunately or unfortunately, don't. Rather, we have no choice but to live in the real world, a world of difficult questions and deep ambiguities. But the real world is also a fascinating place of brilliant color and real diversity. For the religious believer, it's a place where beliefs are shared and discussed with fellow believers of different creeds and faiths, as well as with those who don't claim any particular faith at all. Now, nobody can deny that the real world is a rough world to call home, and fundamentalist thinking remains a constant temptation. Still, the wise words of the great sage Stan Marsh from "The Biggest Douche in the World" continue to ring true: "The big questions in life are hard." Or as Keith Ward humbly puts it, "Philosophy has no equations, predictions, or conclusive confirmations. That is precisely why some of us become philosophers in the first place."[10]

# Notes

1. Charles S. Peirce, "The Fixation of Belief," *Popular Science Monthly* 12 (1877): 1–15.
2. Hans-Georg Gadamer, *Truth and Method* (New York: Continuum, 2006). For a more technical discussion of Gadamer and the history of hermeneutic philosophy, see Jean Grondin, *Introduction to Philosophical Hermeneutics*, trans. Joel Weinsheimer (New Haven: Yale University Press, 1994). We would also recommend the recent and very accessible introductory text from Monica Vilhauer, *Gadamer's Ethics of Play: Hermeneutics and the Other* (New York: Lexington Books, 2010).
3. Friedrich Schleiermacher, *On Religion: Speeches to Its Cultured Despisers*, trans. Richard Crouter (Cambridge: Cambridge University Press, 1996), 21.
4. Keith Ward, *Is Religion Dangerous?* (Grand Rapids, MI: William B. Eerdmans Publishing Co., 2007), 125–126.
5. Reinhold Niebuhr, *The Nature and Destiny of Man* (Louisville: Westminster John Knox Press, 1966), vol. 1, 201–202.
6. John Locke, *An Essay Concerning Human Understanding* (1690), book 4, chapter 19, sections 6–8.
7. For two notable and differing discussions of this issue, see Alvin Plantinga, *Where the Conflict Really Lies: Science, Religion, and Naturalism* (Oxford: Oxford University Press, 2011) and David Ray Griffin, *God, Power, and Evil: A Process Theodicy* (Louisville, KY: Westminster John Knox Press, 2004).
8. Blaise Pascal, *Penseés* (New York: E.P. Dutton Publishers, 1958), 265.
9. Jacques Ellul, *Living Faith: Belief and Doubt in a Perilous World*, trans. Peter Heinegg (New York: Harper & Row Publishers, 1980), 268.
10. Keith Ward, *The Independent*, Feb. 10, 2009.

# Part IV

# RESPECTING MY AUTHORITAH! IN SOUTH PARK

# Juvenile Hijinks With Serious Subtext

## Dissent and Democracy in South Park

*David Valleau Curtis and Gerald J. Erion*

To first-time viewers, *South Park* might seem to offer little more than crude animation and tasteless jokes expressed with an immature, offensive vulgarity. But Douglas Rushkoff argues in his book *Media Virus!* that sophisticated criticisms of culture often lurk beneath the surface of cartoons, comics, and video games.[1] Such is the case with *South Park*, a show that often conveys a veiled social criticism illuminating principles of democratic political philosophy, including ideas from such great thinkers as Karl Popper and Thomas Jefferson.

For example, consider *South Park*'s treatment of overzealous political activists. Though the show's core characters of Kyle Broflovski and Stan Marsh fill moderate roles, many of the remaining cast members are extremist caricatures who serve as objects for some of the sharpest jokes on *South Park*. Eric Cartman, for instance, often plays a buffoonish exaggeration of a right-wing conservative. Meanwhile, Hollywood celebrities like Rob Reiner appear as liberal fanatics whose political views have little connection to the mainstream. And religious extremists of all types receive particularly harsh treatment. Indeed, anyone familiar with the show knows that this is one of the main reasons why *South Park* is so regularly targeted for censorship, boycott, or outright cancellation.

Maybe extremists receive such unflattering portrayals on *South Park* because they threaten the very free expression that makes the

*The Ultimate South Park and Philosophy: Respect My Philosophah!*, First Edition.
Edited by Robert Arp and Kevin S. Decker.
© 2013 John Wiley & Sons, Inc. Published 2013 by John Wiley & Sons, Inc.

show possible. *South Park* co-creator Trey Parker, for example, hints at this point during an extended interview with his partner Matt Stone on the PBS program *Charlie Rose*: "What we say with the show is not anything new, but I think it is something that is great to put out there. It is that the people screaming on this side and the people screaming on that side are the same people, and it's OK to be someone in the middle, laughing at both of them."[2] But *South Park* doesn't silence the radicals and fanatics it targets. Instead, it allows them to express their views, which are then held up for consideration and subsequent ridicule. So, while extremists are tolerated on *South Park*, they are not permitted to suppress the sort of free expression that is so crucial to the show itself.

In this chapter, we'll explore themes like freedom of expression and what makes for a democratic society by examining characters and situations collected from a variety of *South Park* episodes. Along the way, we'll consider some of the important democratic concepts and arguments presented by thinkers like Popper and Jefferson. Of particular interest are the roles of free expression and unfettered intellectual inquiry—even when they're offensive—in a democratic society. In the end, we'll see that Popper and others understand this sort of freedom to be absolutely *essential* to a healthy democracy.

## Karl Popper, the Open Society, and Its Enemies

An Austrian by birth, Karl Popper (1902–1994) made major contributions to philosophical thinking about knowledge and science. However, it's his demolition of the ideas behind totalitarian government in *The Open Society and Its Enemies* that concerns us here, since we can see dimensions of his critique in many *South Park* episodes.

Popper's problem with totalitarianism is based on the difference between what he calls *closed societies* and *open societies*. Popper's closed societies have social customs that are especially rigid and resistant to criticism. The key to a closed society is "the lack of distinction between the customary or conventional regularities of social life and the regularities found in 'nature'; and this goes often together with the belief that both are enforced by a supernatural will."[3] As a result, the rules and customs of closed societies are relatively clear and uncontroversial. "The right way is always determined by taboos, by magical tribal institutions which can never become objects of critical consideration."[4] It's no surprise, then, that ways of life in closed societies rarely change. When changes do occur, they are more like "religious conversions" or "the introduction of new magical taboos" than careful, rational attempts to improve the lives of the society's members.

On the other hand, Popper's *open society* has customs open to the "rational reflection" of its members.[5] In an open society, reflection and public discussion are important and can ultimately change the society's taboos, rules, and codified laws. In fact, this power extends even to whole governments. Popper claims that the key mark of a democracy is its ability to facilitate wholesale governmental changes without violence.[6]

Popper's critique of closed totalitarian societies is in large part a practical one. To Popper, the most successful societies are able to apply the ideal of uninhibited criticism that lies at the heart of the scientific method to new social problems they might face. As Bryan Magee writes, "because problem solving calls for the bold propounding of trial solutions which are then subjected to criticism and error elimination, [Popper] wants forms of society which permit of the untrammeled assertion of differing proposals, followed by criticism, followed by the genuine possibility of change in the light of criticism."[7] So, open societies are preferable because they permit—or even better, *promote*—a free and critical exchange of ideas. This ultimately leaves them more flexible than closed societies, and they're more capable of creatively dealing with the problems that inevitably confront them.

Of course, not every society is an open society, nor is every open society as open as it should be. Given his experiences in Europe just before World War II, Popper was particularly interested in why democracies are sometimes attracted to the closed totalitarianism of, for instance, Nazism or Fascism. As a result, he devotes considerable attention to this in both *The Open Society* and his later book *The Poverty of Historicism*. The bulk of Popper's work here investigates the political philosophies of Plato and Karl Marx, but what's more important is that Popper understands those on both the extreme right wing and the extreme left wing of the political spectrum as "enemies of the open society." Representatives of both extremes have difficulty tolerating the free and open public discussion that is so necessary in a democracy. Moreover, both left and right are impatient with the imperfections of the democratic process, and both are too quick to reject the possibility that their views might be mistaken.

## South Park and the "Enemies"

Despite the over-the-top themes of most *South Park* episodes, it's likely that co-creators Parker and Stone would share Popper's distrust of political extremism. Time and time again, they develop characters and circumstances that ridicule various "enemies" of the open society. For Parker and Stone, as much as for Popper, democracy is endangered by extremist threats from both the political right and the political left. Recall Parker's claim during the *Charlie Rose* interview that the "people screaming on this side and the people screaming on that side are the same people, and it's OK to be someone in the middle, laughing at both of them." While the strategy of Parker and Stone is not so much to argue with extremists as to mock them, there is no question that the duo consistently singles out fanatics of all sorts for especially vicious treatment.

Consider Cartman. Anti-democratic and authoritarian, Cartman is often portrayed as a ridiculous, albeit unusually young, right-wing fanatic. In an interview with NPR's *Fresh Air*, Parker explains, "We always thought of him as a little Archie Bunker."[8] For example, Cartman brings the dramatic presentation style of conservative television personality Glenn Beck to South Park Elementary's morning announcements in "Dances with Smurfs." He also embraces the role of a xenophobic border patrol agent for a backyard game of "Texans versus Mexicans" in "The Last of the Meheecans." In fantasizing about a career in law enforcement, Cartman yearns not to help people or serve his community, but to have others, as he drawls, "respect my authoritah." (To our horror and amusement, Cartman actually manages to get himself deputized in "Chickenlover.") And Cartman's unchecked interest in making money leads him to webcast fights between cocaine-addicted infants in "Crack Baby Athletic Association." For these and countless other extreme actions, Cartman rarely makes it through an episode without being ridiculed or otherwise punished.

Parker and Stone satirize the political left, too, especially when left-wing politics lead to the sort of hypocrisy inconsistent with an open society. For example, *South Park* often targets liberal efforts sometimes tagged as "political correctness." This is especially true of politically correct attempts to limit offensive language, such as the slurs and epithets in "With Apologies to Jesse Jackson" and "The F Word." But *South Park* targets heavy-handed efforts to control behavior as well. In "Ike's Wee Wee," Mr. Mackey attempts to convince Kyle, Stan, and the rest of Mr. Garrison's class that smoking, alcohol, and drugs are bad. Alas, his presentation doesn't reveal a sophisticated understanding of substance abuse or addiction. Instead, in a rather paternalistic and condescending lecture, Mr. Mackey simply tells the children: "Smoking's bad; you shouldn't smoke. And, uh, alcohol is bad; you shouldn't drink alcohol. And, uh, as for drugs, well, drugs are bad; you shouldn't do drugs."

The left-wing liberalism of many Hollywood celebrities also receives brutal treatment on *South Park*. Indeed, Parker and Stone seem to reserve some of their most merciless attacks for outspoken stars like Tom Cruise, who is portrayed as a litigious hypocrite, fervent cult leader, and closeted homosexual in episodes like "Trapped in the Closet," "200," and "201." Indeed, Cruise was allegedly so upset by "Trapped in the Closet" that he threatened to back out of a promotional blitz for Viacom's *Mission Impossible III* if the episode was rebroadcast. After "Trapped" was pulled, Parker and Stone responded with a satirical statement issued to *Daily Variety*.

So, Scientology, you may have won THIS battle, but the million-year war for earth has just begun! Temporarily anozinizing our episode will NOT stop us from keeping Thetans forever trapped in your pitiful man-bodies. Curses and drat! You have obstructed us for now, but your feeble bid to save humanity will fail! Hail Xenu!!![9]

Cruise is not the only liberal star subjected to *South Park*'s unflattering portrayal; scores of celebrities join forces in a class-action lawsuit against the town in "200." One of the plaintiffs is U2's Bono, who's upset by his portrayal as an emotionally fragile limelight seeker whose humanitarian work fronts for his overinflated ego (in "More Crap"). Likewise, Rob Reiner appears willing to lie, cheat, and sacrifice Cartman's life in order to further his heavy-handed anti-tobacco agenda in "Butt Out." Barbara Streisand's moralizing criticism of both *South Park* and Mike Judge's *Beavis and Butthead* led Parker and

Stone to portray her as a Godzilla-like robotic monster in "Mecha-Streisand." And in "Trapper Keeper," Rosie O'Donnell's proposal to resolve an unsettled kindergarten election with questionable vote recount strategies leads Mr. Garrison to erupt:

> People like you preach tolerance and open-mindedness all the time, but when it comes to Middle America, you think we're all evil and stupid country yokels who need your political enlightenment! Well, just because you're on TV doesn't mean you know crap about the government!

*South Park* clearly exhibits a pattern of criticism of extremist "enemies of the open society," whether right-wing fascist types or sanctimonious liberal celebrities. Some episodes are even constructed to target both the left and right *simultaneously*. "Dances With Smurfs," for example, mocks Glenn Beck's paranoia while attacking the pious liberalism of Hollywood blockbuster films *Avatar* and *Dances with Wolves*. "Whale Whores" satirizes both the whalers and the protesters fighting them. "1%" targets Occupy Wall Street activists while also lampooning the Tea Party's animosity toward President Barack Obama. (For good measure, "1%" also critiques the typically shallow political reporting of mainstream television news outlets that struggle to cover such movements, including Occupy Red Robin.) And "About Last Night …" mocks both the overblown elation of Obama supporters and the overblown fears of his Republican opponents in the aftermath of the 2008 election. As Stone explains in his previously mentioned *Fresh Air* interview, "I guess our political attitude is, '*South Park*'s bigger than both the Republicans and the Democrats.'" Parker then follows up:

> So many episodes are, like, this side of an issue and that side of an issue, and they're all yelling at each other and calling each other evil and stupid, and the boys are in the middle, going, God, just both of you shut up. There's a reason the show's like that, because that's basically who we are.[10]

## Not Tolerating a Tolerance for Intolerance

Popper's contributions to democratic political philosophy also include a component dubbed the *paradox of tolerance*. According to Popper, the sort of tolerance required to keep a democracy healthy requires, ironically, an *intolerance for intolerance*. In other words, those who refuse to let others ask questions and speak their minds ought to be prevented from doing so; otherwise, the open discussion so essential to a healthy democracy will become impossible to maintain. As he puts it, "If we extend unlimited tolerance even to those who are intolerant, if we are not prepared to defend a tolerant society against the onslaught of the intolerant, then the tolerant will be destroyed, and tolerance with them."[11]

*South Park*'s special concern with criticizing and countering intolerance might explain its surprisingly nasty treatment of groups like the Church of Scientology. Popularized by the endorsement of such celebrities (and *South Park* foils) as Tom Cruise and John Travolta, the Church of Scientology also suffers from the public perception that it silences former members and others who criticize its beliefs and practices. In fact, Isaac Hayes, a Scientologist who had long provided a voice for the beloved character Chef, left the show in 2006 because of its treatment of Scientology in episodes like "Trapped in the Closet." (We can only imagine his reaction had he stuck around for "The Return of Chef," an episode produced just after his departure in which Chef joins a cult-like group called "The Super Adventure Club." His lines in "The Return of Chef" were voiced by splicing together bits of his singing and dialogue from earlier episodes in a distinctly awkward but amusing way.)

*South Park*'s willingness to criticize intolerance earned the show a Peabody Award in April of 2006. According to Peabody Awards Program director Horace Newcomb, "We see [*South Park*] as a bold show that deals with issues of censorship and social and cultural topics. My line on *South Park* is that it properly offends everybody by design and by doing so it reminds us all that it's probably a good idea to be tolerant."[12]

## Thomas Jefferson and the Foundations of Modern Democracy

Before we conclude, let's connect Popper's ideas to earlier American thinkers, especially since Popper viewed himself as part of this tradition. Students of American history may notice similarities between Popper's views on free and open expression and those of the great scholar and US President Thomas Jefferson (1743–1826). Jefferson is known as the primary author of the American Declaration of Independence (1776), but he was also one of the foremost intellectuals of the Revolutionary era. Under the influence of some of the same thinkers who later inspired Popper—especially Francis Bacon (1561–1626) and John Locke (1632–1704)—Jefferson pursued a wide range of philosophical interests throughout his life. He was, by all accounts, deeply committed to freedom of thought and expression, a commitment that showed itself in his steadfast defense of religious freedom and tolerance.

While it might be easy for us to take religious freedom for granted today, Jefferson lived in times after the very long and very bloody conflict that engulfed Europe following the Protestant Reformation. He knew well the high social, political, and personal costs of religious discrimination, coercion, and war. Jefferson's preeminent contribution to the defense of religious liberty was his *Virginia Bill for Establishing Religious Freedom*, a document first drafted in 1777 and passed into law in 1786. Jefferson was so proud of the Bill that it was one of the three items that he listed in his self-penned "Epitaph" of 1826.[13]

Rereading the Bill today, it's easy to discern a Popper-like conviction that free and unfettered inquiry is the only good method for gaining knowledge, whether in science, politics, religion, or any other area. "Truth," Jefferson writes, "is great and will prevail if left to herself; [...] she is the proper and sufficient antagonist to error, and has nothing to fear from the conflict unless by human interposition disarmed of her natural weapons, free argument and debate." Jefferson continues, "Errors ceas[e] to be dangerous when [truth] is freely permitted to contradict them." There's also something of a divine hand in free inquiry here, as when Jefferson proclaims that "God hath created the mind free." He concludes with the bold universal declaration that "the rights hereby asserted are of the natural rights of mankind."[14] All this prompts Julian Boyd to write in his editor's footnotes to the Bill: "The Preamble to [Jefferson's] Bill provided philosophical justification, as of natural right, not merely to the ideas of religious toleration and separation of state and church but also for the right of the individual to complete intellectual liberty—'the opinions of men are not the object of civil government, nor under its jurisdiction.'"[15]

Given our earlier discussion of *South Park*'s treatment of the Church of Scientology, and given the show's infamous and insensitive ridicule of Christianity, Judaism, Islam, Mormonism, and other faiths, these are points worth remembering. According to Jefferson, living in the aftermath of tremendous religious violence, "free argument and debate" are the proper means for settling contentious issues. And, as we saw, Popper adds that "rational reflection" supplemented by open public discussion is the most effective way to solve complex social problems. As for *South Park*'s creators, consider Stone's comments during his interview with Parker on *Charlie Rose*: "Where we live is, like, the liberalest liberal part of the world. There's a groupthink, and you only get to some new truth by argument and by dissent, and so we just play devil's advocate all of the time." So *South Park* should be understood as part of a wider intellectual context that champions free—and sometimes offensive—investigation and expression. Instead of limiting discussion about difficult issues when it becomes uncomfortable, Popper, Jefferson, Parker, Stone, and others would be willing to tolerate such discussion for its greater benefits.

## Notes

1.  Douglas Rushkoff, *Media Virus! Hidden Agendas in Popular Culture* (New York: Ballantine Books, 1994), 100–125, 179–209.
2.  *Charlie Rose*, Sept. 26, 2005.
3.  Karl Popper, *The Open Society and Its Enemies* (London: G. Routledge and Sons, 1945), 168.
4.  Ibid., 168.
5.  Ibid., 169.
6.  "Prediction and Prophecy in the Social Sciences," in Karl Popper, *Conjectures and Refutations* (New York: Basic Books, 1962), 344–345. See also Popper's "Public Opinion and Liberal Principles" contained in the same volume, 346–354.
7.  Bryan Magee, *Karl Popper* (New York: Viking, 1973), 70–71.
8.  "South Park Celebrates 14 Years of Fart Jokes," *Fresh Air*, Mar. 24, 2010.
9.  Michael Fleming, "Inside Moves: Is 'South Park' Feeling Some Celebrity Heat?," *Variety Daily*, Mar. 17, 2006: 3.
10. "South Park Celebrates 14 Years of Fart Jokes," *Fresh Air*, Mar. 24, 2010.
11. Popper, *The Open Society and Its Enemies*, 546.
12. Interview with Josh Grossberg, "'South Park,' 'Galactica' Peabody'd," *E! Online*, April 5, 2006.

13.  The other two items were his writing of the Declaration of Indepen-
     dence and his founding of the University of Virginia; it is interesting to
     note the omission from this list of his two terms as President of the
     United States. See the "Epitaph" in Jefferson's *Writings*, ed. Merrill
     D. Peterson (New York: Literary Classics of the U.S., 1984), 706–707.
14.  All quotations from *Writings*, 346–348.
15.  From Julian P. Boyd (ed.), *The Papers of Thomas Jefferson* (Princeton,
     NJ: Princeton University Press, 1950), vol. 2, 547.

# 12

# Of Marx and Mantequilla

## Labor and Immigration in "The Last of the Meheecans"

### Jeffrey Ewing

If Marx had seen the *South Park* episode "The Last of the Meheecans," he may have started his magnum opus *Das Kapital* by paraphrasing Craig Tucker, possibly wearing a blue hat topped with a yellow puffball: "The proletariat is one of those classes who economists can never remember whether they were there or not." Marx, however, grounded his work in recognizing the central importance of labor to human production. The "labor theory of value," a cornerstone of Marx's criticism of capitalist economics, centers on the importance of human labor to the dominant Western system of economic production. The most important statement by Marx about the labor theory of value and economics is in *Das Kapital*, first published in 1867. What Marx seems to be missing is a statement of the impact of race, ethnicity, and gender on the value of "labor-power" under capitalism. One hundred and forty-four years later, its key "missing element" was brought to public attention, very surprisingly, in the *South Park* episode "The Last of the Meheecans." This episode weaves a tale of immigration and labor through the story of Mantequilla, aka Butters, aka the leader of the Great Migration to Mexico of 2011 in a way that highlights how ethnicity and race, specifically, affect the "value of labor-power," a central part of Marx's theory. What can Marx teach us about Mantequilla? And what can Mantequilla teach us about Marx?

*The Ultimate South Park and Philosophy: Respect My Philosophah!*, First Edition.
Edited by Robert Arp and Kevin S. Decker.
© 2013 John Wiley & Sons, Inc. Published 2013 by John Wiley & Sons, Inc.

## Work, Proletariat Work

To Marx, human labor is important in several ways. Labor is the way in which humans create the social and cultural world, and, at the same time, the means by which they create themselves. Labor is also how people interact with non-human nature to meet their needs. Historically, the capitalist economic system (or "mode of production" in Marxian terms) contrasts with pre-capitalist economic systems because human labor makes *commodities*, goods produced specifically for sale on the market. In Marx's theoretical framework, these commodities have two kinds of value: *use* value (how useful they are as a means to something) and *exchange* value (roughly based on the amount of labor and the skill required to produce the commodity). For Marx, the key of looking at economic systems through the lens of the labor theory of value is this: under capitalism, all goods are produced for sale on the market, and their prices are ultimately determined by the "value" of the labor used to produce them.

Under capitalism, however, more than products and raw materials are put up for sale on the market. Labor power is treated as a commodity (of a kind), but unlike other commodities, the value of labor power is directly related to "the value of the means of subsistence necessary for the maintenance of the laborer."[1] Needs and wants of workers vary, though, from place to place, and, as Marx writes, "the number and extent of his so-called necessary wants, as also the modes of satisfying them, are themselves the product of historical development, and depend therefore to a great extent … on the conditions under which, and consequently on the habits and degree of comfort in which, the class of free laborers has been formed."[2]

Marx thinks this introduces "a historical and moral element" into "the determination of the value of labor-power."[3] The value of labor power to the capitalist, while depending on a host of historical factors, ultimately comes down to this: as human organisms, society will only survive if enough workers survive to maintain it. But this also means that the value of labor can be reduced if capitalists find a way to do more with less, and this drastically lowers workers' standards of living.

## Of Jobs and Meheecans

But maybe the labor theory of value doesn't capture the whole story. "Production" means the application of human labor power to either non-human nature or to the products of other human labors, and it's through control over this human labor power that social classes and class power are maintained. Race and gender, both systems of dominating others, intersect with class but operate differently. Both race and gender depend upon the way *bodies* are interpreted in terms of language, behavior, and social institutions, and the socially constructed *meaning* of what it is to have that kind of body.[4] In other words, in Marx's labor theory of value, human work has a particular value to capitalists, and it could take on board dominating relations of race and gender, for societies give different *meanings* to bodies in racialized and gendered ways. Though Marx himself didn't frame his labor theory of value in that way, the convergence of labor power, race, and gender is highlighted in "The Last of the Meheecans."

Racialized populations are often assumed to take up activities and kinds of work that they're seen as more or less "fit for." Where particular people are judged like this to be "less fit" for other kinds of labor, they are less likely (thanks to market logic) to get employed in those areas. Of course, the occupations fit only for groups who fall at the bottom of these dominating social orders are held to have less worth and deserve lower rewards. A capitalist wouldn't even need to personally be a chauvinist to gain from applying this logic, at least if it increases profit harmonized with local norms, meets market demands, and damages labor unity. Is this perfectly consistent change to Marx's own theory of the value of labor power implied in "The Last of the Meheecans"?

The episode begins with the South Park boys playing "Texans versus Mexicans," where the "Texans" (led by Cartman) construct a "border fence" that the "Mexicans" attempt to cross. The faux-Mexicans are led first by Butters, who adopts the "Meheecan" name Mantequilla, but Kyle takes over due to Butters' "inability to lead." The Mexicans succeed, winning the game, but at a sleepover at Cartman's, the boys realize Mantequilla never successfully crossed the border, and the game isn't over. The episode ends with Mantequilla— now recognized as a national hero for restoring Mexican national pride—in a standoff at the border with Cartman.

In "Meheecans," stereotypes about class, labor, and "Mexicans" are hard to miss, from the very first game of "Texans versus Mexicans." Cartman yells at his teammates for letting the Mexican team through: "If you let yourselves get distracted for even one minute, we're gonna be overrun with these jobless, no good ..." and is interrupted before he finishes his sentence. Even in the very beginning of the episode, the stereotypical connection of Mexicans or Mexican-Americans and joblessness is made. When Butters finds himself lost and unable to find the border, he wanders and sings to himself a song whose main lyric is "Work, Mexican, work," alluding to the idea that illegal Latino immigrants are good for nothing in America except cheap, hard labor.

Subtleties of dialogue offer racialized images of Mexicans and Mexican-Americans. Cartman, represents the hyper-patriotic, chew-spitting townie who sees Mexicans as shiftless and lazy, while Butters represents Mexican-Americans, and casually sings to himself a song showing an equally stereotypical image of the Mexican as doomed to perpetual labor. These images conflict, which brings two questions to mind—first, which is correct? Are Mexican-Americans lazy, shiftless, and jobless, or are they the hard-working backbone of much of the American workforce? And second, why do these opposite perceptions of Mexicans and Mexican-Americans and labor exist? Why is the racialization of Mexican-Americans so ambiguous on the topic of labor?

## Window… Wiiiiiindow: The (Mis)uses of Meheecan Labor Power

When Butters/Mantequilla is taken in by the couple who hit him with their car, they take him to their home to recover, assuming him to be a Mexican immigrant who has lost his "amigos" and family crossing the border. The woman begins to "teach" Mantequilla English words, like "Guest room. Bed, bed. Pillow." Soon she directs him to the window, saying to her husband, "He'll have so much more opportunity here than he ever would in Mexico!" Then, to Mantequilla: "Window. Window," as she gives him a bottle of Windex. "Windex. Windex, Mantequilla. Paper towel." His value as a "Mexican," for them, is his capacity to perform their domestic labor.

Mantequilla's situation gets worse rather than better. Later they give him a "present" they've "scraped some money together" for—a leaf blower. The husband asks, "How do you like that, Mantequilla? Your very own leaf blower! Ha-ha! I have no idea how it works, but I'm sure you do, huh? Say, how would you like to go in the back yard and play?" Mantequilla uses his gift later to clean the back yard of leaves: now his value as a Mexican is as an (unpaid) laborer. Their assumption about his ability to use a leaf blower seems to stem from him having some innate "Mexican" *knowledge* as a function of being a "Mexican laborer." Mantequilla soon sings a more elaborate version of his "Work, Mexican, work" song, complete with backing singers. They sing:

| | |
|---|---|
| SINGERS: | Work, Mexican, work. |
| BUTTERS: | All week long, bossman say ... |
| SINGERS: | Work, Mexican, work. |
| BUTTERS: | Sing your song, earn your pay. |
| BOTH: | Work, Mexican, work. Work, Meheecan ... |
| SINGERS: | Sweat. |
| BUTTERS: | Meheecan. |
| SINGERS: | Toil. |
| BUTTERS: | Meheecan, it's your ... |
| BOTH: | ... lot in life. |
| BUTTERS: | While people play in the sun all day ... |
| BOTH: | Work, Mexican, work. |

Butters' showier version of the song equates the life of a Mexican/ Mexican-American with perpetual work (sweat and toil), while non-Mexicans/Mexican-Americans get to play in the sun and enjoy life, complete with a "bossman" or dominating employers demanding ever more labor from Mexicans and Mexican-Americans.

Mantequilla's song and his treatment by the couple show that there's a racialized association between being Mexican or Mexican-American and being inclined to, and happy with, hard, perpetual work by *nature* or *custom*. For Mantequilla, perpetual "sweat" and "toil" is what "bossman say," and this is underscored by the fact that so many whites can "play in the sun all day" *because* of Mexican and Mexican-American work. Soon the husband finds his wife crying and asks her what's wrong. She says: "It's Mantequilla. We've tried giving him everything, but I don't think he's happy. Tonight I told him he could do whatever he wanted before bed—wash the dishes, mop up our bathroom—but you know what he said? 'I need to go home.' I tried telling him, 'your home is here, Mantequilla! ¡Tu casa es aquí!' But I don't think he feels it."

His misery isn't the result of being treated as a pack animal within their home (indeed, he could clean *whatever he* wanted—let's forget for a second that he doesn't have the option *not to clean*). The couple's prescription is that Mantequilla belongs with "his own kind," and so they drop him off at a Mexican restaurant.

This sets off a chain reaction when Mantequilla convinces the restaurant employees to return to Mexico, and they proceed to tell their friends and family (all in varied service industry jobs) to do the same. Unlike the white family who can't tell Mantequilla *isn't actually Mexican*, Butters doesn't fool the workers at the Mexican restaurant for *un minuto*. To them, it's strange that there is "a white American kid who wants to be Mexican" but they still conclude, "Mantequilla is RIGHT! Why did we even come to this country? It SUCKS HERE, MAN!" This starts a mass migration of Mexican-Americans past the border from the US to Mexico and the border patrol has to reverse its normal operations in order to keep Mexican-Americans from leaving the US. As a confused TV anchorman says: "You've heard of Mexican salsa, but Mexican pride? The phenomenon is called 'Orgullo de Mantequilla,' where Mexicans are realizing it actually is starting to suck more here in the US. The borders are being flooded with Latin Americans trying to get back to their own countries." The mass migration results when recognition blossoms about how terrible it is to be a population that's "super-exploited" because of their racialization within the US society and economy. "The Last of the Meheecans" shows two things: first, that Mexican and Mexican-American labor is just as important as it is disrespected in US society; second, the racialization of this population in the US involves two conflicting stereotypes—that Mexicans and Mexican-Americans are lazy *and* that they excel at demeaning, difficult service work.

## Marx, Race, and Nation

Marx isn't known for his in-depth treatment of race or ethnicity, but he also doesn't ignore these topics. Marx scholar Kevin Anderson suggests that Marx's writings "on oppressed nationalities and ethnic groups ... became central to Marx's assessment of the working-class movements of the two most powerful capitalist societies, Britain and the United States. He concluded that labor movements in core capitalist countries that failed to support adequately progressive nationalist movements on the part of those affected by their governments, or failed to combat racism toward ethnic minorities within their own societies, ran the danger of retarding or even cutting short their own development."[5] The charge has been made, though, that Marx's earliest writings on issues of nation and ethnicity reveal a certain "Eurocentrism." In the *Communist Manifesto*, for example, Marx and Friedrich Engels write:

> The bourgeoisie, by the rapid improvement of all instruments of production, by the immensely facilitated means of communication, draws all, even the most barbarian nations into civilization. The cheap prices of its commodities are the heavy artillery with which it batters down all Chinese walls, with which it forces the barbarians' intensely obstinate hatred of the foreigners to capitulate. It compels all nations, on pain of extinction, to adopt the bourgeois mode of production; it compels them to introduce what it calls civilization into their midst, i.e. to become bourgeois themselves. In one word, it creates a world after its own image.[6]

Marx's thoughts about colonialism evolve, though, in his progressive studies of Polish and Irish national liberation movements, as well as slavery and the American Civil War.

Issues of national independence were deeply connected with class struggles for Marx. For example, in the *Communist Manifesto* Marx says that with "the supremacy of the proletariat," class exploitation will end, but so will "the exploitation of one nation by another."[7] Engels, too, noted the importance of national liberation movements for class struggles within the dominant European countries. Engels supported the 1846 Polish insurrection, arguing that "by opposing Russia, the Poles were also undermining the major external support of the Prussian monarchy, and 'henceforth the German people and the Polish people are irrevocably allied'."[8] For the Polish uprising of 1863, Marx had drafted an unsigned, short statement of support:

> In this fateful moment, the German working class owes it to the Poles, to foreign countries and to its own honor to raise a loud protest against the German betrayal of Poland, which is at the same time treason to Germany and to Europe. It must inscribe the *Restoration of Poland* in letters of flame on its banner, since bourgeois liberalism has erased this glorious motto from its own flag. The English working class has won immortal historical honor for itself by thwarting the repeated attempts of the ruling classes to intervene on behalf of the American slaveholders by its enthusiastic mass-meetings ... If police restrictions prevent the working class in Germany from conducting demonstrations on such a

scale for Poland, they do not in any way force them to brand themselves in the eyes of the world as accomplices in the betrayal, through apathy and silence.[9]

Marx also offers unconditional support for the abolition of American slavery in several newspaper articles. In 1860, Marx wrote that "in my view, the most momentous thing happening in the world today is, on the one hand, the movement among the slaves in America, started by the death of [John] Brown, and the movement among the slaves in Russia, on the other."[10] Issues of race and nation were deeply important to Marx.

Less well known is that fact that Marx also exulted about Abraham Lincoln's reelection on behalf of the First International, which he helped organize:

> While the working men, the true political power of the North, allowed slavery to defile their own republic; while before the Negro, mastered and sold without his concurrence, they boasted it the highest prerogative of the white-skinned laborer to sell himself and choose his own master; they were unable to attain the true freedom of labor or to support their European brethren in their struggle for emancipation, but this barrier to progress has been swept off by the red sea of civil war.[11]

This language is matched in a 1866 letter from Marx to Paul Lafargue, a French socialist and journalist. Marx talks about recent Congressional victories of radical Republicans in the US, in which he notes that "the workers of the North have finally understood very well that labor in the white skin cannot emancipate itself where in the black skin it is branded"[12] For Marx, interracial unity was a condition for the revolutionary overcoming of class society, and clearly the existence of racialized slavery (or racialized subjugation of any kind), defines both the nation in which it occurs and the dominant race of that nation. Most importantly, it's an obstacle to the freedom of the entire working class.

## All You Have to Lose Is Your *Encadenamientos*

The Marx best known for *Das Kapital* kept issues of nation, ethnicity, and race mostly outside of his analysis of the value of labor power in an explicit manner. But it's clear that he treated such value as socially determined, a process based on the actual social needs of a population of workers, given what that population is used to in their place, time, and circumstances. But as Marx started to analyze the political issues of his day, he highlighted issues of national liberation, opposed colonization and slavery, and advocated interracial solidarity. Marx and Engels both criticized the use of national and racial divisions by ruling classes to divide laborers from each other, emphasizing that international and interracial unity among laborers must be achieved in order for collective freedom from class society to be achievable. Marx's labor theory of value is about due, as a result, for a reevaluation in terms of the socially constructed division of people based on their value as members of a particular nation, ethnicity, race, or gender. As soon as Butters becomes racialized when he's interpreted as a Meheecan, he's treated as though his nature is to clean and engage in hard domestic labor. "The Last of the Meheecans" hilariously illustrates the connection between race, ethnicity, and nation, on the one hand, and class and labor power, on the other. It does this in the very way that Marx's labor theory of value connects to his thoughts on nationalities and races. And it leaves us with but one conclusion: Meheecans of the World Unite!

## Notes

1. Karl Marx, S. Moore, and E.B. Aveling, *Capital: A Critique of Political Economy*, ed. F. Engels and E. Untermann (New York: Modern Library: 1936), 190.
2. Ibid.
3. Ibid.
4. A lot of has been written on the social construction of race and gender, but the events of "The Last of the Meheecans" truly begin when Butters/ Mantequilla is *falsely* taken to be from Mexico. His "Mexican" identity as Mantequilla is the product of assumptions about him as part of a "racialized" population, and when this happens, his behaviors, traits, history, and limitations are filtered through a racist lens.
5. Kevin Anderson, *Marx at the Margins: On Nationalism, Ethnicity, and Non-Western Societies* (Chicago: The University of Chicago Press, 2010), 3.
6. Marx and Engels, *The Communist Manifesto*. Retrieved from http://www.marxists.org/archive/marx/works/1848/communist-manifesto/ch01.htm#007, accessed Feb. 12, 2013.

7.  Anderson, *Marx at the Margins*, 58.
8.  Ibid., 60.
9.  Ibid., 66.
10.  Ibid., 85.
11.  Ibid., 110.
12.  Ibid., 114.

# 13

# "Vote or Die, Bitch"
## Does Every Vote Count in a Two-Party System?

### John Scott Gray

Patrick Henry famously exclaimed, "Give me liberty or give me death!" Some people might argue that this statement could be a motto worthy of the American democratic experience. As evidence, they might also point to how our free elections put officials in positions of power, and then take them out, in a non-violent fashion. The passing of political power as representative of the will of the people rests on questionable assumptions, though. For one, the American founders gave the power of the vote to very few of the new nation's inhabitants, allowing a small number of men to select office-holders in the legislative branch. Also, American democracy rests on the moral idea that every vote counts and counts equally. This can be questioned by looking at statistics, especially in light of the 2000 and 2004 presidential election controversies.

*South Park* dealt with these issues in the 2004 episode "Douche and Turd," parodying the American election process in the attempt to ratify a new school mascot. After the initial selection of nominees, the boys are forced to select between a Giant Douche and a Turd Sandwich in a run-off. Stan doesn't care about the issue and decides not to vote. This decision leads to the introduction of Puff Daddy, who enlightens Stan about his "Vote or Die" campaign. Stan is forced to consider the value of the election process and in the end casts a vote for the Turd Sandwich, who loses in a landslide. How important was Stan's vote,

*The Ultimate South Park and Philosophy: Respect My Philosophah!*, First Edition.
Edited by Robert Arp and Kevin S. Decker.
© 2013 John Wiley & Sons, Inc. Published 2013 by John Wiley & Sons, Inc.

given that the election went soundly against his choice? Would the vote have been more valuable had the final margin of victory been closer? Also, how important is a vote that is between only two viable and equally unsavory options?

Questions like these are the subject of *political philosophy*, which evaluates political institutions and the ways in which they're constructed. In light of *South Park*'s parody of the election process, this chapter engages with these questions by looking at how the power to vote has been extended in the United States over the past 200 years and discussing the voting irregularities that arose in the 2000 and 2004 presidential elections. This chapter will also consider the problem of choice within a two-party system, given the South Park PETA member's comment that every election is "always between a giant douche and a turd sandwich."

## Enfranchised? So What!

In the twentieth and twenty-first centuries, Americans have taken the ability to vote for granted. Any student of history knows that the founders viewed voting as a privilege worthy of only the best citizens society had to offer, with only white male landowners able to cast ballots. Such voting *directly* elected only members of the House of Representatives, with the presidency decided by the Electoral College and US Senators appointed by the various state legislatures. In the process of amending the Constitution, ten of the 17 amendments proposed after the Bill of Rights either directly or indirectly dealt with elections. Of these changes, the most important was the Fifteenth Amendment (1870), giving freed male slaves the right—at least in principle—to vote. Also noteworthy were the Seventeenth Amendment (1913), making the election of senators a direct election; the Nineteenth Amendment (1920), giving women the right to vote; and the Twentieth-Sixth Amendment (1971), making the minimum voting age 18.[1]

Given the suffering and hardships so many people had to endure in order to ensure their right to vote, one might think that nearly every eligible American would choose to exercise their right. But, just like Stan in "Douche and Turd," many Americans choose not to vote. Nearly 40% of the *eligible* voters chose not to vote in the general election of 2004, and over a million *actual* voters didn't cast a ballot for that presidential race. While the general trend in voter turnout has been downward since the 1960s—with voting-age turnout at 63.1% in 1960—the numbers for the Bush–Kerry election are surprising given the controversy that surrounded the 2000 election. Data from the "United States Elections Project" show that tens of millions of possible voters now fail to make the trip to their local ballot box, with only 60.7% of the voting-eligible population voting in the fall of 2004 and 62.2% in 2008 (at the time of writing, data from 2012 are still being analyzed, but it appears that the turnout percentage will drop slightly from 2008).[2] Maybe Stan's desire not to vote is a part of this trend because of lack of interest in the two nominees, or maybe he shared real voters' feelings that a single vote did not matter in the larger scheme of things. Is the trend that Stan represents symbolic of a growing sense of apathy, or is something more going on?

In polls held after the 2000 presidential election was resolved, many people thought that the voters had little to say in nominating presidential candidates and in the final selection of the chief executive. We might write this sentiment off as being due to the controversial ballot counting in Florida and the contentious court proceedings that ultimately upheld the initial results, giving the state's electoral votes—and the presidency—to George W. Bush. Political commentators, however, are able to point to more general reasons for this disillusionment. They include the fact that the elections are often decided by millions of votes (at least in terms of the popular vote), the way in which the Electoral College separates actual voters from the process of determining the new president, the length of the process, and the many ways in which the elections can be contested. There's also widespread uncertainty about the counting of the votes, with some estimates saying that as many as 3% of the ballots cast nationwide during the 2000 election were invalidated because of some irregularity.[3]

Stan's also left feeling that his vote didn't matter, given that his candidate lost by a margin of 1410 votes to 36. His father disagrees, and his mother says that you can't judge the validity of an election by whether or not a given candidate wins. Still, Stan's helplessness is felt, as we just saw, by millions of voters. Considering the size of winning margins, we might understandably feel as if our votes didn't matter in landslides, but this can also be true of close races. Logically speaking, very few races are so close—that is, tied or won by a one-vote margin—so that a single vote can actually change the outcome.

## Going to (Electoral) College

Whether or not your individual vote matters in elections decided by large margins, the role of the Electoral College further alienates many voters.[4] The Electoral College is the system created by the Founders to elect an individual to the presidency. The decision is based on groups of electors, who are chosen by each political party that gains a large enough share of the vote. The percentages of electors are determined by the majority popular vote in each state. The number of electors assigned to each state is equal to the number of representatives in the House and Senate, with the exception of Washington DC, whose electors are based on their population.[5] Currently, 48 states award *all* of the Electoral College votes to the candidate that won a simple plurality of the votes in that state.

In fact, presidential candidates now run two different types of campaigns. The "sure thing" states receive little attention or fanfare while the "swing" states get saturated with ads and appearances by the candidates. According to political scientist Thomas Patterson, "Residents of competitive states are exposed to a vigorous campaigning ... Residents of other states get to see only part of the campaign, and their votes are discounted, which diminishes their interest in going to the polls."[6] Because most presidential elections boil down to roughly ten "battleground" states such as Ohio, Florida, and Pennsylvania, potential voters in other states may be less motivated to take action, both in terms of campaign volunteering or voting. No other large democracy uses an Electoral College system to select its head of state, and most other democracies don't delegate the authority to individual states in order to decide the national executive, but instead conduct the election on a national level, with uniform balloting procedures.[7] It's not uncommon to hear that the American voter's growing apathy is due to a feeling of powerlessness. In essence, the Electoral College turns more than half of the country into mere spectators.

The Electoral College is just one of America's *disincentives to vote*. These disincentives—or the costs of voting to the potential voter—include early network projections on election night declaring who's won the election before many polls have even closed. Early poll closing times are another factor, with 26 states requiring people to vote before 7:30 p.m. Estimates seem to show that turnout in these states is 3% lower than in states whose polls close at 8:00 p.m. or later. Beyond this, the complicated voter registration process, which is handled independently by each state, also confuses the matter for many. The frequency and number of elections in the United States, including primaries, general elections, run-offs, midterms, odd-year locals, and special elections, is said to lead to "voter fatigue." Furthermore, the fact that elections are held on Tuesdays instead of on holidays or weekends (unlike many other democracies) further compounds the problem.[8]

## Liberty or Death?

We owe John Locke (1632–1704), one of the most influential philosophers of all time, a debt for introducing to political philosophy the inalienable rights to life and liberty that are so much a part of our founding documents, like the Declaration of Independence. In his *Second Treatise of Government*, Locke argued that political authority comes from the consent of the people. If Locke is correct, isn't voting the primary avenue for granting consent? When Stan refuses to vote for one of the two new school mascots, in essence he's rejecting the authority of both of the candidates to represent him. Although Stan might be alone in his protest in South Park, he's joined by nearly half of all Americans eligible to vote every presidential year—and by nearly two-thirds during midterm elections.

John Stuart Mill (1806–1873) would likely have agreed with Locke and so he'd see the trend of more people choosing not to cast ballots as particularly problematic. Ahead of his time, Mill argued for granting suffrage to under-represented and non-represented groups, arguing that voting deepens community interconnectedness and involvement, and also provides greater legitimacy to political institutions themselves. Mill said that for these institutions, at "every stage of their existence they are made what they are by human voluntary agency ... It needs, not their simple acquiescence, but their active participation."[9] For Mill, the case of tens of millions of Americans simply not being motivated to get involved in the process is worthy of close inspection.

Mill's primary concern was the protection of individual liberty. In his essay *On Liberty*, Mill argued that political systems need to represent the interests of the people yet not fall prey to the "tyranny of the majority." This is what often happens when the majority sees its view as right regardless of how unjust the consequences might be to minorities. Mill based his political philosophy on the simple premise that government should never interfere with the liberty of individuals unless interference is needed to prevent harm to others. These basic limits would help foster liberty, but Mill wouldn't have favored limits that discouraged individuals from participating in the selection of their representatives.[10]

Although in the US people feel free to choose not to vote, Stan feels immense pressure from both his family and friends. When Stan originally declares he isn't going to vote, Kyle reminds him of Puff Daddy's "Vote or Die" campaign, mimicking the real Sean "Puff Daddy" Comb's T-shirt campaign to get young voters involved. In the world of *South Park*, Puff Daddy and his posse immediately rush to the scene to convince Stan of the importance of his vote. Puff Daddy particularly emphasizes the "die" option by whipping out a gun from his back pocket, cocking it, and pointing it squarely at Stan. The threats of violence from Puff Daddy, as well as the decision by the people of South Park to banish Stan from the town for not voting, mirror the social pressure, rather than a sense of civic duty, that motivates many people to vote.[11]

"Vote or Die" and other campaigns like "Rock the Vote" tend to be directed at younger voters. There's good reason for this, as citizens who lived through great national crises like World War II and the Cold War are slowly being replaced by the X and Millennial (sometimes referred to as Y) generations. Older generations are seen as more civic-minded due to their life experiences, but potential X- and Y-gen voters tend to be more private and individualistic, and are less tied to traditional conceptions of civic duty, especially political activism. A lot of data support these claims: in 1972, the voting rate of adults under 30 years hovered around 50%, yet it was barely above 30% by the 2000 election.[12] While the numbers did increase to near their 1972 levels in the 2004 election, the states that showed the largest jump in under-30 voting were the battleground states discussed above. This shows that youth in neglected states still aren't going to the polls in overwhelming numbers. Even in the 2008 election, which continued a recent upward trend in presidential election turnout, with 62.2% of the voting-eligible population voting, we still saw over 80 million eligible voters simply choose not to go to the polls (and

2012 could be as low as 61% according to some projections). Midterm, primary, and local elections still maintain much poorer turnout percentages.

## Vote for Me, and Only for Me

Stan is plagued by people telling him to vote only because they believe he'll vote for their mascot. Kyle tells Kenny, "We have got to make Stan understand the importance of voting, because he'll definitely vote for our guy." At one point, after Puff Daddy's first intervention, Stan temporarily decides to cast a vote, a move cheered on by Kyle until he realizes that Stan is actually voting for Cartman's candidate. Kyle criticizes Stan's decision, and Stan replies, "I thought I was supposed to make my own decision." Kyle responds, "Well yeah, but not if your decision is for Turd Sandwich! What the hell is wrong with you?" Cartman also seems to take politicking to the extreme as he and Butters use candy to try and sway undecided voters, including Clyde, to their Turd Sandwich candidate. He even offers to help Stan vote, promising a steak dinner after the process is completed. Stan resists this ploy, though, and refuses to be manipulated into making a choice.

Not even kindergartners are safe from pressure and tricks. In the episode "Trapper Keeper" the class is called upon to elect a new class president, but a stalemate ensues when Flora is unable to choose between Filmore and Kyle's little brother, Ike. The vote is tied at six each, and Mr. Garrison tells Flora that she will cast the winning vote. He can't read her hand-written ballot, so he asks her whom she picked. When Flora says that she doesn't know, Mr. Garrison forces the issue, telling her that she has to pick one. As Flora tries to decide, the other kids argue, trying to get her to cast her deciding vote for their pick. The situation escalates when Rosie O'Donnell, Filmore's aunt, comes on the scene to help make sure "that the kids that voted for my nephew don't get cheated," and calls for recount after recount. Mr. Garrison stands up to Rosie: "Half the kids in the class didn't vote for your nephew, so what about them? You don't give a crap about them because they're not on your side!" In the end, Filmore drops out because he doesn't want to play the stupid game anymore, letting Ike become class president. Ike promptly declares that he pooped his pants, and the class begins to finger-paint.

## You Wanna (Third) Party?

Stan's resistance to voting has mainly to do with his feelings about the two candidates. In the end he admits "I learned that I'd better get used to having to pick between a douche and a turd sandwich because it's usually the choice I'll have." Perhaps if Stan or Flora didn't feel that their choices were limited to those two options, they might feel more inclined to vote. In American politics, there are alternate choices represented by third parties (including the Green, Libertarian, Constitution, and Natural Law parties), but these options are usually not seen as legitimate. The games of presidential politics are dominated by the two major parties, given how elections are structured in terms of winner-takes-all and how debates are closed to other parties.

The debates are controlled by the Commission on Presidential Debates, which was created in 1987 with the support of the two major parties. The rules of the Commission require that a third-party candidate must perform strongly in the polls, must possess strong organizational resources, and must be seen as having a viable campaign with a realistic chance of winning the election in order to be included in the televised debates. This policy begs key questions about what "viable" campaigns and "realistic" chances are. It's these rules that excluded Ross Perot from the 1996 debates, even though he had an impressive showing in the previous election.[13] Ralph Nader has also had great difficulty with the Commission, and he was excluded from the debate process even though some believe that his Green Party candidacy may have swung the election away from Al Gore in 2000.[14]

Stan's choice between the douche and the turd is captured in a song played as he finally votes:

> Let's get out the vote!
> Let's make our voices heard!
> We've been given the right to choose
> between a douche and a turd.
>
> It's democracy in action!
> Put your freedom to the test.
> A big fat turd or a stupid douche.
> Which do you like best?

This distasteful duality of choice is even more troublesome for voters who see their vote as a type of self-expression or self-definition. According to political scientists Geoffrey Brennan and Loren Lomasky, "If individuals do genuinely vote merely as an act of self-expression ... Surely individuals need a larger repertoire of political positions than two in order to define themselves and/or express their political affections."[15] Our two-party system appears to have too little room for third parties. But if we attempted election reform along the lines of a proportional representation system (instead of winner-take-all), third parties might get more attention. In a proportional representation system, the percentage of votes received by a party determines the percentage of seats they obtain in the legislature. Even if proportional representation were only applied to the Electoral College system, so that the percentage of the vote in each state would translate into the fraction of electoral votes received for that candidate, more people might be less alienated by the election process.

More political parties might also undermine the atmosphere of partisan vitriol that exists today. The 2008 post-election episode "About Last Night ..." captures that atmosphere, with Randy Marsh and his friends chanting loser to the neighbors across the street, believing that "everything is going to be awesome now ... this is the greatest day of our lives!" The "losers" across the street, including Mr. Garrison and Butters' parents, think that Obama's "change" will mean the end of civilization, so they make an ark in the side of a mountain to try to survive when society breaks down. This clear division is even seen in the hospital, where the nurse determines if incoming patients partied too hard or had tried to kill themselves by asking if they supported Obama or McCain. This kind of divisive extremism can leave those in the middle feeling that they're without representation in the political process. In a thought-provoking twist, this two-party dualism is itself mocked as the episode plays out, with Obama and McCain actually working together in a plot to use the presidential escape tunnel from the White House to steal the Hope Diamond.

## Stability in a Political Storm

Despite all this, you have to marvel at the stability of the American system. During the uncertain days that followed election day in 2000, little political unrest and no major physical violence took place. Our political structure continued to work and, ultimately, most Americans accepted the winner as legitimate, even if they did not agree with his selection. This respect for the system might simply be due to American reverence for national institutions. This respect might also be due to a faith that we are, rightly or wrongly, better off in our system than we would be in any other.

Americans who choose not to vote on election day may simply be too distracted by the day-to-day events of busy lives. They may choose not to vote as a form of protest against a system or against candidates that they object to. They may not cast ballots because, quite simply, they don't believe their vote matters. The question is, then, is this is a true democracy, given how few voters determine its course? Contemporary philosopher Jürgen Habermas has said that the right to vote, "interpreted as a positive liberty, becomes the paradigm for rights in general not just because it is constitutive for political self-determination but because its structure allows one to see how inclusion in a community of equal members is connected with the individual entitlement to make autonomous contributions."[16] More work must be done in political philosophy to investigate the reasons for the absence of so many voters from our political community, as well as ways to alleviate the problems that are involved.

## Notes

1. The text of the Constitution can be found in most US government textbooks, such as Steffen Schmidt, Mack Shelley, and Barbara Bardes, *American Government and Politics Today* (Belmont, CA: Wadsworth, 2001). The Constitution can also be found online at: http://www.senate.gov/civics/constitution_item/constitution.htm, accessed Feb. 15, 2013.
2. Michael McDonald, "Up, Up and Away! Voter Participation in the 2004 Presidential Election," *The Forum: A Journal of Applied Research in Contemporary Politics* 2 (2004): 6–22. Complete data from the project can be found at: http://elections.gmu.edu/voter_turnout.htm, accessed Feb. 15, 2013.
3. Discussion of these assertions can be found in Thomas Patterson, *The Vanishing Voter* (New York: Alfred A. Knopf, 2002). For further discussions of recent voter behavior, see Alan Abramowitz, *Voice of the People: Elections and Voting in the United States* (New York: McGraw-Hill,

2004); André Blais, *To Vote or Not To Vote? The Merits and Limits of Rational Choice Theory* (Pittsburgh: University of Pittsburgh Press, 2000); Geoffrey Brennan and Loren Lomasky, *Democracy and Decision: The Pure Theory of Electoral Preference* (New York: Cambridge University Press, 1993); Donald Green, *Get Out the Vote!* (Washington, DC: Brookings Institution Press, 2004); Steven Schier, *You Call This an Election? America's Peculiar Democracy* (Washington, DC: Georgetown University Press, 2003). Robert S. Erikson and Christopher Wlezien's book, *The Timeline of Presidential Elections: How Campaigns Do (and Do Not) Matter,* looks at the ways in which the campaign process impacts voter behavior (Chicago: University of Chicago Press, 2012).

4. For an explanation and discussion of the United States Electoral College, see Robert Bennett, *Taming the Electoral College* (Stanford: Stanford University Press, 2006).

5. Schmidt, Shelley, and Bardes, *American Government and Politics Today,* 325–327.

6. Patterson, *The Vanishing Voter,* 144.

7. Schier, *You Call This an Election?,* 9.

8. See Patterson, *The Vanishing Voter,* chapter 5 and Blais, *To Vote or Not to Vote?,* chapter 1.

9. J.S. Mill, *Considerations on Representative Government* (Buffalo: Prometheus Books, 1991), 12–13.

10. J.S. Mill, *On Liberty* (New York: Penguin Books, 1975).

11. Blais, *To Vote or Not To Vote?,* 8.

12. Patterson, *The Vanishing Voter,* 21.

13. Ibid., 172.

14. Nader drew over 97,000 votes in Florida. This crucial state decided in favor of Bush by just over 500 votes.

15. Brennan and Lomasky, *Democracy and Decision,* 119–120.

16. Jürgen Habermas, *Between Facts and Norms: Contributions to a Discourse Theory of Law and Democracy* (Cambridge, MA: The MIT Press, 1996), 271.

# Socioeconomic Darwinism from a South Park Perspective

## Dale Jacquette

*War to palaces, peace unto cabins—that is the battle cry of terror which may come to resound throughout our country. Let the wealthy beware!*
> —*The Times*, June 1844; quoted by Friedrich Engels

*Yeah, that's three homeless! Suck on that!*
> —Eric Cartman, "Night of the Living Homeless"

It is one of the great dilemmas of our industrialized culture, playing itself out in economic events as it does periodically, in an appalling way. We expect marketplace competition to result in the better quality, availability, and affordability of a wider range of goods. Many of these commodities are not only worth having, but also we owe their presence on the market to corporations in mutual competition. In case you hadn't noticed, corporations have become indispensable to what we today consider a civilized life.

Corporations also appear by their very nature to be instruments for concentrating wealth in fewer and fewer hands at the top of the economic food chain. That kind of wealth equals power and presents temptations of corruption, among them limitless petty and grand larcenies and any number of related crimes that might privilege corporate profits regardless of the social costs. All of us with a stake

*The Ultimate South Park and Philosophy: Respect My Philosophah!*, First Edition.
Edited by Robert Arp and Kevin S. Decker.
© 2013 John Wiley & Sons, Inc. Published 2013 by John Wiley & Sons, Inc.

in the social contract should inquire into the nature of corporations, about what they are, and whether corporations are potentially greater goods outweighing corporate misbehavior. We should also ask whether corporations can be morally as well as legally responsible when they act in socially irresponsible ways. Those are exactly the questions that a number of *South Park* episodes address. The answers given by the bad-boy fourth-graders, comrades in all things, have controversial philosophical as well as social and political dimensions.

## Class Warfare Over the One-Percent Fat Fucking Pigs

It's cool or it sucks, unless it's kinda' both. The boys' honesty when they're exposed to harsh social realities, and their candid reactions to their own micro-culture of growing up in an absurd post-industrial America, are all the more revealing for their lack of ulterior motives. Each episode sees them reflect on daily life, spiced up with bizarre imaginative cartoon elements, occasional aliens, a pterodactyl or two, biological mishaps, nuclear meltdowns, celebrity politicians, and an endless stream of adult behavior that can only be classified as stranger than weirdness.

So it is with the South Park kids' encounter with American economic realities. These are comic-dramatized with the usual irony, sarcasm, idealization, and end-of-the-hour moralizing that we have come to associate with a satisfying *South Park* episode. Several stories from the South Park archives offer comment on the concentration of wealth in the so-called "1%," the disappearance of the middle-class American dream, joblessness, homelessness, the Occupy Wall Street movement, and the glorious naked greed of an astonishing culture of "me first" acquisitiveness that assumes we have to "get ours" or lose out, while everyone else thinks and acts the same. The boys, of course, think this sucks—ass.

Surprisingly, the episode "1%" sends the message that social inequalities and corporate wrongdoing are nothing but whiny sloganeering on the part of those who aren't successfully playing the "amass wealth" game. The greater majority suffer for the misdeeds of the few—of one person, in this case: Cartman. He's the 1% at the bottom of his local social pyramid. He's so badly out of physical shape that he not only brings down his whole class average, but that of his entire school in a nationwide competition, making it the lowest in the country. Could that really happen? Suffice it to say that in a school with as many students as South Park Elementary is depicted as having, it wouldn't be mathematically possible for even a fat fucking pig like Cartman single-handedly to bring the entire school down, even if all the other students were exactly average in fitness according to the tests.

The philosophical point is that the so-called 1%, whether Cartman or the super-wealthy, are easy to scapegoat until we remember that social groups making up the 99% will inevitably take sides against each other. This shatters their solidarity and, with it, their political will and political power, which is exactly what happens in the *South Park* episode. An 83% soon begin opposing the remaining 17%, specifically the fourth grade. Because of the sins of one member of the fourth grade, the entire school is being made to suffer mandatory PE class instead of recess for four months. The fifth graders are angry and become increasingly threatening and militant.

Jean-Jacques Rousseau (1712–1778) seems to have anticipated the moral of this *South Park* adventure in his book *The Social Contract*:

> If we enquire wherein lies precisely the greatest good of all, which ought to be the goal of every system of law, we shall find that it comes down to two main objects, *freedom* and *equality*: freedom because any individual dependence means that much strength withdrawn from the body of the state, and equality because freedom cannot survive without it.[1]

The sense of equality at the school is broken because penalties aren't falling where they could do the most good: on Cartman's sorry carcass. The penalty suffered by South Park Elementary reveals another conflicting concept of justice. The federal government setting the parameters for the nationwide physical fitness tests is bound by statute never to single out and confront any individual students who have humiliating test results or to make them the particular individual focus of corrective measures. As one regular extra, Jimmy Valmer, remarks, "How can a meager 17% ruin things for 83%"? The answer is that *Cartman* makes all the difference to their test results. To this, Jimmy then reasonably replies that Cartman is only 17% of the problem, and the argument trails off.

Later, as the Occupy Red Robin incident winds down, the cheesy television announcer, as usual trying to induce a false sense of urgency at the fast food restaurant chain, mentions a further fracturing of the protests into 30%, 26%, "and even little brackets of 5%s here and there." So now who's in which group? And with what percentage? To which side of things do I belong? Does it matter if it's one number or another? The entire question eventually seems meaningless, even if the issues about rights and social equality behind the statistics, not to mention the mindless and socially irresponsible selfish greed, are real and concerning enough. Along with the government representative, Jimmy meets the "crippled kid," who identifies him and the other boys as a delegation from the "Fatty-boom-balatty School" (later also eulogized as the "Boom-boom-chubby-choom-choom School"). Jimmy, having read the policy and heard his classmates described by the government representative as "fat fucking pigs," challenges the President's Council on Fitness rep through his endearing lisp with the knowing pronouncement, "I warn you, this could turn very ugly."

On this fatal prophecy, class warfare erupts on a South Park scale, with protestors occupying the Red Robin, while nonetheless creating no disruption to its daily business. Nor can Trey Parker and Matt Stone resist a scatological pun in claiming that another splinter group has broken away to occupy the Red Robin *restroom*, where the sliding sign on the door plainly indicates in red, "OCCUPIED." There is the sound of a toilet flushing, the door panel slides back to the green "UNOCCUPIED," and a confused boy emerges to cameras and microphones. The event prompts the reporter to remark: "Tom, the movement is finished. But from the time it took, it must have been a pretty decent-sized movement." (This is where we are looking for philosophical insight.)

A cartoon version of freelance video journalist Michael Moore also puts in an unflattering cameo outside the Red Robin, with his signature baseball cap and flabby gut hanging out of his T-shirt, screaming solidarity with the 99% into a megaphone. Surely, this is the kind of disorganized mishmash of social theory and frontal politics that Rousseau has in mind, again in *The Social Contract*:

> It is said that Japanese mountebanks can cut up a child under the eyes of spectators, throw the different parts into the air, and then make the child come down, alive and all of a piece. This is more or less the trick that our political theorists perform—after dismembering the social body with a sleight of hand worthy of the fairground, they put the pieces together again anyhow.[2]

Or maybe not. I had wanted to use the word "mountebank" in something
I was writing for a long time, and this is *Japanese* mountebanks!

## Zombie See, Zombie Do Among
## the Economic Undead

Cartman, meanwhile, finds a way to blame President Barack Obama.
He tells his feather-headed, over-indulgent, fawning mother in his
sniffly voice: "People voted for Obama, so now that everything sucks,
they can't blame him, so they have to blame *me-eee*!"

There's a twisted logic to Cartman's reasoning, coupled with his
usual delusions of grandeur and overweening paranoia. He seeks
sanctuary with the young black neighbor kid Token Williams, thinking
he'll be safe in Token's house because of his theory that "in this day
and age, black people are just impervious to being fucked with."
That's our Cartman.

What it comes down to, in transparently legible technicolor, is
*personal, individual, responsibility* for action. At the beginning of the
episode "Night of the Living Homeless," a mounting wave of people
who've lost their jobs, homes, and families take on the dimensions
of a popular zombie horror movie. The boys are out on the street
and literally stumble over a homeless person in a fetal position. "Spare
any change?" they're asked by more ambulatory homeless, to which
Cartman responds, "No, fuck off!" Then, closing the door behind them,
he adds, "This is bullcrap. Somebody has to be responsible!" Cartman
nevertheless knows exactly what to do upon his first encounter with
the shelter-challenged. He assumes that the other boys are fully behind
him as he dons a cape and crash helmet, and prepares to charge admission
for skateboarding over one hapless victim who's lying down at the end
of a ramp. Cartman doesn't even clear him as he bounces painfully
over the man's undernourished ribs.

Yet kind-hearted Kyle may have unknowingly started an avalanche
when he gives a homeless guy $20. That, at least, is the opinion of the
ruggedly handsome Head of Homeless Studies, who warns the community
on TV, "If we give them anything, there could be more!" "They feed
on our change," he tells the boys when they visit his laboratory. He
drops some coins in the cup of a bearded ragged man chained to the
wall, observing, "It has already completely forgotten that I have just

given it change. It just wants … more change." Nor does Kyle receive any thanks for his charity, only the request, "Do you have any more?" Now a scene of the economically undead unfolds, with helicopter news reporting of people trapped on rooftops at a shopping mall, and the media warning everyone to "Stay indoors and protect your change."

Even Kyle's dad gets caught up in the frenzy. Trying to escape from the mall roof through the street, he finally showers coins from his pockets to the unappeasable horde, only to realize that he has no change for the bus. Almost immediately, he plays zombie, staggering around like the others asking for change. "He has become one of them," his neighbors remark, watching through binoculars. Steve Garrett, from the library, pounds frantically on the door and pleads to be let inside. "For God's sake, they're coming!" he shouts. "One of them is a war veteran. We're gonna *have* to give *him* some change!" One of the stragglers at just that moment realizes his unpaid mortgages have resulted in the loss of his home. He starts to fret over what he'll do with all his *stuff*, getting increasingly frantic as the enormity of the situation dawns. He reasons out loud that he could rent a locker if he could put together some money, and starts asking the others for change, whereupon he gets his cartoon head blown off by a cartoon shotgun—the only reliable remedy for the marauding, unpropertied, living dead, just as it is for the "real" zombie onslaught in the Pennsylvania countryside.

## Corporate CEOs as Underpants Gnomes

The worldwide economic problem from a *South Park* perspective is not to be laid at the door of big corporations. The 1998 episode "Gnomes" manages to praise the abstract concept of corporations while serving up a scathing parody of blind corporate greed in same episode's central economic parable. The gnomes are elfin underpants thieves. With pointless industry they steal underpants from bedroom drawers and, eventually, from inattentive people right out from within their trousers.

The gnomes are enormously proud of their business sense. They're keen to share and show off their corporate model to the South Park boys. At first, only Tweek, the blond-haired son of a local family-owned-and-operated coffee shop, has seen the gnomes. He can't sleep at night, when the gnomes are active, because his parents keep feeding him strong brewed coffee. The other kids deny the gnomes' existence, thinking that Tweek is just a little overwrought and failing to understand the effects of coffee on his frayed nervous system. Finally, late at night, the gnomes are seen in Tweek's house by the other boys. Cartman smacks one of them with a stick and eventually the gnome decides to share the secrets of their trade.

The gnomes have a daring three-plank business plan, which begins in Phase 1: Collect underpants, and terminates in Phase 3: Profit. For Phase 2 the gnomes have nothing but a big fat question mark. They have no clue as to how they are supposed to profit from the pilfered briefs, and so no idea why they're stealing the garments in the first place. They never even pause to consider, in their eager energetic efforts to corner the market on mostly used underpants, why they are devoting their time and talent to the enterprise. What's it for? Why are we doing all this rather than anything else? These are questions that non-gnome corporations caught up in the corporate rat race might also ask themselves.

After Tweek's family-owned-and-operated coffee shop is challenged by a hostile takeover bid from Harbuck's Coffee, the boys inadvertently raise the cause of small business versus corporate giants. They're supposed to do a presentation to the entire school board in a last-ditch effort to prove that Mr. Garrison isn't a "complete dickhole," but is teaching his students something socially relevant. The gang would actually prefer to have him fired, but Mr. Hat threatens them with horrible things if they don't make him look good. The boys meet at Tweek's house to plan their course of action, and on Tweek's first recommendation they do a presentation on the underpants gnomes. When the gnomes fail to materialize, and they can't come up with anything else after running themselves ragged and actually chewing on coffee grounds to keep themselves awake, Mr. Richard Tweek ropes them into speaking on how big corporations are ruining America. When Mr. Tweek complains about Harbucks' plan to open a coffee shop right next to his, Harbucks' representative John Postum says, "Hey, this is a capitalist country, pal—get used to it."

That basic fact of American life seems indeed to be part of the episode's final message. Mr. Tweek is merely a laid-back, friendly neighborhood coffee slinger, who stands in front of rainbows and waxes poetic about the virtues of hand-selected, fresh ground and home-brewed coffee beans: "Like the morning after a rainstorm." We can see from a mile away that he's going to get absorbed by the starving paramecium Harbucks. Frazzled as he is on a high caffeine intake, unable to bear the slightest pressure of responsibility, Tweek has no comic distance as Richard Tweek occasionally threatens to sell the boy into slavery. The Tweeks get the other boys so revved up on their first exposure to coffee that they spend all their time running in circles and bouncing off the walls. Richard Tweek actually writes their speech for them, which they deliver to the tremendous approval of the school board. Now, as often happens, the South Park kids have really started something: the case is taken to the mayor, there's live news coverage, and the boys are interviewed. Postum from Harbucks is on point, and the boys on counterpoint. The moderator is anything but moderate, introducing Postum on camera as "Mr. Douchebag," "Mr. Assface," and "a big, fat, smelly, corporate guy from New York." Ignoring Postum's efforts to remind everybody of the social acceptability of *anything* that sells on the market, the moderator asks the boys, "What's your principal argument?" There follows an embarrassing pause, because they don't have a clue what to say. They didn't research the presentation themselves, and they don't know their own argument or any of the supporting facts. Out of strike-first desperation as much as sassy bravado, and because we're due for a mild shock in the episode at about this point, we hear them defiantly conclude, "This guy sucks ass." As triumphantly, as inexplicably, the boys are told, "Your argument wins!"

Sales temporarily plummet for Harbucks as a result of the negative publicity. The company responds by bringing out its heavy artillery in the form of mascot Camel Joe. The lovable character demonstrates his social conscience when he offers a variety of kiddie coffee drinks to get the youngsters hooked. Meanwhile, the gnomes continue methodically thieving underpants, now sometimes in broad daylight, humming their catchy little work song like Santa's busy elves or the diligent merry seven dwarfs, whenever they surface, swelling the coffers of their subterranean underpants cavern cache:

> Time to go to work,
> Work all day,
> Search for underpants hey!
> We won't stop until we have underpants!
> Yum yum yummy yum yay!

> Time to go to work,
> Work all night,
> Search for underpants yay!
> We won't stop until we have underpants!
> Yum tum yummy tum day!

It can be surprisingly hard to get this melody out of your head, especially if you watch the episode over and over again as part of your research for writing something like this chapter. You'll find yourself humming it in the most unlikely places and at the most inappropriate times.

Parker and Stone seem to be saying that the CEOs of leviathan corporations are just like the underpants gnomes. They have no sense of what they're pursuing or why; they can only answer, "Profit" or "Underpants." Both parties don't know what to do with their acquisitions, which might as well be vintage wines or rare coins or rare vintage underpants made out of coins and full of wine. Corporate CEOs have no grasp of what wealth should be doing and how it should be used, except to endlessly expand the corporation's market share. Like Cartman, they're just greedy gullets, the 1% whose exploits inflict costs on countless other persons who may be just lucky enough to keep body and soul together. Still, those are all the results of individual decisions and actions for which individuals rather than corporations are personally responsible.

## Moral in a Nutshell

As has already been emphasized, as if we needed any reminding, "This is a capitalist country, and we had better get used to it." If collecting wealth is the game and if you're playing it, whether you like it or not, then why not play it to the hilt? We can always figure out what to do with the money afterwards.

So, do we figure out what to do after we have it *all*? Or just as much as we think we can tuck away? Ah, but that's not playing the game after all; it's giving up before the end. The Russian writer Leo Tolstoy, in his (1886) short story of the same name, asks "How Much Land Does a Man Need?" His answer is that the only land that anyone *needs* in the end is just about the one by two meters needed to bury a standard-size coffin. Death is the great equalizer, which the boys are just old enough to sense. A lifetime's economic struggles end with the same needs for every person, whether the downtrodden victim of economic injustice or the most hard-nosed economic profiteer. The *South Park* creators seem to be saying on final analysis that it's senseless to blame corporations for the decisions of individual assholes working in corporations.

Kyle blubbers out his trademark sobbing earnest conclusion, this time that corporations are *good*. "Good?" The mayor and school board are incredulous. At the gang's school board presentation, they'd just forcefully reached the opposite judgment. Now Kyle explains, "Because without big corporations we wouldn't have things like cars and computers and canned soup." Of course, our species has slogged along without these things for about 50,000 years. Still, they're good, many of these canned soups, and it's hard to imagine soup getting canned except by a corporation. All these positive benefits come as one big package deal, along with medical advances and space travel and consumer electronics. So, if you want laser eye surgery and miracle cancer treatments, then you'd better belly up for shitty electronics and even shittier dining at the Red Robin. If we are tempted to retreat to the opposite position of, "Just look at all the evil corporations have done!" then we've missed the precious morsel of philosophical content to be juiced from these *South Park* episodes: this is that the corporation in and of itself—the *idea* of a corporation—is not something that sucks, but on the contrary is something cool. The problem is always with individuals who use corporations to do things that suck. It's those misbehavers who must be held personally responsible for their individual decisions, even when their actions are committed through corporate agency. Corporations can then be as cool as they are meant to be, when the people who work for them are also cool, rather than sucking ass, as many of them most assuredly do.

Stan immediately adds, "Even Harbucks Coffee started off as a small, little business. But because it made such great coffee, and because they ran their business so well, they managed to grow and grow until it became the corporate powerhouse it is today. And that is why we should all let Harbucks stay!" M'kay, so maybe it's not exactly the pull-yourself-up-by-your-bootstraps appeal of Bernard Mandeville's classic *Fable of the Bees* (1714), or even Ayn Rand's stultifyingly dismal novel *Atlas Shrugged* (1957). But I think that once again we may have all learned something today. How can you dismiss your own senses, as when Mr. Tweek finally tries a Harbucks' French Roast? Unable to stop himself from loving it, he instantly launches his own homespun Harbucks' commercial: "It's subtle and mild. Mild, like that first splash of sun on an April morning. This coffee is coffee the way it should be." One townsman chirps, "Hey, this is pretty damn good," provoking another's response, "Yeah, it doesn't have that bland, raw, sewage taste that Tweek's coffee has."

The corporations, as Mr. Tweek likes to say, have his balls in a vice grip, a salad shooter, and a juice maker. He's offered to manage the very Harbucks that would have driven his family business to ruin. Although he jokes that he won't need the money after he sells his son into slavery, he leaves it open whether he'll work for the giant coffee chain before whose superiority he prostrates himself in good-humored capitulation.

It is nonsense, *South Park* says, to blame corporations for the wrong-doing of individuals. Corporations are good in and of themselves. Individual persons who use corporate tools to do bad things need to be held responsible as individuals, regardless of whether legal and economic penalties apply to a business as corporate entity. Corporations, as Mr. Tweek observes, have seized upon some favorite parts of our anatomies in the grip of hazardous kitchen appliances, where we can expect they won't be treated very gently or respectfully. Nor is this any less true for the fact that we don't have much choice, just as long as we continue to want and are willing to work all our lives in exchange for the kinds of things that only corporations can provide.

## Notes

1. Jean-Jacques Rousseau, *The Social Contract*, trans. Maurice Cranston (New York: Penguin Books, 1968), 96.
2. Ibid., 71.

# Part V

# LIBER-ARIANISM IN SOUTH PARK

# Cartman Shrugged
## South Park and Libertarian Philosophy

*Paul A. Cantor*

*Tho' ye subject bee but a fart, yet will this tedious sink of learning ponderously philosophize.*

— Mark Twain, 1601

Critics of *South Park*—and they are legion—bitterly complain about its relentless obscenity and potty humor. And they have a legitimate point. But if one wanted to mount a high-minded defense of the show's low-minded jokes, one might go all the way back to Plato (427–347 BCE) to find a link between philosophy and vulgarity. Toward the end of his dialogue the *Symposium*, a young Athenian nobleman named Alcibiades offers a striking image of the power of Socrates. He compares the philosopher's speeches to a statue of the satyr Silenus, which is ugly on the outside, but which, when opened up, reveals a beautiful interior: "if you choose to listen to Socrates' discourses you would feel them at first to be quite ridiculous; on the outside they are clothed with such absurd words and phrases ... His talk is of pack-asses, smiths, cobblers, and tanners ... so that anyone inexpert and thoughtless might laugh his speeches to scorn. But when these are opened ... you will discover that they are the only speeches which have any sense in them."[1]

These words characterize equally well the contrast between the vulgar surface and the philosophical depth of the dialogue in which

*The Ultimate South Park and Philosophy: Respect My Philosophah!*, First Edition.
Edited by Robert Arp and Kevin S. Decker.
© 2013 John Wiley & Sons, Inc. Published 2013 by John Wiley & Sons, Inc.

they are spoken. The *Symposium* contains some of the most soaring and profound philosophical speculations ever written. And yet in the middle of the dialogue the comic poet Aristophanes comes down with a bad case of hiccups that prevents him from speaking in turn. By the end of the dialogue, all the characters except Socrates have consumed so much wine that they pass out in a collective drunken stupor. In a dialogue about the spiritual and physical dimensions of love, Plato thus suggests that, however philosophical we may wax in our speeches, we remain creatures of the body and can never entirely escape its crude bodily functions. In the way that the *Symposium* moves back and forth between the ridiculous and the sublime, Plato seems to be making a statement about philosophy—that it has something in common with low comedy. Both philosophy and vulgar humor fly in the face of conventional opinion.

## High Philosophy and Low Comedy

I'm not sure what Plato would have made of *South Park*, but his Silenus image fits the show quite well. *South Park* is one the most vulgar shows ever to appear on television, and yet it can at the same time be one of the most thought-provoking. Its vulgarity is of course the first thing we notice about it, given its obsession with farting, pissing, shitting, vomiting, and every other excretory possibility. As Plato's dialogue suggests, it's all too easy to become fixated on the vulgar and obscene surface of *South Park*, rejecting out of hand a show that chose to make a Christmas icon out of a talking turd named Mr. Hankey. But if you're patient with *South Park*, and give the show the benefit of the doubt, you'll find that it takes up one serious issue after another, from environmentalism to animal rights, from assisted suicide to sexual harassment, from presidential elections to US foreign policy. And the show approaches all these issues from a distinct philosophical position, known as libertarianism, the philosophy of freedom. If anything, the show can become too didactic, with episodes often culminating in a character delivering a speech that offers a surprisingly balanced and nuanced account of the issue at hand.

In thinking about *South Park*, we should recall that some of the greatest comic writers—Aristophanes, Chaucer, Rabelais, Shakespeare, Jonson, Swift—plumbed the depths of obscenity even as they rose to the heights of philosophical thought. The same intellectual courage that emboldened them to defy conventional proprieties empowered them to reject conventional ideas and break through the intellectual frontiers of their day. Without claiming that *South Park* deserves to rank with such distinguished predecessors, I will say that the show descends from a long tradition of comedy that ever since ancient Athens has combined obscenity with philosophy. There are almost as many fart jokes in Aristophanes' play *The Clouds* as there are in a typical episode of *The Terrance and Phillip Show*. In fact, in the earliest dramatic representation of Socrates that has come down to us, he's making fart jokes as he tries to explain to a dumb Athenian named Strepsiades that thunder is a purely natural phenomenon, not the work of the great god Zeus:

> First think of the tiny fart that your intestines make.
> Then consider the heavens: their infinite farting is thunder.
> For thunder and farting are, in principle, one and the same.[2]

## Speaking the Unspeakable

The people who condemn *South Park* for being offensive need to be reminded that comedy is by its very nature offensive. It derives its energy from its transgressive power—its ability to break taboos, to speak the unspeakable. Comedians are always pushing the envelop, probing to see how much they can get away with in violating the speech codes of their day. Comedy is a social safety valve. We laugh precisely because comedians momentarily liberate us from the restrictions that conventional society imposes on us. We applaud comedians because they say right out in front of an audience what, supposedly, nobody is allowed to say in public.

Paradoxically, then, the more permissive American society has become, the harder it has become to write comedy. As censorship laws have been relaxed, and people have been allowed to say and show almost anything in movies and television—above all to deal with formerly taboo sexual material—comedy writers like the creators of *South Park*, Trey Parker and Matt Stone, must have begun to wonder if there is any way left to offend an audience.

The genius of Parker and Stone has been to see that in our day a new frontier of comic transgression has opened up because of the phenomenon known as *political correctness*. Our age may have tried to dispense with the conventional pieties of earlier generations, but it has developed new pieties of its own. They may not look like the traditional pieties, but they're enforced in the same old way, with social pressures and sometimes even legal sanctions punishing people who dare to violate the new taboos. Many of our colleges and universities today have speech codes, which seek to define what can and can't be said on campus, and in particular to prohibit anything that might be interpreted as demeaning someone because of his or her race, religion, gender, handicap, and a whole series of other protected categories. Sex may no longer be taboo in our society, but sexism now is. *Seinfeld* was probably the first television comedy that systematically violated the new taboos of political correctness. The show repeatedly made fun of contemporary sensitivities about such issues as sexual orientation, ethnic identity, feminism, and handicapped people. *Seinfeld* proved that being politically incorrect can be hilariously funny in today's moral and intellectual climate, and *South Park* was quick to follow its lead.

The show has mercilessly satirized all forms of political correctness—anti-hate crime legislation, tolerance indoctrination in the schools, Hollywood do-gooding of all kinds, environmentalism and anti-smoking campaigns, the Americans with Disabilities Act and the Special Olympics—the list goes on and on. It's hard to single out the most politically incorrect moment in the history of *South Park*, but I'll nominate the spectacular "cripple fight" in the fifth season episode of that name, and indeed just look at the politically incorrect name to describe what happens when two "differently abled," or rather "handicapable," boys named Timmy and Jimmy square off for a violent—and interminable—battle in the streets of South Park. The show obviously relishes the sheer shock value of moments such as this. But more is going on here than transgressing the boundaries of good taste just for transgression's sake.

## A Plague on Both Your Houses

This is where the philosophy of libertarianism enters the picture in *South Park*. The show criticizes political correctness in the name of freedom. That's why Parker and Stone can proclaim themselves equal opportunity satirists; they make fun of the old pieties as well as the new, savaging both the right and the left insofar as both seek to restrict freedom. "Cripple Fight" is an excellent example of the balance and even-handedness of *South Park*, and the way it can offend both ends of the political spectrum. The episode deals in typical *South Park* fashion with a contemporary controversy, one that has even made it into the courts: whether homosexuals should be allowed to lead Boy Scout troops. The episode makes fun of the old-fashioned types in the town who insist on denying a troop leadership to Big Gay Al (a recurrent character whose name says it all). It turns out that the ostensibly straight man the Boy Scouts choose to replace Big Gay Al is a pedophile who starts abusing the boys immediately by photographing them naked. As it frequently does with the groups it satirizes, *South Park*, even as it stereotypes homosexuals, displays sympathy for them and their right to live their lives as they see fit.

But just as the episode seems to be simply taking the side of those who condemn the Boy Scouts for homophobia, it swerves in an unexpected direction. Big Gay Al himself defends the right of the Boy Scouts to exclude homosexuals on the principle of freedom of association. An organization should be able to set up its own rules and the law should not impose society's notions of political correctness on a private group. This episode represents *South Park* at its best—looking at a complicated issue from both sides and coming up with a judicious resolution of the issue. And the principle on which the issue is resolved is *freedom*. As the episode shows, Big Gay Al should be free to be homosexual, but the Boy Scouts should also be free as an organization to make their own rules and exclude him from a leadership post if they so desire.

This libertarianism makes *South Park* offensive to the politically correct, for, if applied consistently, it would dismantle the whole apparatus of speech control and thought manipulation that do-gooders have tried to construct to protect their favored minorities. Libertarianism is a philosophy of radical freedom, and particularly celebrates the free market as a form of social organization. As a philosophy, it descends from, among other sources, the thinking of the Scottish Enlightenment in the eighteenth century. Moral philosophers from that period such as Adam Smith (1723–1790) argued for free trade and the reduction of government intervention in the economy. Libertarianism is especially grounded in the work of the Austrian School of economics, above all the writings of Ludwig von Mises (1881–1973) and Friedrich Hayek (1899–1992), who offer the most cogent defense of unfettered economic activity as the key to prosperity and progress.[3] The term *libertarianism* was popularized by Murray Rothbard (1926–1995), a student of Mises, who developed the most radical critique of state interference in economic and social life, a philosophy of freedom that borders on anarchism.[4]

With its support for unconditional freedom in all areas of life, libertarianism defies categorization in terms of the standard one-dimensional political spectrum of right and left. In opposition to the collectivist and anti-capitalist vision of the left, libertarians reject central planning and want people to be left alone to pursue their self-interest as they see fit. But in contrast to conservatives, libertarians also oppose social legislation; they generally favor the legalization of drugs and the abolition of all censorship and anti-pornography laws. Parker and Stone publicly identify themselves as libertarians—which explains why their show ends up offending both liberals and conservatives. Parker has said: "We avoid extremes but we hate liberals more than conservatives, and we hate them."[5] This does seem to be an accurate assessment of the leanings of the show—even though it is no friend of the right, *South Park* is more likely to go after left-wing causes. In an interview in *Reason*, Matt Stone explained that he and Parker were on the left of the political spectrum when they were in high school in the 1980s, but in order to maintain their stance as rebels, they found that, when they went to the University of Colorado, Boulder, and even more so when they arrived in Hollywood, they had to change their positions and attack the prevailing left-wing orthodoxy. As Stone says: "I had Birkenstocks in high school. I was that guy. And I was sure that those people on the other side of the political spectrum [the right] were trying to control my life. And then I went to Boulder and got rid of my Birkenstocks immediately, because everyone else had them and I realized that those people over here [on the left] want to control my life too. I guess that defines my political philosophy. If anybody's telling me what I should do, then you've got to really convince me that it's worth doing."[6]

## Defending the Undefendable

The libertarianism of Parker and Stone places them at odds with the intellectual establishment of contemporary America. In the academic world, much of the media, and a large part of the entertainment business, especially the Hollywood elite, anti-capitalist views generally prevail.[7] Studies have shown that business people are usually portrayed in an unfavorable light in movies and television.[8] *South Park* takes particular delight in skewering the Hollywood stars who exploit their celebrity to conduct liberal or left-wing campaigns against the workings of the free market (Barbra Streisand, Rob Reiner, Sally Struthers, and George Clooney are among the celebrities the show has pilloried). *South Park* is rare among television shows for its willingness to celebrate the free market, and even to come to the defense of what is evidently the most hated institution in Hollywood, the corporation. For example, in the ninth season episode "Die Hippie Die," Cartman fights the countercultural forces who invade South Park and mindlessly blame all the troubles of America on "the corporations."

Of all *South Park* episodes, the second season "Gnomes" offers the most fully developed defense of capitalism, and I will attempt a comprehensive interpretation of it in order to demonstrate how genuinely intelligent and thoughtful the show can be. "Gnomes" deals with a common charge against the free market—that it allows large corporations to drive small businesses into the ground, much to the detriment of consumers. In "Gnomes" a national coffee chain called Harbucks—an obvious reference to Starbucks—comes to South Park and tries to buy out the local Tweek Bros. coffee shop. Mr. Tweek casts himself as the hero of the story, a small business David battling a corporate Goliath. The episode satirizes the cheap anti-capitalist rhetoric in which such conflicts are usually formulated in contemporary America, with the small business shown to be purely good and the giant corporation shown to be purely evil. "Gnomes" systematically deconstructs this simplistic opposition.

In the conventional picture, the small business operator is presented as a public servant, almost unconcerned with profits, simply a friend to his customers, whereas the corporation is presented as greedy and uncaring, doing nothing for the consumer. "Gnomes" shows instead that Mr. Tweek is just as self-interested as any corporation, and he is in fact cannier in promoting himself than Harbucks is. The Harbucks representative, John Postem, is blunt and gruff, an utterly charmless man who thinks that he can just state the bare economic truth and get away with it: "Hey, this is a capitalist country, pal—get used to it." The irony of the episode is that the supposedly sophisticated corporation completely mishandles public relations, naively believing that the superiority of its product will be enough to ensure its triumph in the marketplace.

The common charge against large corporations is that, with their financial resources, they're able to exploit the power of advertising to put their small rivals out of business. But in "Gnomes," Harbucks is no match for the advertising savvy of Mr. Tweek. He cleverly turns his disadvantage into an advantage, coming up with the perfect slogan in his circumstances: "Tweek offers a simpler coffee for a simpler America." He thereby exploits his underdog position, while preying upon his customers' nostalgia for an older and presumably simpler America. The episode constantly dwells on the fact that Mr. Tweek is just as slick at advertising as any corporation. He keeps launching into commercials for his coffee, accompanied by soft guitar mood music and purple advertising prose; his coffee is "special like an Arizona sunrise or a juniper wet with dew." His son may be appalled by "the metaphors" (actually they are similes), but Mr. Tweek knows just what will appeal to his nature-loving, yuppie customers.

"Gnomes" thus undermines any notion that Mr. Tweek is morally superior to the corporation he's fighting, and in fact the episode suggests that he may be a good deal worse. Going over the top as it always does, *South Park* reveals that the coffee shop owner has for years been overcaffeinating his son Tweek (one of the regulars in the show) and is thus responsible for the boy's hypernervousness. Moreover, when faced with the threat from Harbucks, Mr. Tweek seeks sympathy by declaring: "I may have to shut down and sell my son Tweek into slavery." It sounds as if his greed exceeds Harbucks'. But the worst thing about Mr. Tweek is that he isn't content with using his slick advertising to compete with Harbucks in a free market. He also goes after Harbucks politically, trying to enlist the government on his side to prevent the national chain from coming to South Park. "Gnomes" thus portrays the campaign against large corporations as just one more sorry episode in the long history of businesses seeking economic protectionism—the kind of business/government alliance Adam Smith criticized in *The Wealth of Nations*. Far from the standard Marxist portrayal of monopoly power as the inevitable result of free competition, *South Park* shows that it results only when one business gets the government to intervene on its behalf and restrict free entry into the marketplace.

## The Town of South Park versus Harbucks

Mr. Tweek gets his chance to enlist public opinion on his side when he finds out that his son and the other boys have been assigned to write a report on a current event. Offering to write the paper for the children, he inveigles them into a topic very much in his self-interest: "how large corporations take over little family owned businesses," or, more pointedly, "how the corporate machine is ruining America." Kyle can barely get out the polysyllabic words when he delivers the ghostwritten report in class: "As the voluminous corporate automaton bulldozes its way ..." This language obviously parodies the exaggerated and overinflated anti-capitalist rhetoric of the contemporary left. But the report is a big hit with local officials and soon—much to Mr. Tweek's delight—the mayor is sponsoring Proposition 10, an ordinance that will ban Harbucks from South Park.

In the ensuing controversy over Prop 10, "Gnomes" portrays the way the media are biased against capitalism and the way the public is manipulated into anti-business attitudes. The boys are enlisted to argue for Prop 10 and the man from Harbucks to argue against it. The presentation is slanted from the beginning, when the moderator announces: "On my left, five innocent, starry-eyed boys from Middle America" and "On my right, a big, fat, smelly corporate guy from New York." Postum tries to make a rational argument, grounded in principle: "This country is founded on free enterprise." But the boys triumph in the debate with a somewhat less cogent argument, as Cartman sagely proclaims: "This guy sucks ass." The television commercial in favor of Prop 10 is no less fraudulent than the debate. Again, "Gnomes" points out that anti-corporate advertising can be just as slick as corporate. In particular, the episode shows that the left is willing to go to any length in its anti-corporate crusade, exploiting children to tug at the heartstrings of its target audience. In a wonderful parody of a political commercial, the boys are paraded out in a patriotic scene featuring the American flag, while the "Battle Hymn of the Republic" plays softly in the background. Meanwhile the announcer solemnly intones: "Prop 10 is about children. Vote yes on Prop 10 or else you hate children." The ad is "paid for by Citizens for a Fair and Equal Way to Get Harbucks Out of Town Forever." *South Park* loves to expose the illogic of liberal and left-wing crusaders, and the anti-Harbucks campaign is filled with one non-sequitur after another. Pushing the last of the liberal buttons, one woman challenges the Harbucks representative: "How many Native Americans did you slaughter to make that coffee?"

Prop 10 seems to be headed for an easy victory at the polls until the boys encounter some friendly gnomes, who explain corporations to them. At the last minute, in one of the most didactic of the *South Park* concluding message scenes, the boys announce to the puzzled townspeople that they have reversed their position on Prop 10. In the spirit of libertarianism, Kyle proclaims something rarely heard on television outside of a John Stossel report: "Big corporations are good. Because without big corporations we wouldn't have things like cars and computers and canned soup." And Stan comes to the defense of the dreaded Harbucks: "Even Harbucks started off as a small, little business. But because it made such great coffee, and because they ran their business so well, they managed to grow until they became the corporate powerhouse it is today. And that is why we should all let Harbucks stay."

At this point the townspeople do something remarkable—they stop listening to all the political rhetoric and actually taste the rival coffees for themselves. And they discover that Mrs. Tweek (who has been disgusted by her husband's devious tactics) is telling the truth when she says: "Harbucks Coffee got to where it is by being the best." Indeed, as one of the townspeople observes: "It doesn't have that bland, raw sewage taste that Tweek's coffee has." "Gnomes" ends by suggesting that it's only fair that businesses battle it out, not in the political arena, but in the marketplace, and let the best product win. Postem offers Mr. Tweek the job of running the local franchise and everybody is happy. Politics is a zero-sum, winner-take-all game, in which one business triumphs only by using government power to eliminate a rival, but in the voluntary exchanges a free market makes possible, all parties benefit from a transaction. Harbucks makes a profit, and Mr. Tweek can continue earning a living without selling his son into slavery, but above all the people of South Park get to enjoy a better brand of coffee. Contrary to the anti-corporate propaganda normally coming out of Hollywood, *South Park* argues that, in the absence of government intervention, corporations get where they are by serving the public, not by exploiting it. As Ludwig von Mises makes the point: "The profit system makes those men prosper who have succeeded in filling the wants of the people in the best possible and cheapest way. Wealth can be acquired only by serving the consumers. The capitalists lose their funds as soon as they fail to invest them in those lines in which they satisfy best the demands of the public. In a daily repeated plebiscite in which every penny gives a right to vote the consumers determine who should own and run the plants, shops and farms."[9]

## The Great Gnome Mystery Solved

But what about the gnomes, who, after all, give the episode its title? Where do they fit in? I never could understand how the subplot in "Gnomes" related to the main plot until I was lecturing on the episode at a summer institute and my colleague Michael Valdez Moses made a breakthrough that allowed us to put together the episode as a whole. In the subplot, Tweek complains to anybody who will listen that every night at 3:30 a.m. gnomes sneak into his bedroom and steal his underpants. But nobody else can see this remarkable phenomenon happening, not even when the other boys stay up late with Tweek to observe it, not even when the emboldened gnomes start robbing underpants in broad daylight in the mayor's office. We know two things about these strange beings: (1) they are gnomes and (2) they are normally invisible. Both facts point in the direction of capitalism. As in the phrase "gnomes of Zurich," which refers to bankers, gnomes are often associated with the world of finance. In the first opera of Richard Wagner's Ring Cycle, *Das Rheingold*, the gnome Alberich serves as a symbol of the capitalist exploiter—and he forges the Tarnhelm, a cap of invisibility.[10] The idea of invisibility calls to mind Adam Smith's famous notion of the "invisible hand" that guides the free market.[11]

In short, the underpants gnomes are an image of capitalism and the way it is normally—and mistakenly—pictured by its opponents. The gnomes represent the ordinary business activity that's always going on in plain sight of everyone, but which they fail to notice and fail to understand. The people of South Park are unaware that the ceaseless activity of large corporations like Harbucks is necessary to provide them with all the goods they enjoy in their daily lives. They take it for granted that the shelves of their supermarkets will always be amply stocked with a wide variety of goods and never appreciate all the capitalist entrepreneurs who make that abundance possible.

What is worse, the ordinary citizens misinterpret capitalist activity as theft. They focus only on what businesses take from them—their money—and forget about what they get in return, all the goods and services. Above all, people have no understanding of the basic facts of economics and have no idea of why businesses deserve the profits they earn. Business is a complete mystery to them—it seems to be a matter of gnomes sneaking around in the shadows and mischievously heaping up piles of goods for no apparent purpose. Friedrich Hayek noted this long-standing tendency to misinterpret normal business activities as sinister:

> Such distrust and fear have led ordinary people to regard trade as suspicious, inferior, dishonest, and contemptible ... Activities that appear to add to available wealth, 'out of nothing,' without physical creation and by merely rearranging what already exists, stink of sorcery ... That a mere change of hands should lead to a gain in value to all participants, that it need not mean gain to one at the expense of the others (or what has come to be called exploitation), was and is nonetheless intuitively difficult to grasp ... Many people continue to find the mental feats associated with trade easy to discount even when they do not attribute them to sorcery, or see them as depending on trick or fraud or cunning deceit.[12]

Even the gnomes don't understand what they are doing. Perhaps *South Park* is suggesting that the real problem is that entrepreneurs themselves lack the economic knowledge that they would need to explain their activity to the public and justify their profits. When the boys ask the gnomes to tell them about corporations, all they can offer is this enigmatic diagram of the stages of their business:

| *Phase 1* | *Phase 2* | *Phase 3* |
|---|---|---|
| Collect Underpants | ? | Profit |

This chart basically encapsulates the economic illiteracy of the American public. They can see no connection between the activities business people undertake and the profits they make. What entrepreneurs actually contribute to the economy is a big question mark to them.[13] The fact that entrepreneurs are rewarded for taking risks, for correctly anticipating consumer demands, and for efficiently financing, organizing, and managing production is lost on most people. They would rather complain about the obscene profits of corporations and condemn their power in the marketplace.

The "invisible hand" passage of Smith's *Wealth of Nations* reads like a gloss on the "Gnomes" episode of *South Park*:

> As every individual, therefore, endeavours as much as he can both to employ his capital in the support of domestick industry, and so to direct that industry that its produce may be of the greatest value; every individual necessarily labours to render the annual revenue of the society as great as he can. He genuinely, indeed, neither intends to promote the publick interest, nor knows how much he is promoting it. By preferring the support of domestick to that of foreign industry, he intends only his own security, and by directing that industry in such a manner as its produce may be of the greatest value, he intends only his own gain, and he is in this, as in many other cases, led by an invisible hand to promote an end which was no part of his intention. Nor is it always the worse for the society that it was no part of it. By pursuing his own interest he frequently promotes that of the society more effectively than when he really intends to promote it. I have never known much good done by those who affected to trade for the publick good.[14]

"Gnomes" exemplifies this idea of the "invisible hand." The economy does not need to be guided by the very visible and heavy hand of government regulation for the public interest to be served. Without any central planning, the free market produces a prosperous economic order. The free interaction of producers and consumers and the constant interplay of supply and demand work so that people generally have access to the goods they want. Like Adam Smith, Parker and Stone are deeply suspicious of people who speak about the public good and condemn the private pursuit of profit. As we see in the case of Mr. Tweek, such people are usually hypocrites, pursuing their self-interest under the cover of championing the public interest. And the much-maligned gnomes of the world, the corporations, while openly pursuing their own profit, end up serving the public interest by providing the goods and services people really want.

## The Wal-Mart Monster

Having had the audacity to defend Starbucks, in its eighth season *South Park* went on to rally to the cause of Wal-Mart—under an even more thinly disguised name in an episode called "Something Wall Mart This

Way Comes." This episode is brilliantly cast in the mold of a cheesy horror movie, as the sinister power of a Wal-Mart-like superstore takes over the town of South Park amid lengthening shadows, darkening clouds, and ominous flashes of lightning. The Wall Mart exerts "some mystical evil force" over the townspeople. Try as they may, they cannot resist its bargain prices. Just as in "Gnomes," a local merchant starts complaining about his inability to compete with a national retail chain. In mock sympathy, Cartman plays syrupy violin music to accompany this lament. When Kyle indignantly smashes the violin, Cartman simply replies: "I can go get another one at Wall Mart—it was only five bucks."

Widespread public opposition to the Wall Mart develops in the town and efforts are made to boycott the store, ban it, and even burn it down (the latter to the uplifting strain of "Kumbaya"). But like any good monster, the evil Wall Mart keeps springing back to life and the townspeople are irresistibly drawn to its well-stocked aisles at all hours ("Where else was I going to get a napkin dispenser at 9:30 at night?"). All these horror movie clichés are a way of making fun of how Wal-Mart is demonized by intellectuals in our society. They present the national chain as some kind of external power, independent of human beings, which somehow manages to impose itself upon them against their will—a corporate monster. At times the townspeople talk as if they simply have no choice in going to the superstore, but at other times they reveal what really attracts them—lower prices that allow them to stretch their incomes and enjoy more of the good things in life. To be even-handed, the episode does stress at several points the absurdities of buying in bulk just to get a bargain—for example, ending up with enough Ramen noodles "to last a thousand winters."

In the grand horror movie tradition, the boys finally set out to find the heart of the Wall Mart and destroy it. Meanwhile, Stan's father, Randy, has gone to work for the Wall Mart for the sake of the 10 percent employee discount, but he nevertheless tries to help the boys reach their objective. But as they get closer, Randy notes with increasing horror: "The Wall Mart is lowering its prices to try to stop us," and in the end he deserts the children when he sees a screwdriver set marked down beyond his wildest dreams. He cries out: "This bargain is too great for me," as he rushes off to a cash register to make a purchase. When the boys at last reach the heart of the Wall Mart, it turns out to be a mirror in which they see themselves. In one of the show's typical didactic moments, the spirit of the superstore tells the children: "That is the heart of Wall Mart—you, the consumer. I take many forms—Wall Mart, K-Mart, Target—but I am one single entity—desire." Once again, *South Park* proclaims the sovereignty of the consumer in a market economy. If people keep flocking to a super-store, it must be doing something right, and satisfying their desires. Randy tells the townspeople: "The Wall Mart is us. If we like our small-town charm more than the big corporate bullies, we all have to be willing to pay a little bit more." This is the free market solution to the superstore problem—no government need intervene. The towns-people accordingly march off to a local store named Jim's Drugs and start patronizing it. The store is so successful, it starts growing, and eventually mutates into—you guessed it—a superstore just like Wal-Mart. *South Park* has no problem with big businesses when they get big by pleasing their customers.

Parker and Stone acknowledge that they themselves work for a large corporation, the cable channel Comedy Central, which is owned by a media giant, Viacom. In the *Reason* interview, Stone says: "People ask, 'So how is it working for a big multinational conglomeration?' I'm like, 'It's pretty good, you know? We can say whatever we want. It's not bad. I mean, there are worse things.'"[15] Anti-corporate intel-lectuals would dispute that claim, and point to several occasions when Comedy Central pulled *South Park* episodes off the air in response to various pressure groups, including Viacom itself.[16] But despite such occasional interference, the fact is that it was Comedy Central that financed the production of *South Park* from the beginning and thus made it possible in the first place. Over the years, the corporation has given Parker and Stone unprecedented creative freedom in shaping a show for television—and not because the corporate executives are partisans of free speech and trenchant satire but because the show has developed a market niche and been profitable. *South Park* doesn't simply defend the free market in its episodes—it is itself living proof of how markets work to create something of artistic value and, in the process, benefit producers and consumers alike.[17]

## Notes

1. *Symposium*, 221E–222A. Quoted in the translation of W.R.M. Lamb, *Plato: Lysis, Symposium, Gorgias*, Loeb Classical Library (Cambridge, MA: Harvard University Press, 1925), 239.
2. *The Clouds*, lines 392–394. Quoted in the translation of William Arrowsmith, *The Clouds* (New York: New American Library, 1962), 45.

3. Mises' most famous book is *Human Action: A Treatise on Economics* (New Haven, CT: Yale University Press, 1949) and Hayek's is *The Road to Serfdom* (Chicago: University of Chicago Press, 1944).

4. Rothbard articulates his libertarian philosophy most fully in *The Ethics of Liberty* (New York: New York University Press, 2002) and *For a New Liberty: The Libertarian Manifesto* (New York: Macmillan, 1978). Perhaps the clearest introduction to the economic principles underlying libertarianism is Henry Hazlitt, *Economics in One Lesson* (San Francisco: Laissez-Faire Books, 1996).

5. As quoted in Brian C. Anderson, *South Park Conservatives: The Revolt against Liberal Media Bias* (Washington, DC: Regnery Publishing, 2005), 178.

6. Nick Gillespie and Jesse Walker, "*South Park* Libertarians: Trey Parker and Matt Stone on Liberals, Conservatives, Censorship, and Religion," *Reason*, 38:7 (2006): 66.

7. For an analysis of why such groups turn against capitalism, see Ludwig von Mises, *The Anti-Capitalistic Mentality* (Princeton, NJ: D. Van Nostrand, 1956), especially pp. 30–33 for the turn against capitalism in Hollywood.

8. A perfect example of Hollywood's negative portrayal of businessmen is the cruel banker Mr. Potter in the classic *It's A Wonderful Life* (dir. Frank Capra, 1946). For a comprehensive survey of the portrayal of businessmen in American popular culture, see the chapter "The culture industry's representation of business" in Don Lavoie and Emily Chamlee-Wright, *Culture and Enterprise: The Development, Representation and Morality of Business* (London: Routledge, 2000), 80–103. Here are some representative figures from media studies: "Of all the antagonists studied in over 30 years of programming, businessmen were twice as likely to play the role of antagonist than any other identifiable occupation. Business characters are nearly three times as likely to be criminals, relative to other occupations on television. They represent 12 percent of all characters in identifiable occupations, but account for 32 percent of crimes. Forty-four percent of all vice crimes such as prostitution and drug trafficking committed on television, and 40 percent of TV murders, are perpetrated by business people" (84).

9. Mises, *Anti-Capitalistic Mentality*, 2.

10. George Bernard Shaw offers this interpretation of Alberich; see his *The Perfect Wagnerite* (1898) in George Bernard Shaw, *Major Critical Essays* (Harmondsworth, UK: Penguin, 1986), 198, 205.

11. For the way H.G. Wells uses invisibility as a symbol of capitalism, see my essay "*The Invisible Man* and the Invisible Hand: H.G. Wells's Critique of Capitalism," in *Literature and the Economics of Liberty:*

*Spontaneous Order in Culture*, ed. Paul A. Cantor and Stephen Cox (Auburn, AL: Ludwig von Mises Institute, 2009), 293–305.

12. Friedrich Hayek, *The Fatal Conceit: The Errors of Socialism* (Chicago: University of Chicago Press, 1988), 90, 91, 93.

13. Several e-mail responses to an earlier version of this chapter argued that the gnomes' diagram makes fun of the sketchy business plans that flooded the initial public offering (IPO) market in the heyday of the dot.com boom in the 1990s. Having helped write a few such documents myself, I know what these correspondents are referring to, but I still think that my interpretation of this scene fits the context better. If the gnomes' business plan is simply satirizing dot.com IPOs, then it has no relation to the rest of the episode.

14. Adam Smith, *An Inquiry into the Nature and Causes of the Wealth of Nations*, 2 vols. (1776; rpt. Indianapolis, IN: Liberty Classics, 1981), vol. 1, 456.

15. Gillespie and Walker, "*South Park* Libertarians," 63.

16. The episodes in question were pulled only from the repeat rotation; they were allowed to air originally and they are now once again available in the DVD sets of the series.

17. A version of this chapter was published under the title "Cartman Shrugged: *South Park* and Libertarianism" in *Liberty* 21:9 (2007): 23–30. For a fuller version of my analysis of *South Park*—including comparisons to works by Rabelais and Mark Twain, as well as a discussion of the controversy surrounding the show's effort to present an image of Muhammad in one episode—see chapter 6 of my book *The Invisible Hand in Popular Culture: Liberty vs. Authority in American Film and TV* (Lexington: University Press of Kentucky, 2012).

# Sitting Downtown at Kentucky Fried Chicken

## One Toke Over the Line

*Kevin S. Decker*

Sometimes when I get wrapped up in a television show, I ask the question, "Would I want to live where this show takes place?" The future of the *Star Trek* universe and *Community*'s Greendale Community College are pretty high up the list of desirable destinations. However, the eponymous small town of South Park is probably the last place I'd want to live. It goes without saying that, in the South Park basin in Colorado, the normal rules of logic, social relations, physics, and of course, good taste, don't apply. More importantly, the people of South Park don't have any of the traits needed to hold a society together, much less create institutions and practices that would allow its citizens to flourish. South Parkers are venial, self-centered, stupid, incompetent, enamored of scatological humor, and, like some Tourette's patients, seemingly unable to prevent themselves from speaking obscenely.

Somewhere, Trey Parker and Matt Stone just heard that and said, "Thank *you*!"

## Libertarianism and Legislating Lifestyles

Like many episodes of *South Park*, "Medicinal Fried Chicken" drags real political scenarios into the cold, hard light of the Rocky Mountains. In this particular case, the issues include the normalization of

*The Ultimate South Park and Philosophy: Respect My Philosophah!*, First Edition.
Edited by Robert Arp and Kevin S. Decker.
© 2013 John Wiley & Sons, Inc. Published 2013 by John Wiley & Sons, Inc.

the use of cannabis, ostensibly for combatting glaucoma, chronic pain, cancer, epilepsy, and other medical needs. At present in the US, medical marijuana has been legalized (in terms of possession, cultivation, or both) in 16 states and the District of Columbia; in 2000, Colorado legalized the possession of up to two ounces of usable cannabis and allowed dispensaries to be established.[1] But the issue of addiction in "Medicinal Fried Chicken"—and the observation that Americans seem keen to be addicted to *something*, legal or not—also stretches to the American movement to provide environments in which healthier eating is encouraged by banning fast food chains from establishing new restaurants, particularly in low-income areas. Such laws typically provoke a firestorm of controversy regarding rights and freedoms— even a kid like Cartman is highly passionate about the fast food issue when, in Randy's car, he says, "Uh sorry, sorry. I just, you know, when I've been waiting too long for the Colonel's chicken I get easily agitated. You're a fuckin' asshole Kenny!"

In this chapter, I'd like to challenge the received interpretation of the moral message behind "Medicinal Fried Chicken" and many other *South Park* episodes, the message that legislating lifestyles is immoral at worst and ridiculous at best. This message is encapsulated by the moral perspective known of libertarianism, which takes individual rights in political and social scenarios to be not only basic, but also to trump many other moral considerations. In the discussion of the legalization of addictive substances—whether pot or fried chicken— Americans very quickly jump to the tension between individual rights and community standards, a conflict that may be insoluble and is certainly interminable. The US has been beset in recent years by political calls for "reform" that recommend the dismantling of rules and regulations because they unfairly bind people's (and corporations') freedom of action. But, as legal scholar Cass Sunstein points out: "Because they resolve cases in advance, rules are disabling, but they are enabling, too. Like the rules of grammar, they help make social life possible ... Rules facilitate private and public decisions by establishing the frameworks within which they can be made, freeing up time for other matters."[2] Not only is Sunstein correct, but rule-less Americans are becoming less and less competent to run their own lives while still maintaining a minimal common good; at least that's the point I'll try to make. This fact is making the US more like South Park, and this is something we all have a good reason to avoid.

# In Harm's Way?

The touchstone in social philosophy for discussion of the relation between community standards and individual rights is John Stuart Mill's (1806–1873) *On Liberty*, a long Victorian essay about the proper compass of liberty. At the center of all of Mill's arguments is the *liberty principle*, that "the appropriate region of human liberty" is found in "a sphere of action in which society, as distinguished from the individual, has, if any, only an indirect interest: comprehending all that portion of a person's life and conduct which affects only himself or, if it also affects others, only with their free, voluntary, and undeceived consent and participation."[3]

In trying to preserve a space for individualism, Mill claimed that the best forms of social organization make possible "liberty of tastes and pursuits, of framing the plan of our life to suit our own character, of doing as we like, subject to such consequences as may follow, without impediment from our fellow creatures, *so long as what we do does not harm them*, even though they should think our conduct foolish, perverse, or wrong."[4] In Mill's native Britain, civil rights were guaranteed by a long string of legislative and judicial decisions dating back to the Magna Carta of 1215; in the United States, many such rights are codified in the Bill of Rights seconded to the American Constitution. Intriguingly, Mill didn't defend civil liberties on the grounds that they were based in the inalienable rights of individuals— a concept that his godfather and fellow philosopher Jeremy Bentham had called "nonsense on stilts." Rather, Mill saw the health and well-being of society as a whole as bound up with the individual freedom of its citizens.

For his time, Mill was a radical, but he was also a member of the social elite. His vision of an educated society enjoying music and poetry is an inherently sustainable one, but it's not clear that this vision would work well in a huge, diverse nation such as the US in the twenty-first century. And, in this question, the one question that Mill never asked is an extremely important one: where do individuals' "tastes and pursuits" come from?

*South Park* is a case study in how problems emerge when Mill's views are plunged into the libertine, consumerist culture of contemporary America. While Mill provides a passionate defense of the maximal liberty of the individual in a society that was increasingly reliant on collective labor and productive of mass media, his arguments are mainly about the beneficial consequences—primarily increased chances for finding truth and growth—that such liberal, open societies are likely to incur. He doesn't deal in any detail with the question of what occurs when one person's liberty interferes with another. In particular, Mill fails to make it clear exactly what *harm* consists in. For example, in the episode "South Park is Gay!" Mr. Garrison and Mr. Slave take Kyle to New York to kill the cast of *Queer Eye for the Straight Guy*. This is clearly a situation of *immediate harm* and Mill would invoke the power of the state to stop them, because no matter how annoying the cast of *Queer Eye* is, their own rights to their lives are not in dispute. However, in another Mr. Garrison and Mr. Slave episode, "The Death Camp of Tolerance," we see a case of *indirect* harm when Garrison, in an effort to get fired by the school board for being gay, subjects Mr. Slave to a course of sexual sadism in front of his kids. This is not a case of physical, but of potential psychological or moral harm. Whether harm is inflicted in this case is dependent upon each child's experience, character, and psychological makeup. While many, if not most, parents would agree that children have a right not to be exposed to offensive behavior, Mill would say that merely being offended isn't being harmed. So it all comes down to whether or not witnessing the sexual sadism actually harms the children.

## Drugs Are Bad, M'Kay

For tensions between an individual's good and the common good in the drug legalization debate, let's look at a 1989 exchange between Milton Friedman and William J. Bennett. Bennett, who was at the time director of the Office of National Drug Control Policy, responded to an open letter in the *Wall Street Journal* written by Friedman, a libertarian economist who won the Nobel Prize in 1976. Bennett's view of the *war on drugs* was uncompromising. "In my judgment," he wrote, "and in the judgment of virtually every serious scholar in the field, the potential costs of legalizing drugs would be so large as to make it a public policy disaster."[5] Friedman was also concerned about the worst effects of drug abuse, but more concerned about how the pursuit of drug dealers and users turns the "tragedy" of drug use for addicts into a "disaster" for society: "Every friend of freedom ... must be as revolted as I am by the prospect of turning the United States into an armed camp, by the vision of jails filled with casual drug users and of an army of enforcers empowered to invade the liberty of citizens on slight evidence."[6]

You may agree, as I do, with Friedman's opposition to the war on drugs. As a libertarian, though, Friedman's argument seems to be fueled by two highly debatable presuppositions: first, that any state intervention in the lives of individuals will result in a net loss of freedom in "an armed camp," and second, that in situations where individual rights and liberties come into conflict with claims in defense of a common good or a common security, the former must win out. Perhaps, however, you're more likely agree with Bennett, who calls himself "an ardent defender" of American laws against drug abuse because this latter practice is morally wrong. "A true friend of freedom understands that government has a responsibility to craft and uphold laws that help educate citizens about right and wrong."[7] One of the most significant differences between Bennett's position and Friedman's is that Bennett sees the exposure of Americans (particularly children) to the *moral* consequences of drug abuse as an *immediate*, not an indirect harm. But there are many reasons to oppose the widespread abuse of drugs other than moral ones, some of which we'll deal with soon.

## Mary Jane, M.D.

What about medicinal marijuana? This might seem to require a different approach, since the argument isn't that everyone has a right to do what they will with their own body, but rather that, as a relatively harmless, natural, and inexpensive drug, marijuana use ought to be allowed on a limited basis. Why? For the purposes of supplying its active ingredient, THC, for: pain relief for sufferers of nerve damage; "nausea, spasticity, glaucoma, and movement disorders;" and stimulation of appetite in people who have wasting diseases, including HIV.[8]

Interestingly enough, Mary Jane is relatively non-addictive. A much-quoted 1999 study of "Marijuana and Medicine" notes that of the 76% of the general US population who have tried tobacco, 32%

had become addicted. Compare that with the 46% who tried cannabis versus the 9% who become addicted and the 2% who tried the second most addictive drug after tobacco, heroin, 23% of whom became addicted.[9] Heroin also topped the British medical journal *The Lancet*'s 2007 schedule of "Drug Rankings by Harm." On a 0 to 4 point scale of possible risks, heroin scored 2.78 for physical harm, 3.0 for dependence, and 2.54 for "social harm." On the same three criteria, tobacco scored 1.24, 2.21, and 1.42, respectively, while cannabis rated 0.99, 1.51, and 1.50.[10]

Despite this, there are many who don't support even the limited introduction of what is currently a Schedule I drug into society, citing the wider availability of pot as a clear and present danger to youth, as a smoke-and-mirror campaign to legalization of non-medicinal marijuana, and as carrying significant health risks. "No medicine prescribed today is ever smoked," one opponent points out. "Marijuana contains over 400 chemicals, and when smoked it easily introduces cancer-causing chemicals to the body."[11] Given both the pros and cons, it's absurd that Randy Marsh would put his long-term health at risk simply to get weed legally at the former KFC, but his choice illustrates the lengths to which the denizens of South Park (and many real-life Americans) are willing to go to in order to satisfy their hedonistic urges. And, of course, there's the fact that women like really big balls.

## I'll Make Sure You're Hooked Up for Life

A perfect libertarian state would legalize drugs like marijuana, regulating them as just another commodity like prescription drugs or automobiles, and only punish its citizens for the consequences of selling or using drugs that violate basic rights to life, liberty, and property.

Property is of particular interest to libertarians, who often claim that the reason why coercion by state or society is wrong is because individuals, first and foremost, "own their own bodies" and can do with them as they please. It's odd to say that our bodies are our property, since it takes a body to claim and protect actual property; also, we quite reasonably don't let people do just anything they please with their property. It also remains to be seen what relationship owning property has to the moral status of people: after all, "owning their own body" is cold comfort to the homeless and penniless who are interested in also having their interests represented in a liberal democracy.

Centering itself on individuals and their property, a libertarian society would model itself upon the capitalist ideal of the perfectly free market, in which the value of every social good and commodity is determined by the law of supply and demand. Such a "minimal state" has only two areas of concern: stopping the use of force or fraud between citizens, and confronting external threats from other nations. No "big government," no welfare, little regulation. And at first glance, the plot of "Medicinal Fried Chicken" provides support for this rosy picture. When the Kentucky Fried Chicken restaurants in South Park and Salina are closed down because of the Colorado law banning unhealthy, fast-food restaurants in low-income areas, Cartman soon falls to buying buckets of Extra Crispy in dark alleys and eventually goes into business with Billy to bring black-market chicken from Corbin, Kentucky. Cartman at first gets into the illegal "original recipe" trade because he's addicted to KFC; only later does he see the profit in it after visiting the Colonel himself in Corbin.

Likewise, perhaps the most important factor in the debate over the legalization of marijuana is the question of the drug's addictive properties. If a substance is addictive—not just narcotics and other outlawed drugs, but also tobacco, alcohol, and perhaps even caffeine and sugar—then it has the possibility of producing either physical dependency through changes in the addict's biochemical states, or the drastic modification of psychological habits, or both. In either case, addiction causes changes to the human brain that start at the reward-processing centers and expand to "complex cognitive functions, such as learning (memory, conditioning, habits); executive function (impulse inhibition, decision making, delayed gratification); cognitive awareness (interoception); and emotional functions (mood, stress reactivity)."[12] It's been widely recognized that the moral agency of addicts is diminished as their autonomous decision-making capacities are whittled down by avoidance or withdrawal symptoms, the belief that they can only be happy when they're high, or their sense of right and wrong is altered by the intense need to procure money or favors to secure their supply. More importantly, the addictive properties of drugs are the basis for a serious challenge to libertarians about the sources of "taste and desire," as Mill put it. Just so long as corporations and special interest groups have an adequate understanding of human psychology, they can manipulate the way in which people utilize their freedom without the issue of coercion as the violation of human rights ever being raised. In this way, the freedom of the libertarian state could be merely "formal," with no one actually being free.

## Fuck You, You Intersubjective Fuck!

The ease with which people like Stan's poker buddies can be controlled by their addiction to drugs serves as a metaphor for the huge flaw in the libertarian's way of thinking about individuals and their rights. Sometimes called the *myth of the omnicompetent individual*, the libertarian picture of human nature is one that contains some curious distortions in that it assumes (against considerable evidence) that the individual is the best judge of their own self-interest and that *only* individuals, and not groups, communities, state, or societies— have intrinsic moral worth.[13]

But what libertarians seem to ignore is that there is a "feedback loop" between individualism and socialization in human development. George Herbert Mead (1863–1931) was an American social psychologist and philosopher who turned the libertarian presupposition on its head, instead arguing for the "temporal and logical pre-existence of the social process to the self-conscious individual that arises in it."[14] For Mead, when we look at the developmental process that allows a non-self-conscious child to eventually become a moral agent, capable of understanding and asserting their individuality and their rights, we see that the process is framed by *intersubjectivity*, or what Mead calls "taking the attitude of the other." In his study of the use and meaning of human signs and symbols, Mead discovered that there are points of qualitative transformation in the experience of individuals, points when they can see themselves as others see them or, more basically, when they can fluidly interpret the meaning of gestures or symbols in the context of a larger system of meanings.

In "Medicinal Fried Chicken," a good example of the *failure* of the intersubjective experience is when giant-testicled Randy is smoking "Purple Lurple" out in the open and is noticed by Office Barbrady and Jimbo:

RANDY:  Uh that is nice! That is *nice*!
JIMBO:  Randy! Jesus, Randy. Your balls!
RANDY:  I KNOW. SMOKIN' POT RIGHT IN FRONT OF A COP. PRETTY SWEET, HUH?

JIMBO:   No, I mean, your actual balls!
RANDY:   OH, YEAH. TESTICULAR CANCER. HERE, HERE, YOU WANT
         SOME? OH WAIT, YOU'RE HEALTHY! HEY BUST HIS ASS,
         OFFICER! [*LAUGHS*]

Randy is unable to see himself as Jimbo does (and frankly, who would want to?). In both *South Park* and the real world, the important point is that gestures and symbols "are certain stages in the cooperative activities which mediate the whole process."[15] This means that without an existing social system for individuality to blossom from, an individual will fail to develop self-consciousness and be unable to "realize" herself.

But Mead shouldn't be taken to imply that individuals are simply *functions* of community life, nor are they insignificant when compared to the collective force of community morals and perspectives. Instead, Mead writes:

> The individual not only has rights, but he has duties; he is not only a citizen, a member of the community, but he is one who reacts to this community and in his reaction to it … changes it. The 'I' is the response of the individual to the attitude of the community as this appears in his own experience.[16]

Mead often emphasizes that voluntary action and responsibility are necessary conditions for the work of intelligence. The ability to choose *is* important, but we shouldn't have any illusions that choices are "free," like being unconstrained by myriad cultural, political, and economic currents. These are things we have no personal control over, but which determine what we consider to be the alternatives for any given choice. This fact seems to be largely ignored by libertarians. Mead's response to them is telling:

> The demand is [for] freedom from conventions, from given laws. Of course, such a situation is only possible where the individual appeals, so to speak, from a narrow and restricted community to a larger one, that is, larger in the logical sense of having rights which are not so restricted.[17]

Of course, this is precisely what libertarians do in their conception of the "omnicompetent individual," who needs to be free of a certain set of restrictions for their full autonomy to be recognized. By abstracting away the political and social history that determines even *what we will choose about*, the libertarian pinpoints the only kind of liberty worth having.

## "I Just Want You to Look at *Me* When We Make Love, and Not Just at My Balls."

Individuals in their freedom and autonomy are of interest to libertarians, so much so that they ignore the power of institutions and social practices that don't operate through force or fraud to cause direct harm, but *can* constrain individual autonomy and channel choices in particular directions. This can be simple persuasion, or it can be insidious influence. Here we should mention not only the addictive substances in drugs and fast food key to the plot of "Medicinal Fried Chicken," but also education, advertising and the media, gender stereotypes, economic class, homophobia, political correctness and institutionalized racism. Frankly, libertarianism seems much the last holdout of the WASP (White Anglo-Saxon Protestant) moral *status quo*, as C.C. Findlay, a critic of the omnicompetent individual ideal points out:

> It is worth noting that, during [the first] five or six decades [of the twentieth century], the traits that defined "competent" and "man" created characters that were inevitably white ... and Anglo-American. Social changes, beginning with the civil rights movement in the '50s, the sexual empowerment of women in the '60s, and the political upheaval that culminated in the '70s with Watergate, undermined the uncritical acceptance of white male infallibility and supremacy.[18]

By contrast, the "identity" or "new social movements" that Findlay speaks about typically base their social criticism on how the power of choice of individuals is formed by the recognition they receive from the communities they live in. As the civil rights movement and ethnic cleansing in Bosnia and Rwanda have showed, lack of recognition of others makes society a worse place to live. For I can't recognize someone as an individual by simply avoiding interference with their life, liberty, or property; this is simply treating them as an abstraction. Instead, recognition requires that I engage in public activities that build social esteem—for instance, supporting Big Gay Al at the South Park Community Center after he was fired as scoutmaster for his sexual preference.

Libertarians are also mute on the subject of *collective responsibility*, which is more and more of a question as countries like the US fail to live up to their national responsibilities, like universal healthcare, or their global responsibilities, like clamping down on climate change. As an example to illustrate this, let's say that Kyle and his friends return to the Atlantis Casino and Waterpark seen in "Jewpacabra." Each child chooses to express his unhappiness with the resort by defecating in the shark tank. While doing this four times in the tank might make a shark or two sick, it doesn't cause direct harm to anyone else.

But if every visitor to Atlantis does the same thing (ignoring for a moment the fact that trashing the shark tank is likely a violation of the owners' property rights), the tank will quickly be polluted, so that the sharks die, and no one can enjoy riding the waterslide down through the tank anymore. If I've paid for this privilege, then I'm directly harmed when it's taken away from me. If I've never been to this unique attraction, then I'm indirectly harmed because I no longer have the opportunity to do so. But who's harmed me? No *one* polluter is responsible for all the trash, and *each* individual polluter is responsible for just a tiny part of the problem. The lesson is this: a community (like the Atlantis Casino and Resort or South Park) is justified in searching for ways to predict and regulate the far-reaching public harms that individuals are *collectively responsible* for, because individuals aren't omnicompetent. They simply can't see the long-term effects of their own actions multiplied by many other imitators.

## Douchebag Prisoners' Dilemma

Political science professors and economists confront these kind of issues on a daily basis, calling them "coordination" or "collective action problems." One of the best-known hypothetical coordination problems is called the Prisoner's Dilemma. Imagine that two thieves have planned to break into South Park's Tantalus V. Observatory (what Dr. Adams calls the plane-*arium*) to steal an expensive laser projector. They were caught breaking in, and are now being questioned in two separate interrogation rooms about their plan. Both thieves know that their punishment will be lighter if they're only convicted of breaking and entering and not the plan to steal the laser projector. Officer Barbrady tells each of them that their best option is to rat out the other and, if they do so, they will escape punishment. If Barbrady can't get a confession from either, he'll have to charge them only with breaking and entering. Each prisoner has only two options: to confess or to keep quiet.

If both thieves keep mum, they'll serve a minimum sentence for breaking and entering. If one thief rats out the other, the one who spills the beans will walk free, while the other who kept tight-lipped will serve a maximum sentence for attempting to steal the projector. But if *both* thieves confess to the plan, they'll serve less than the maximum sentence.

Why is this a "coordination problem"? Because of their lack of ability to communicate. Each thief will initially realize that his best option is to keep quiet, but in the absence of a knowing wink or a hushed conversation between them, they'll also suspect that their confederate will confess, in which case they'll receive the worst punishment while the other goes scot-free. If it's true that, as they say, "there is no honor among thieves," it's unlikely that trust alone will convince both of them to keep quiet.

Note that these thieves are, in a purely formal sense, perfectly *free* to make the decision of confessing or not. Nonetheless, this is a situation that few of us would like to be in. It's not just because our best hope would come from the communication that's denied us, but also because of certain flaws in our psychology that all of us share after millions of years of evolution of human cognitive abilities. In the case of the Prisoner's Dilemma, what is likely to make both thieves confess is a certain human short-sightedness (or "myopia") about potential costs and benefits of our decisions. "Myopia may take the form of decisions," Cass Sunstein explains, "whose short-term net benefits are high but whose long-term costs dwarf their long-term benefits."[19] The thieves are much more likely to rat out each other, and both will sit in prison for longer than if they had kept silent.

Coordination problems confront us everywhere in daily life through situations that meet two conditions: (1) people would be better off if they coordinated their activities than if they just "went it alone," but (2) the same people realize that they'll be worse off if only a handful of individuals participate in the coordination. When Jimbo, Travis, and Nelson acknowledge that they have a common interest in widening the door at the former KFC (to at least elephant-size-testicle-width), they organize a protest, albeit an ultimately unsuccessful one. Similarly, unions, consumer organizations, food co-ops, parents'

KEVIN S. DECKER

playgroups, and letter- and email-writing campaigns attempt to overcome the costs of fragmented, individual action by uniting people for a common cause.

## "Sharon, You Got a Scrotum Coat? Lucky!"

Despite these communal acts of accepting responsibility for each other, less-than-omnicompetent individuals don't organize others in every such case, even when it's in their own best interest. It would also be naive to think that there are centers of economic and social power that wouldn't take advantage of such coordination problems. In these cases, government "for, of, and by the people" will still retain a role in securing substantive, and not merely formal, liberty. Libertarians don't trust government, and perhaps rightly so, but they also fail to realize that *we are the government*. When we say that democracy requires "self-government," this implies that we are required to try to choose the best for ourselves, and to frame that choice in terms that will be amenable to many, if not all, others.

If the example of "Medicinal Fried Chicken" shows anything, it is that those of who don't want to live in *South Park* need to face a difficult fact about human nature and freedom: "Apparently, societies that seek to give everyone the same chance at freedom can only do so at some cost to freedom itself."[20] At some point, we have to realize that the cost of respecting individuals' freedom to make mistakes and exercise poor judgment is a worse kind of paternalism than intervening to prevent these costs from escalating. In many ways, the only character who makes any sense in "Medicinal Fried Chicken" is the clerk at the medicinal marijuana dispensary, who in response to the mountain-oyster-hoppity-hop picketers, yells, "Look, can't we skip all this and just make pot legal? Everyone is just abusing this medicinal system anyway, it's ridiculous!"

## Notes

1. See the data compiled by the National Organization for the Reform of Marijuana Laws (NORML) at its website. Retrieved from http://norml.org/, accessed Feb. 22, 2013.

2. Cass Sunstein, "Problems with Rules," *California Law Review*, 83:4 (1995): 972.
3. J.S. Mill, *On Liberty* (London: Longman, Roberts & Green, 1859), 12.
4. Ibid.; italics added.
5. William J. Bennett, "A Response to Milton Friedman," *The Wall Street Journal*, September 19, 1989, A30.
6. Milton Friedman, "An Open Letter to Bill Bennett," *The Wall Street Journal*, September 7, 1989, A14.
7. Bennett, "A Response to Milton Friedman," A30.
8. National Organization for the Reform of Marijuana Laws, "Marijuana Should Be Legalized for Medical Purposes," in *Drug Legalization*, ed. Karen F. Balkin (Farmington Hills, MI: Greenhaven Press, 2005), 170.
9. Institute of Medicine, "Marijuana and Medicine: Assessing the Science Base" (Washington, DC: National Academy Press), 3.16.
10. David Nutt, Leslie A. King, William Saulsbury, and Colin Blakemore, "Development of a rational scale to assess the harm of drugs of potential misuse," *The Lancet*, 269 (2007): 1051.
11. Gregory M. Gassett, "Marijuana Should Not Be Legalized for Medical Purposes," in *Drug Legalization*, 186.
12. Nora D. Volkow, "Treating Addiction as a Disease: The Promise of Medication-Assisted Recovery," National Institutes of Health/National Institute on Drug Abuse. Retrieved from http://www.drugabuse.gov/about-nida/legislative-activities/testimony-to-congress/ (see June 2010), accessed Feb. 22, 2013.
13. The myth derives from John Dewey, *The Public and Its Problems* (New York: Henry Holt, 1927).
14. G.H. Mead, *Mind, Self and Society*, ed. Charles W. Morris (Chicago: University of Chicago Press, 1934), 186.
15. Ibid.
16. Ibid., 196.
17. Ibid., 199.
18. C.C. Finlay, "The Omnicompetent Man in Speculative Fiction." Retrieved from http://www.ccfinlay.com/omnicompetent-man.html, accessed Feb. 22, 2013.
19. Sunstein, "Problems with Rules," 974.
20. Michael Ignatieff, *The Needs of Strangers* (New York: Viking Penguin), 137.

# Cat Urine, Medicinal Fried Chicken, and Smoking

## South Park's Anti-Paternalistic Libertarianism

### Shane D. Courtland

Central to the political view called libertarianism is the idea that people should be able to do what they want to do in a society, as long as the rights of others aren't violated in the process. So, if you're an adult and want to go to Hooters and check out the action, no one—be it a fellow citizen or the government itself—should stop you from going. As John Stuart Mill (1806–1873) states in *On Liberty*, "Over himself, over his own body and mind, the individual is sovereign."[1] On the other hand, the owners of Raisins (an obvious *South Park* reference to Hooters) probably should be thrown in jail because they're exploiting pre-teen girls by sexualizing them. Libertarians tolerate lots of actions, but they won't put up with straightforward exploitation, sexual predation, murder, theft, rape, or any other action that harms someone.

When interviewers for *Reason* asked Stone and Parker if they could be described as libertarians, they both agreed. In fact, Stone replied, "I think it is an apt description for me personally, and that has probably seeped into the show."[2] In many episodes Stone and Parker advocate Mill's idea of personal sovereignty over oneself and they criticize *paternalism*, or government infringement upon individual sovereignty. They also do this while mocking the behaviors that are wrongfully prohibited. In true libertarian fashion, it's not as though they disagree when Mr. Mackey asserts to third graders, "Drugs are bad, m'kay." Instead, they would cleverly add, "… but government interference in

*The Ultimate South Park and Philosophy: Respect My Philosophah!*, First Edition.
Edited by Robert Arp and Kevin S. Decker.
© 2013 John Wiley & Sons, Inc. Published 2013 by John Wiley & Sons, Inc.

such matters for rational adults is unhelpful and unjustified, m'kay." In this chapter, we'll examine some of Stone and Parker's "seepage," looking at episodes that provide excellent cases of the core ideas of libertarianism.

## Self-Ownership and Paternalism

As Murray Rothbard (1926–1995) writes, "The central core of the libertarian creed, then, is to establish the absolute right to private property of every man: first, in his own body."[3] Besides Mill, we see the emphasis of this right to exclusive self-ownership and sovereignty in the writings of John Locke (1632–1704), specifically in his *Two Treatises of Government*.[4]

Self-ownership has always been at the center of libertarianism, and all libertarians hold that each individual has a private sphere that should be immune from outside interference. As long as the individual doesn't violate the rights of others—through physical or psychological harm—he is to be left to his own devices. Anyone who happens to disagree with his choices can try to persuade him, but it's unacceptable to coerce him. Since the individual owns himself, his will is sovereign over matters that only regard him. This idea is echoed in Friedrich Hayek's (1899–1992) notion that "freedom thus presupposes that the individual has some assured private sphere, that there is some set of circumstances in his environment with which others cannot interfere."[5] Or, as contemporary libertarian Tibor Machan states, "The bottom line of libertarianism is that individual members of human communities are sovereign, self-ruling, or self-governing agents whose sovereignty any just system of laws must accommodate."[6]

Opposed to this core libertarian value is *paternalism*, which allows government authorities (or some private citizens) to interfere with a person's private life in order to protect or advance that individual's interests. Those doing the interfering are acting like a parent or guardian (*pater* is Latin for "father"), while the individual, whose sovereignty gets compromised, is viewed as a child in need of guidance. With paternalism, then, interference by others in the affairs of an individual is okay even if that individual never violates the rights of others. Modern-day China is a clear example of a paternalistic society, given its censorship of certain Internet sites and other policies.[7]

It shouldn't be a surprise that libertarians are hostile to paternalistic policies. John Hospers (1918–2011), for example, writes that libertarians are "vigorously anti-paternalistic, believing as they do that people should absorb the consequences of their own actions, and that in any case the State has no right to legislate what people should do as long as their actions harm no one else."[8] Since the creators of *South Park* are self-identified libertarians, it shouldn't come as a surprise that anti-paternalistic themes are seeded throughout various episodes. When interviewers for *Reason* asked Matt Stone to define *libertarian*, he stressed his overriding motivation for resisting those who sought "control over his life."[9] Of course, just as there are many libertarians, there are many different libertarian arguments for why paternalism is inappropriate. In South Park it's no different, and we can witness various instances of these arguments. Let's examine two types here: consequentialist and deontological.

## Consequentialist Reasons to Avoid Paternalism

One reason for rejecting paternalism is that it causes unintended bad consequences. In the episode "Major Boobage," South Park is beset with a "serious" drug problem. It comes to the attention of the adults that their children might be "huffing" cat urine. When a male cat marks his territory, he sprays a concentrated blast of urine. If you were to inhale such a blast (a.k.a., "cheesing"), that would, according to Mr. Mackey, "get you really high, m'kay? Re-really, reeeally high." Since the adults are terrified that their children will become cheesing-crazy-people (a clever reference to *Reefer Madness*), they take action. Kyle's dad, Gerald, spearheads a law to address this epidemic. At a public gathering, Gerald announces, "I have written up a bill that would make having a cat illegal in the city of South Park ... With my super lawyer powers, we can rid our town of cats, so that our kids never get high again!" With Gerald's solution, the state coercively takes cats from their owners in order to prevent individuals from harming themselves.

One of the problems associated with paternalism is its outright futility. If an individual has an overriding desire to self-harm, it's not clear that any law will prevent him from doing so. Take, for example, drugs in prison. Here's a place where liberty is *overtly* compromised—prisoners are perpetually locked-up and forcibly denied civil liberties, albeit for good reasons. Even in this environment, it's hard to prevent addicts from finding their drug of choice. In our normal (non-prison) environment, where we possess various liberties, it would be even more futile to attempt to prohibit such drugs.

This futility also holds in the town of South Park. Kenny is seriously addicted to cheesing and his friends are concerned that he might be at it again. Stan is skeptical and claims, "Yeah, and where is he gonna find cats anyway? They've been outlawed." Kyle responds, "Pot's illegal too, but people still manage to find it ... I'll bet Kenny's at home cheesing right now." Sure enough, Kenny found Cartman's horde of cats. In fact, eventually even Gerald recognizes this problem. He laments, "Cats aren't the problem. We made cats illegal and then I cheesed for the first time in ten years." The point is that it's incredibly difficult, if not impossible, to prevent people who, like Kenny and Gerald, are seriously motivated to seek pleasures that also harm them from accomplishing that end. Employing the coercive power of the state won't be effective at preventing addicts from getting drugs.

Here's another problem. Notice that when Gerald is employing the power of the state, his goal isn't merely to stop cheesing—he wants to prevent individuals from *ever* getting high, period. This is impossible, as Gerald comes to realize. At the end of the episode he states, "Kids are always gonna find a new way to get high. Like sniffing glue or licking toads, or fermenting feces or huffing paint." The episode ends with Kenny getting high smelling flowers!

When states (or others) seek to prevent individuals from harming themselves via illicit substances, they're placed into a problematic dilemma. As Rothbard notes:

> Once again: Every man has the right to choose. Propagandize against cigarettes as much as you want, but leave the individual free to run his own life. Otherwise, we may as well outlaw all sorts of possible carcinogenic agents—including tight shoes, improperly fitting false teeth, excessive exposure to the sun, as well as excessive intake of ice cream, eggs, and butter which might lead to heart disease. And, if such prohibitions *prove unenforceable*, again the logic is to place people in cages so that they will receive the proper amount of sun, the correct diet, properly fitting shoes, and so on.[10]

A paternalistic government policy might ban *some* of the substances that could be used to self-harm. However—and here's the dilemma—on one hand, if they only ban some (like cats or marijuana), they'll fail to achieve their end. Someone will just switch to another harmful substance. On the other hand, the government might ban *all* unhealthy substances. This, however, would probably be impossible to enforce.

If they *could* enforce such a policy, this would lead to life in a cage more compromising to liberty than any known prison! A list of actions and substances that would need to be prohibited would be very long. Take, for example, Kevin Decker's chapter in this book. Decker argues that it is acceptable for the state to paternalistically ban (or coercively regulate) any item that might undermine autonomy. This includes *any* item that can be construed as "addictive." According to Decker, this is "not just narcotics and other outlawed drugs, but also tobacco, alcohol, and perhaps even caffeine and sugar ..."[11] In addition, Decker implies that such paternalistic policies could legitimately be extended to "not only the addictive substances in drugs and fast food ... but also education, advertising and the media, gender stereotypes, economic class, homophobia, political correctness and institutionalized racism."[12] Hopefully individuals are not claustrophobic—because the state's ability to act paternalistically could make our cages small indeed.

Another consequence of paternalism can be seen in "Medicinal Fried Chicken." Due to the unhealthy nature of Kentucky Fried Chicken (KFC) and the fact that it's marketed primarily to the poor, the state of Colorado closes all KFCs and renders its products illegal. Cartman, a hardcore KFC "addict," is forced to seek alternate means to satiate his fried chicken fix. This pushes Cartman into a newly formed black market. In an overt "Scarface" parody, Cartman becomes a KFC dealer with direct ties to Colonel Sanders. Eventually, the Colonel feels betrayed by Cartman and violently destroys Cartman's organization. Although Cartman survives, many meet a bloody end.

A common libertarian criticism of paternalism is that the interference with an individual's sovereignty creates more harm than non-interference would. Despite the fact that a state might make a particular substance illegal, the demand for it doesn't disappear. Organizations like drug cartels and prostitution rings form to satisfy the ongoing demand. Since these organizations' products are illicit, crime and violence flow from these markets operating outside the law. Since black markets limit supply, forcing the operation to remain underground, the price of illicit goods is higher, primarily because demand remains the same. Cartman discovers this the hard way. After eating "the Colonel's popcorn chicken and honey-mustard sauce," he is informed that his snack costs 85 dollars. Cartman, of course, lacks the money to pay. His addiction, coupled with such high cost, pushes Cartman to join the KFC cartel. As Rothbard notes, this connection between high costs and crime is common with black markets: "Crimes are committed by addicts driven to theft by the high price of drugs caused by the outlawry itself! If narcotics were legal, the supply would greatly increase, the high costs of black markets and police payoffs would disappear, and the price would be low enough to eliminate most addict-caused crime."[13]

Since addicts like Cartman can't afford to sustain their addictions, they seek quick means to enrich themselves, which also tend to be illegal. These include theft, blackmail, and prostitution. Libertarians argue that by legalizing illicit substances, supply will increase and, as a result, crime will decrease. After all, how often is criminal activity associated with tobacco addiction? Imagine, on the other hand, what would happen if you could only get tobacco at 85 bucks a pack!

Black markets also often lead to violence. When there's a dispute in a free market, the parties involved seek legal remedies, and disputes between legitimate companies rarely turn violent because all parties can have their case heard under the law. This isn't true for businesses that operate in the black market. Any disagreements over product quality or fulfillment of contract are resolved through *extra*-legal (nudge, nudge, wink, wink) means. In "Medicinal Fried Chicken," when Cartman is making a drug deal, he samples some supposed KFC gravy and remarks, "This is cut with Boston Market gravy!" Immediately, he pulls a pistol and threatens to execute the dishonest dealer. What's particularly interesting is, at that very moment, Officer Barbrady catches them in the act. He asks, "What's going on back there?" and Cartman replies, "Nothin', it's cool." Cartman has been the victim of fraud. If he were dealing in legal goods, he could've informed Barbrady and taken the guy to court. Instead, he had to settle the dispute himself—with a pistol.

Toward the end of the episode, Cartman fails to fulfill an obligation to Colonel Sanders. Again, this can't be resolved via legal means, and (in keeping with the *Scarface* parody) the Colonel sends a death squad to Cartman's headquarters. Cartman escapes, but there are massive casualties. Countless people die, including innocent bystanders. These deaths may have been avoidable had KFC not been forced into a black market. Significant violence has been associated with 1920s prohibition, America's and Mexico's war on drugs, and South Park's war on KFC.[14]

Before moving on, let's take stock of the consequentialist reasons for respecting individual sovereignty in lieu of paternalistic policies. If our goal is to prevent one from employing individual sovereignty to self-harm, it's futile paternalistically to coerce that individual. If our society possesses greater civil liberties than a prison, individuals will always be able to find their drug of choice. Even if we could stop a particular drug, people would just find another drug to replace it. In addition, the very act of making some substances illicit fosters the creation of black markets, and these markets inflate prices, thus creating a motive for crime. Also, since they deal in banned substances, individuals cannot resolve their disputes through legal, and subsequently peaceful, means. All of these considerations don't imply, of course, that libertarians are in favor of employing individual sovereignty to commit acts of self-harm. However, since there is no such thing as an *omnicompetent*[15] paternalistic state, the paternalistic "cure" is potentially worse than the disease.

## Deontological Reasons to Avoid Paternalism

Another way to argue in favor of libertarianism is based on the idea that each individual is a rational agent and, because of this, their decisions should be respected. The strongest arguments here come from Immanuel Kant (1724–1804), whose moral theory is referred to as *deontology*. As *deon* is Greek for "duty," this means that others are duty-bound to respect the agency of the individual, even when she does things that might harm herself. On this view, paternalism (even if it were to result in beneficial consequences) is expressly forbidden. You simply can't control an individual, even for his own good, as that control is a direct affront to his status as a rational agent. If someone wants to alter the behavior of a self-harming individual legitimately, all they can do is provide that agent with information and attempt to reason with him. Robert Nozick (1938–2002), author of the libertarian book *Anarchy, State and Utopia*, says, "Individuals are inviolable ... My nonpaternalistic position holds that someone may choose (or permit another) to do to himself *anything*, unless he has acquired an obligation to some third party not to do or allow it."[16]

We must be clear when discussing what it means to "respect an individual's agency." We must respect people because they are *autarchic*, but not necessarily because of their *autonomy*.[17] For an agent to have autarchy, he must fulfill the minimal requirements of rationality. An autarchic person has to be free of inner compulsions (like kleptomania), at a sufficient level of maturity (an adult), and capable of ordered thoughts (sane). Autarchy is the normal state of humanity. Any individual who lacks it is viewed as less than fully human. We don't hold non-autarchic people fully responsible for their actions, nor should we allow them to be fully free from paternalistic influence. Autonomy, on the other hand, is a much stronger concept. It means to live according to a moral law that you prescribe to yourself, like freeing yourself from the pull of base desires. Autonomy is an excellence of character that not every human reaches. When a libertarian, then, respects the agency of an individual, this *doesn't* imply that the agent is autonomous. It only implies that they are autarchic—that is, minimally rational.[18]

When others interfere with a person's personal sovereignty and decision making—even if they only intend to help—this is always an unjustified trespass against the individual's agency. As Machan writes, "In a libertarian system no vice squad is sent to break up prostitution, but prostitutes may be implored to stop their degrading professional practices. Once we send in the vice squad we actually deny the prostitutes their humanity, as if they could not make up their own minds."[19] Prostitution may harm prostitutes, yet to force people to change (via coercive interference) undermines their moral status as agents. The only legitimate way to change someone's behavior is by information, reason, and argumentation.

This sentiment is clearly expressed in the *South Park* episode "Butt Out." After watching an anti-smoking musical they think is moronic, Kyle, Stan, and Cartman rebel by smoking behind the school. When they get caught, they accidently burn the school down. Ironically, their parents are more distraught about the fact they're smokers than that they destroyed the school. Of course, the parents blame their smoking on the influence of tobacco companies. Their parents' strategy, then, is to garner the "help of the greatest anti-smoking celebrity that ever lived"—Rob Reiner.

Reiner seeks to employ the power of the state, proclaiming: "I pushed a law for higher taxes on cigarettes, I lobbied to get images of cigarettes removed from movies and art, I forced smokers out of bars and parks." Reiner claims to use these methods to keep individuals from self-harm via tobacco. As a true paternalist, Reiner laments, "Apparently, people still don't understand how bad smoking is for them. Don't they know how dangerous it is to their health?"[20]

Kyle and Stan provide cogent libertarian responses. First, Kyle says, "You just hate smoking, so you use all your money and power to *force* others to think like you. And that's called fascism, you tubby asshole!" Second, Stan attaches blame to the appropriate parties, asserting that it was their fault they smoked, not the tobacco company's fault: "We should all take personal responsibility instead of letting fat fascists like him tell us what to do!" Both Kyle and Stan affirm their moral status as agents capable of choice. When you respect agency, there are two sides to this coin. On one side, you allow the individual to exercise that agency (by not coercively interfering). On the other side, the individual must take personal responsibility for all actions that flow from his agency.

Compare all of this to the arguments of the show's protagonist, Kevin Harris, vice president of "Big Tobacco." After giving the boys a tour of the cigarette factory, Harris states: "And so for centuries, tobacco production flourished. Nobody was even aware of any dangers back then, until, in 1965, when Congress passed an act forcing all tobacco companies to put the Surgeon General's warning on their packages. So now, everyone knows the dangers of smoking. And some people still choose to do it, and we believe that's what being an American is all about." When pressed about the dangers of smoking, Harris provides information to others, allowing them to make an informed choice. Kyle claims about all this, "That sounds perfectly reasonable." Agents, because of their moral status, ought to be able to choose for themselves. When people (like Reiner) violate this status, both Kyle and Stan see them as fascists. However, when faced with the autarchy-respecting methods of Harris, they see this as "perfectly reasonable."

## The Final Say As to How to Run One's Life

The deontological line of reasoning doesn't invoke consequences. Perhaps taking away a person's choice might lead to better consequences. It's possible that some libertarians may acknowledge this fact (disregarding the arguments of the last section), all the while decrying such coercion as an unforgivable lapse of libertarian principles. As Hospers notes: "Once it is clear that our goals for a person do not coincide with his goals for himself, and once we have used reason and possibly persuasion to convince him (never force), and he still sticks to his own, then as libertarians we must conclude, 'It's his life, and I don't own it … From my point of view, and perhaps even in some cosmic perspective, my ideals for him are better than his own. But his have the unique distinguishing feature that they are *his*; and as such, I have no right to interfere forcibly with them.' Here, as libertarians, we can stand pat."[21]

Since an individual owns himself, he gets the final say as to how to run his life. The observance of libertarian principles requires the respect of an individual's agency. To coerce an agent, even if it's demonstratively for his own benefit, runs afoul of the libertarian conception of self-ownership—a conception that some of the more reflective inhabitants of South Park, like Kyle and Stan (and perhaps Matt Stone and Trey Parker), seem to endorse.

## Notes

1. John Stuart Mill, *On Liberty* (London: Longman, Roberts & Green, 1859), 10.
2. Nick Gillespie and Jesse Walker, "*South Park* Libertarians: Trey Parker and Matt Stone on Liberals, Conservatives, Censorship, and Religion," *Reason*, 38:7 (2006). Retrieved from http://reason.com/archives/2006/12/05/south-park-libertarians/singlepage, accessed Feb. 23, 2013.
3. Murray Rothbard, *For a New Liberty: The Libertarian Manifesto* (New York: Collier Books, 1978), 47. There are two broad versions of libertarianism—right libertarianism and left libertarianism—and both share the value and endorsement of self-ownership. The core difference between these versions centers on the appropriation of property in the natural world. See Peter Vallentyne's entry, "Libertarianism" in the *Stanford Encyclopedia of Philosophy*. Retrieved from http://plato.stanford.edu/entries/libertarianism/, accessed Feb. 23, 2013.

4. John Locke, *Two Treatises of Government: In the Former, The False Principles and Foundation of Sir Robert Filmer, And His Followers, are Detected and Overthrown. The Latter is an Essay concerning The True Original, Extent, and End of Civil-Government* (London: Aronsham Churchill, 1690).

5. Friedrich Hayek, *The Constitution of Liberty* (Chicago: University of Chicago Press, 1960), 13.

6. Tibor Machan, "The Case for Libertarianism: Sovereign Individuals," in *Libertarianism: For and Against*, ed. Craig Duncan and Tibor Machan (London: Rowman & Littlefield, 2005), 3.

7. See, for example, Sun Xiaoxia Guo Chunzhen, "Application of Legal Paternalism in China," *Social Science in China*, 1 (2006): 1–27.

8. John Hospers, "Libertarianism and Legal Paternalism," *The Journal of Libertarian Studies*, 4:3 (1980): 256.

9. Gillespie and Walker, "*South Park* Libertarians."

10. Rothbard, *For a New Liberty*, 112.

11. See chapter 16, by Kevin S. Decker, "Sitting Downtown at Kentucky Fried Chicken: One Toke Over the Line," 200.

12. Ibid., 203.

13. Rothbard, *For a New Liberty*, 111.

14. For more on this, see Doug Husak and Peter de Marneffe, *The Legalization of Drugs: For and Against* (Cambridge: Cambridge University Press, 2005).

15. This is a reference to what Decker refers to as the *myth of the omnicompetent individual*. I am skeptical that any libertarian "assumes (against considerable evidence) that the individual is the *best judge of their own self-interest* ..." ("Sitting Downtown at Kentucky Fried Chicken," 206). One ought to be skeptical of anything that claims to be omnicompetent. Libertarians can acknowledge that both individuals and the state (or society) are imperfect regarding the determination of self-interest. The important consideration is to *which* imperfect entity we should defer— the individual or the state. Libertarians are concerned that if we defer to the state, we invite tyranny. We have seen many examples of tyrannical regimes that employ "autonomy promoting" paternalism as they haul individuals to the gulag to be killed or forcefully re-educated. Decker seems to recognize this concern when he writes, "Libertarians don't trust government, and perhaps rightly so, but they also fail to realize that *we are the government*" (206, emphasis in original). Democracy might help, but it is not sufficient to ameliorate libertarian concerns. There still exists the potential for majority tyranny. In fact, the tyranny of the majority was the core concern at the center of Mill's *On Liberty*.

16. Robert Nozick, *Anarchy, State and Utopia* (New York: Basic Books, 1974), 30–31, 58. For more on the Kantian aspects of self-ownership, see Robert Taylor, "A Kantian Defense of Self-Ownership," *The Journal of Political Philosophy*, 12:1 (2004): 65–78.

17. For an excellent discussion on the distinction between autarchy and autonomy, see Stanley Benn, *A Theory of Freedom* (Cambridge: Cambridge University Press, 1988).

18. Decker at times, in chapter 16 of this book, focuses his criticism on an agent's lack of autonomy. The central plot of "Medicinal Fried Chicken" has Randy Marsh deciding to give himself testicular cancer in order to receive medicinal marijuana. In response to this decision, Decker writes, "Given both the pros and cons, it's absurd that Randy Marsh would put his long-term health at risk simply to get weed legally at the former KFC, but *his choice illustrates the lengths to which the denizens of South Park (and many real-life Americans) are willing to go to in order to satisfy their hedonistic urges*" ("Sitting Downtown at Kentucky Fried Chicken," p. 199, emphasis added). I think libertarians would agree that this is not a rational choice—and, hence, not autonomous. However, it is an autarchic choice that Randy can be held accountable for—and, a choice he ought to be free to make.

19. Machan, "The Case for Libertarianism," 12.

20. Gillespie and Walker, "*South Park* Libertarians." As Matt Stone states, "But things like California's smoking ban and Rob Reiner animate both of us. When we did that Rob Reiner episode, to us it was just common sense. Rob Reiner was just a great target."

21. Hospers, "Libertarianism and Legal Paternalism," 265.

# Part VI

# THERE'S A TIME AND A PLACE FOR EVERYTHING, CHILDREN

# You (Still) Can't Get Married, You're Faggots

## Mrs. Garrison and the Gay Marriage Debate

### *Jacob M. Held*

Gay marriage is an issue that almost everyone has an opinion about. To make matters worse, almost everybody's position, whether for or against, is based on really bad arguments. As with most controversial topics, *South Park* has also had its say. This chapter is going to center around one particular episode of *South Park*, "Follow That Egg!" But since its original airing in late 2005 a lot has happened with respect to gay marriage.[1] California's passage of Proposition 8 in 2008[2] and the Ninth Circuit Court of Appeal's subsequent ruling that the gay marriage ban was unconstitutional[3] have brought gay marriage back into the spotlight for what appears to be an inevitable Supreme Court showdown. Also, North Carolina passed an amendment to constitutionally ban gay marriage in May 2012. Even President Obama has entered the debate by publically supporting same-sex marriage. These recent events show that although the episode may be getting old, the issue and the themes raised in it are as topical as ever.

In "Follow that Egg!" Mrs. Garrison attempts to rekindle her relationship with Mr. Slave, but the reunion doesn't go as planned. Mr. Slave is going to marry Big Gay Al as soon as the Colorado governor signs a bill authorizing same-sex marriages. Mrs. Garrison vows to put an end to the bill, claiming, "Fags are gettin' married over my dead body."[4] She then begins her crusade against gay marriage,

*The Ultimate South Park and Philosophy: Respect My Philosophah!*, First Edition.
Edited by Robert Arp and Kevin S. Decker.
© 2013 John Wiley & Sons, Inc. Published 2013 by John Wiley & Sons, Inc.

with arguments from tradition, the holy sacrament of marriage, and the parental needs of children.

There are many arguments for and against gay marriage. In what follows, I'll look at the most familiar arguments on both sides and demonstrate that they usually miss the point, are entirely irrelevant, or are just bad arguments. In so doing, I hope to map out the landscape of the gay marriage debate and show how barren it is. The only real case for gay marriage is rooted in America's political liberal tradition of "negative liberty."

## My God, Nature, and the Dictionary Say "No!"

There's a basic religious argument against gay marriage that simply says that, according to scripture and/or revelation, homosexuality is a sin, marriage is a holy sacrament between a man and a woman, or *both*. Many religiously minded people take this issue seriously, and they have the right to their religious beliefs. But our government isn't a theocracy and our rights shouldn't be determined by religious traditions. We live under the Constitution, not the book of Leviticus. To be a good citizen, you obey a rule of law, not your pastor or priest. Whatever your god is, whatever book you think communicates this god's laws, and however you interpret those laws is irrelevant to a debate about the distribution of rights and privileges in a democracy.[5] The United States is a secular nation.

So the religious argument may be subjectively comforting to some, but that's about as much as it can convince. That is, unless Jesus Christ actually gets a public access call-in show, where we could actually get his take on the matter! But even then he couldn't simply claim that his position was superior merely because "Jesus says so." He'd still need to justify his view, and he'd have to appeal to reason using facts as evidence for his position. Mrs. Garrison does argue that marriage is a holy sacrament, but even she doesn't push the point. She knows that marriage is a secular issue of rights and privileges, not a theological matter.

Another argument against gay marriage is an argument from definition; it says that marriage is defined as a union between a man and a woman, so gay marriage can't be marriage. This is trivially true. If marriage is defined in this way, then same-sex unions, whatever else they might be, can't be marriage. But the last time I checked, we didn't refer constitutional issues or matters of rights to *Webster's Dictionary*.[6] We need more than a dictionary to understand the issues at hand here. To be charitable, let's presume that what the definition argument really implies is that marriage is *essentially* a union between a man and a woman. But what could this mean? If it's just about gender and Mr. Slave is now legally a woman, if she is going to marry anyone, she has to marry Mrs. Garrison. But surely this isn't consistent with what opponents of gay marriage intend. When they speak of marriage there must be something else, because how can a marriage between Mr. Slave and Mrs. Garrison be acceptable for those who wish to maintain the sanctity of marriage?

What this argument usually boils down to is not just an issue about opposite sexes, but procreation; the essence of marriage is the connection of opposites for procreation.[7] A marriage is essentially a bond between a man and woman because they are the ones who can have children. But this presumes there are moral implications of simple biological or natural facts. If this moral order is one designed by a god, then it's unacceptable, as we saw, for its lack of secularity. If it's not theological, it still would imply that marriage should be illegal for post-menopausal women, sterile couples, or couples who willingly choose not to have children. They all violate the sanctity of marriage by denying its procreative purpose. To avoid this problem, some say it's about the fact that a man and woman *could* have children if everything was working properly, whereas gays can't possibly have children. It's a biological fact about gay relationships that they're not procreative. But still, what about childless couples who choose to be childless and remarriages of post-menopausal women? In fact, this whole argument seems to absurdly boil down to the idea that the possession of complementary sexual organs is the necessary condition for marriage. But this seems incredibly arbitrary when talking about the distribution of rights and privileges. Apparently, just because my wife and I "fit together," we're granted certain rights others aren't; that is, we enjoy the position of a privileged class because of our genitalia—*not* because of our capacity to have children, our love for or commitment to each other, or any other factor that's important to staying married. If I've framed this argument correctly, then not only is the argument circular (marriage is between a man and woman because only a man and woman can get married, and for no other reason than that one is a man and the other a woman), but also it betrays a simple bigotry: "Gays can't get married because they're gay." End of story, no further explanation needed.

But rights are too important to be left to the irrational, emotional, or visceral reactions of others, and the law is not about enforcing the morality of the majority.[8] In fact, this is why the very idea of public referenda on marriage equality is a problem. The public shouldn't be able to vote on who is or is not treated equally. Civil liberties should never be put up to a vote. Doing so subjects the minority to the whims of the majority. Instead, if we grant rights to some and not to others, there should be reasons for this. Reasons are what hold our society together and afford all of us an equal voice.

So there *must* be something more to the position against gay marriage. What about the argument from tradition that marriage has *always* been between a man and a woman? Although this is historically debatable,[9] let's presume it's true. So what? Slavery was a tradition with a long lineage, and so was the oppression of women. Tradition doesn't prove that something is acceptable, just that others have accepted it. But the traditionalists must know this, because they always bolster this argument by claiming that traditional marriage has endured because it works so well and it's a fundamental institution of society. George W. Bush (a.k.a. "Turd Sandwich") has remarked: "Ages of experience have taught humanity that the commitment of a husband and wife to love and to serve one another promotes the welfare of children and the stability of society."[10] Let's go with this appeal to good consequences, because the simple fact that something has been done a certain way for a long time means very little. The argument then becomes: marriage is a fundamental social institution that's too important to lose, and gays will obviously fuck it up. So keep gays away from marriage or we'll all be screwed.[11]

## You Think Kids Can Be Raised by Queers?

So maybe gay marriage will harm society, and this is a reason to prevent it from becoming law. This is a legitimate concern, and one that needs to be addressed. Marriage has played a very important role in society and it's a valuable institution. It should be protected and probably promoted. So, in what way will gay marriage destroy it or prevent heterosexual marriage from continuing to function? Will it erode the institution of marriage itself? Well, whether or not Mr. Slave and Big Gay Al get married has no impact whatsoever on *my* marriage. Yet, opponents of gay marriage argue it will devalue marriage in general. Aside from the questionable implication—that it will undermine marriage because gays marrying make a mockery of it—this doesn't seem plausible.[12] Gays want marriage rights because they value the institution and want in on it. Heterosexuals will still be able to marry (and divorce) as they always have. Maybe it's about the children?

Mrs. Garrison is quick to point out to the governor that if gays are allowed to marry, then they'll also want adoption rights. Think of the children! TV talking head Bill O'Reilly has made the same case, arguing that nature made marriage between a man and woman because they're best suited to raise children.[13] The one small problem with this claim is that all existing data fail to show that kids raised in families with gay parents are harmed, disadvantaged, or otherwise maladjusted by the fact.[14] Some of the concerns themselves seem ludicrous: these children will have a distorted sense of sexual identity, people say.[15] But again, no study has shown this to be the case. People also argue that these children will suffer from social isolation or ridicule. But is this a good argument? The fact that Mrs. Garrison is willing to rip on Stan and Kyle's "freak egg" because it has two daddies is her problem, not the egg's or gay parents' problem. Consider her reasoning: the egg can't be raised by gay parents because, if it is, then she and other people like her will pick on it, causing it to be maladjusted. This then proves that gay parents can't raise healthy children!

In fact, it would undoubtedly be better for a child of gay parents if her parents weren't stigmatized by society, with their commitment publicly recognized and secured through a system of rights and privileges. This advances moral progress rather than giving in to bigotry and hatred. If marriage really is about fitness as parents, then where's the test for straight parents that would guarantee they are qualified to have children? Did Butters' parents have to demonstrate their fitness as parents before they could fuck him up?

The argument that's by far the most popular and many people think is decisive against gay marriage is based on the idea of a "slippery slope." It goes like this: if you won't deny gays the right to marry because gender's not a good reason to limit marriage rights, then you have to reject all limitations on marriage. So if we allow gays to marry, then we'll have to allow polygamy, polyandry, and even incestuous marriage. Who knows, somebody might even want to marry their cat![16] This argument might seem sound because its adherents don't see a way to distinguish between gay marriage and other more "questionable" types of relationships. Allowing one means you must allow them all. But this is not true, for a number of reasons.

First, gay marriage is different from these other types of marriage in this important way: there's no foreseeable harm from gay marriage, whereas polygamy and incestuous marriage harm the social good. We could imagine arguments parallel to those against gay marriage opposing the Supreme Court's ruling in *Loving v. Virginia* (1967) in which the court ruled anti-interracial marriage legislation unconstitutional. But no reasonable person would have taken this seriously. Gay marriage should stand or fall on its own merits, not as a result of the hyped and unjustified fears of its detractors, even if they are such stand-up citizens as Mrs. Garrison.

Yet at the heart of the opponents' arguments is a genuine concern, namely, the good of society. Opposition to gay marriage take two basic forms: the first is to claim that gay marriage just is wrong and unnatural and so it shouldn't be allowed. But revulsion, personal disgust, or visceral reactions aren't moral positions—they are mere reactions, and they're not solid ground for public policy.[17] My rights can't simply depend on your opinion of me or my lifestyle. Unfortunately, just like Mrs. Garrison, people who oppose gay marriage *feel* that it's wrong and construct arguments after the fact to try and rationalize their conclusions. Mrs. Garrison's arguments are simply a way for her to allow her own jealousy into a public policy debate through the back door (tasteless pun intended). The only consideration worth weighing is the claim that gay marriage might have a negative impact on society, whether through undermining the institution of marriage, harming children, or leading to other consequences like sanctioning polygamy and incestuous marriage.

America's liberal heritage is rooted in the notion of "negative liberty" best expressed in John Stuart Mill's (1806–1873) harm principle: "The only purpose for which power can be rightfully exercised over any member of a civilized community, against his will, is to prevent harm to others."[18] Before the government can restrict behavior, Mill thinks, it has to prove that that behavior will cause harm to others. The claim that liberty is freedom from encroachment on my rights and that I have the right to self-determination so long as it harms no one is a foundational principle of American democracy. With respect to natural rights, Thomas Paine (1737–1809) claimed we had "all those rights of acting as an individual for his own comfort and happiness, which are not injurious to the natural rights of others."[19] And civil rights are those secured through a social contract that guarantees our natural rights. The moral condemnation of the majority isn't a good reason to limit the rights of a minority. This is the same reasoning the Supreme Court used to prove the unconstitutionality of anti-sodomy laws.[20] And it's the same reasoning that can demonstrate there's no compelling reason to deny marriage rights to gays.

## They're Going to Allow Queers and Homos to Get Married, Huh?

There are two popular arguments *for* gay marriage. The first starts with the simple claim that what gays are demanding are the same rights that straights have, and that sexual orientation isn't an adequate reason to deny a group of individuals these rights. Denying gays the right to marry is, it is argued, discrimination equivalent to that historically suffered by other minority groups like women and African-Americans.

This argument is based, though, on a fundamental misunderstanding. Gay marriage would require the creation of an entirely new category of rights. The civil rights movement was based on the idea that all people should have the same rights, so if men can vote, then women ought to be afforded the right also. But gay marriage is different, since as it stands, nobody has the right to marry a person *of the same sex*. Straight people don't have that right any more than gay people do. And the right that straights have, to marry one partner of the opposite sex, is shared by gays.[21] Mr. Slave could marry Mrs. Garrison. What proponents of gay marriage want is a new right, one to marry a member of the same sex, presumably through the legal redefinition of marriage. To claim that this is an equal rights issue betrays a fundamental misunderstanding of the issue at stake, the *redefinition* of marriage rights. This is a civil rights issue, but it is not about equal rights.

The other often-made case for gay marriage is that gay marriage will have the same stabilizing and beneficial effect on society that traditional marriage has had: so, if this is a good enough reason to maintain traditional marriage, then there's an equally good reason to promote gay marriage.[22] If this argument's correct, then gay marriage will help stabilize the gay community, promote family values in a community that could benefit from them, provide loving and nurturing homes and families to children who might otherwise not have them, and, in general, benefit society. Mr. Slave and society could only gain by allowing Big Gay Al to marry, and perhaps temper some of Mr. Slave's otherwise less than desirable proclivities (poor Lemmiwinks!). There has been little research on this matter and perhaps all that can be said is this: at worst gay marriage doesn't hurt society and at best it helps.

## Teacher, Our Egg Is Fine—Gays Can Get Married

The best case *for* gay marriage is that there is no compelling, legitimate case *against* it.[23] Really, gays shouldn't have to make the case for themselves; rather, others should have to make a case against them. Mrs. Garrison can't rely on tradition, holiness, or the good of the children to condemn gay marriage. She has to acknowledge that she only wants the ban because she doesn't want to see Mr. Slave married to anybody but her. But without good reason, her personal feelings don't count as a good foundation for her argument.

Of course, marriage is not something that's freely handed out. We put certain restrictions on it. You can only marry one person at a time; they have to be of a certain minimal age and of the opposite sex; and they can't be a close relative. But marriage is also fairly permissive. Rapists and child molesters can get married, and so can transgendered individuals and even gays, so long as they meet the requirements above.[24] These restrictions and allowances are all justified based on the principle of harm: we can't deny the right to marry to felons because there's no compelling reason to exclude them. Arguments about further restricting marriage are based on the desire to regulate harmful practices, so we don't allow polygamy, incestuous marriage, or under-age marriages. But each of these cases can be made on the facts that demonstrable harm would be caused by allowing them.

To allow under-age marriages is to allow the exploitation of children who require protection. To allow incestuous marriages undermines the family structure, since it makes relatives accessible sexual targets and creates insecurity and instability in the family unit. The case against polygamy is similar: it's harmful to women and has negative repercussions for society.[25] But the case of gay marriage is different.

Many of our rights are negative rights; that is, rights to not be interfered with by others. The only justifiable way government can interfere in our right to self-determination is to prevent harm. So if there is no likely harm, there's no reason for government to interfere. Applied to gay marriage, this allows us to say that since gay marriage doesn't carry demonstrable threats to society, in the way some other forms of marriage might, there's no justifiable reason to ban it.

The reason to support the right of gay marriage is the importance of family. Marriage is about creating families, and although the family has traditionally been a man and a woman raising naturally born children, this isn't how it has to be. In "Follow That Egg!" Stan and Kyle were frankly much better parents than Stan and Bebe. Cartman broke his egg. Clearly, being straight isn't enough to be a good parent, just like being gay isn't enough to make a person unqualified to be a parent. Families are the basic units that allow society to cohere and they provide for child rearing and stability. But nothing in this definition demands that the work must be done by the traditional family held up by those who oppose gay marriage. Adoptions and single-parent families can function well, and would do better with governmental support. Families with gay parents have provided stability in the past, too. Although a cliché, it's also true that there are many ways to be a family.[26] In fact, there are many greater threats to marriage than gays wanting it, and better ways to bolster the institution than to build anti-gay discrimination into it. As John Kerry (a.k.a. "Giant Douche") said about the 1996 Defense of Marriage Act, "If this were truly a defense of marriage act, it would expand the learning experience for would-be husbands and wives. It would provide for counseling for troubled marriages … treatment on demand for those with alcohol and substance abuse [problems] … it would expand the Violence Against Women Act."[27] Defending marriage is important, but gay people are not the threat.

Despite all this, I don't think all opponents of gay marriage are bigoted. They probably would not endorse Mrs. Garrison's solution of a "fag drag." Some have genuine and legitimate concerns about the relationship between gay marriage and family, an institution they believe to be at the heart of society. But if all your arguments fail and you're left with merely your visceral reaction, moral indignation and nothing else, you're allowed your opinion but can't reasonably expect that your personal preference be the guiding principle of public policy, especially at the expense of others.

## Being "Butt Buddies" Isn't the Same as Being Married

In "Follow That Egg!" the governor of Colorado comes up with an ingenious solution to the problem of gay marriage. Gays will be able to marry, but it won't be called "marriage." Gays will get the new right they want and opponents won't have the word marriage "tainted" by the inclusion of gays. Gay married couples will instead be called "butt buddies" (and apparently, since nobody cares about dykes, we don't have to worry about them). Mr. Slave lisps, "We want to be treated equally" (yes, he's so gay he can lisp a sentence without a single "s" in it). The governor says that this *is* equality, and everybody's happy, right?

No. This isn't being treated equally in any relevant sense. Gay marriage is based on rights, but the moral message behind it is about family and acceptance. Gays want marriage rights because they want to be included in society. Jonathan Rauch notes: "One of the main benefits of publicly recognized marriages is that it binds couples together not only in their own eyes, but also in the eyes of society at large."[28] It's about social recognition. To use a different word or phrase to set off gay marriage marks it as different and inferior. It doesn't treat gays as equals but, rather, reaffirms their second-class citizenship. Some people who oppose gay marriage are for civil unions—or "butt buddies"—because they acknowledge the importance of rights, but they don't want to include gays in their traditions. This is the height of hypocrisy. To classify gays differently is to deny them equal status as members of the community. It's degrading and humiliating. Marriage as an institution is important, not just because of the rights it affords the members of the marriage, but because of the order it bestows on society through its moral message of commitment. This is an aspect of marriage denied civil unions by its very nature as a relationship that's "not marriage." Separate but equal is never equal, for the simple reason of the stigma attached to what is set apart. If there's a case for gay marriage, it is for gay *marriage* and nothing short of full recognition will do. Until Mr. Slave and Big Gay Al are pronounced "man and man," they're not married, regardless of whether or not they are butt-buddies.

## Notes

1. Currently 20 states and the District of Columbia offer some form of legal recognition to same-sex couples. Only six of these states and DC offer same-sex marriages, although two additional states recognize same-sex marriages issued from out of state. See: http://www.hrc.org/resources/entry/same-sex-relationship-recognition-laws-state-by-state, accessed Feb. 23, 2013.
2. Proposition 8 was a ballot initiative in California that would have amended the Constitution of California so that only marriages between a man and a woman could be recognized by the state. It was passed in the fall of 2008.
3. See *Perry v. Brown*, 134 Cal. Rptr.3d 499 (9th Cir. 2011).
4. In order to quote the show accurately I have to use Mrs. Garrison's own words, but I am offended by her use of the word "Fag." I agree wholeheartedly with Cartman: "Fag" is a hate word, and it's insensitive to butt pirates.
5. Currently straight couples receive over 1100 federal benefits and protections that gay couples are not afforded. See: http://www.hrc.org/files/assets/resources/HRC_Foundation_Answers_to_ Questions_About_Marriage_Equality_2009.pdf, 5, accessed Feb. 23, 2013.
6. Although when put up to state referenda the majority unfortunately, unthinkingly believe *Webster* is authoritative—hence the 30 (with the recent addition of North Carolina) states that have constitutional amendments defining marriage as between one man and one woman and an additional 12 with laws restricting marriage to one man and one woman. See: http://www.hrc.org/files/assets/resources/marriage_prohibitions_2009(1).pdf, accessed Feb. 23, 2013.
7. See Sam Schulman, "Gay Marriage—and Marriage," in James E. White, ed., *Contemporary Moral Problems* (Belmont, CA: Wadsworth Publishing, 2006), 285–293.
8. See Ronald Dworkin, *Taking Rights Seriously* (Cambridge, MA: Harvard University Press, 1978), Chapter. 10, "Liberty and Moralism."

9. Some have argued that historical data show that the equivalent to gay marriage has existed in the past. For a good summary of this position, see Andrew Sullivan, ed., *Same-Sex Marriage: Pro and Con: A Reader* (New York: Vintage Books, 2004), chapter 1, "For the First Time Ever? Same-Sex Marriage in History."

10. George W. Bush, "The President Speaks: President George W. Bush, February 24, 2004" in *Same-Sex Marriage: Pro and Con*, 343.

11. Although, as stewards of the institution of marriage, straights don't have a very successful record.

12. Maggie Gallagher presents this type of argument in her piece, "What Marriage is For: Children Need Mothers and Fathers," in Lewis Vaughn, ed., *Doing Ethics*, 2nd ed. (New York: W.W. Norton and Company, 2010), 434–438.

13. Aside from the questionable premise that nature intends anything (he must mean a god), it presumes that what qualifies one to be a parent is the proper genitals, not any set of parenting skills. He made this comment on "The O'Reilly Factor," air date June 5, 2006, and no doubt countless other times. But at this point should any of us be surprised at what comes out of the mouth of a grown man who thinks that the effect of the gravitational force exerted by the moon on large bodies of water is proof of a divine entity?

14. When faced with this many opponents to gay marriage, like O'Reilly, fall back on the claim that they just don't believe gays can raise kids as well as straights. Apparently facts and logic are irrelevant for the forming of their opinions; all they need are good old fashioned gut reactions. Bullshit goes in, bullshit comes out. Never a miscommunication. Stephen Colbert would be proud of such a strong commitment to truthiness. For this type of view, see: James Q. Wilson, "Against Homosexual Marriage" and Hadley Arkes, "The Role of Nature," in *Same-Sex Marriage: Pro and Con*; Stephen Knight, "How Domestic Partnerships and Gay Marriage Threaten the Family," in Robert M. Baird and Stuart E. Rosenbaum, eds., *Same-Sex Marriage: The Moral and Legal Debate* (Amherst, NY: Prometheus Books, 1996).

15. See Charlotte Patterson, "Children of Lesbian and Gay Parents: Summary of Research Findings," in *Same-Sex Marriage: Pro and Con*, 240–245.

16. This is a fear that former senator and Republican presidential candidate Rick "Man on Dog" Santorum might share.

17. See Dworkin, *Taking Rights Seriously*, chapter 10.

18. John Stuart Mill, *On Liberty and The Subjection of Women* (Hertfordshire: Wordsworth Editions, 1996), 13.

19. Thomas Paine, *Rights of Man in Collected Writings* (New York: Literary Classics of the United States, 1995), 464.
20. See Justice Kennedy's majority opinion in *Lawrence v. Texas*, 539 U.S. 558 (2003).
21. See Richard McDonough, "Is Same-Sex Marriage an Equal-Rights Issue?" *Public Affairs Quarterly*, 19 (2005): 51–63.
22. See Jonathan Rauch, "Who Needs Marriage?" in James E. White, ed., *Contemporary Moral Problems* (Belmont, CA: Wadsworth Publishing, 2006), 294–302.
23. Traditionally, US courts have maintained that any measure that effectively limits or denies citizens their rights must pass one of two tests depending on the nature of the right in question: strict scrutiny or rational basis review. To pass rational basis review, the restriction in question must be rationally or reasonably related to a "legitimate" government interest. To pass strict scrutiny, the restriction in question must serve to further a "compelling" governmental interest, and must be narrowly tailored to achieve that interest. With respect to gay marriage the question becomes: does limiting marriage to straights promote a legitimate or compelling state interest? Such interests usually include preventing foreseeable harms.
24. See M.D.A. Freeman, "Not Such a Queer Idea: Is There a Case for Same Sex Marriages?" *Journal of Applied Philosophy*, 16 (1999): 1–17.
25. I'm not claiming that these are definitive arguments, merely that they have been offered. In fact, I think polygamy is an interesting case that should be revisited, and, given Trey Parker and Matt Stone's fascination with Mormons, *South Park* is bound to take it up at length at some point.
26. See Larry A. Hickman, "Making the Family Functional: The Case for Same-Sex Marriage," in *Same-Sex Marriage: The Moral and Legal Debate*, 192–202.
27. John F. Kerry, "Senate Debate on the Defense of Marriage Act: September 10, 1996," in *Same-Sex Marriage: Pro and Con*, 232.
28. Rauch, "Who Needs Marriage?" 301.

# Cute and Cuddly Animals versus Yummy Animals

*Cynthia Jones*

Lots of *South Park* episodes parody animal rights activism, vegetarianism and veganism, as well as animal experimentation. My personal favorites are "Whale Whores," "Pee," and "Fun with Veal." One recurring theme, especially in "Whale Whores" and "Fun with Veal," is that most people are outraged over the killing of cute and cuddly animals while they're unmoved by the killing of yummy animals. But, at the same time, the animal rights activists portrayed in episodes like "Whale Whores" and "Free Willzyx" are crazy, single-minded animal lovers who will kill people to liberate an animal from a zoo or aquarium. Why are some people vegetarians or vegans and why do some people protest zoos, aquariums, and animal experimentation? And why should we care?

## All Animals Are Created Equal … Not Really! (and the Japanese Hate Whales and Dolphins)

With Japanese whale hunting and a particularly inane real-life Animal Planet show entitled *Whale Wars* gaining media attention, "Whale Whores" finds Stan doing battle with the Japanese whale hunters as the captain of an eco-terrorist ship that attacks the whale and dolphin slaughterers. Of course, the Japanese aren't content with just slaughtering the defenseless whales and dolphins in the ocean. Being very

*The Ultimate South Park and Philosophy: Respect My Philosophah!*, First Edition.
Edited by Robert Arp and Kevin S. Decker.
© 2013 John Wiley & Sons, Inc. Published 2013 by John Wiley & Sons, Inc.

thorough, they head to aquariums and amusement parks to kill captive whales and dolphins there as well.

According to *South Park*, the Japanese hate whales and dolphins because of the United States-provided photo of the *Enola Gay* dropping the atomic bomb on Hiroshima, a photo that clearly shows a dolphin and a whale as pilot and bombardier. When Stan presents the Japanese Prime Minister with a newly doctored photo of the incident that clearly shows a cow and a chicken perpetrating the bombing, the Japanese turn their ire instead to cows and chickens, saving the cuter dolphins and whales and bringing the Japanese animal-killing into line with our more refined American sensibilities about which animals can be gratuitously slaughtered.

"Pee" finds the boys quarantined in a waterpark after the pee-to-water ratio tops 98% and the park explodes. The park has to be quarantined because, as an experiment with three rhesus monkeys clearly demonstrates, exposure to large quantities of pee makes the poor victims really angry and violent. The problem is that the "experiment" involves the researchers peeing on the monkeys and watching their response. Getting peed on while tied up seems to agitate them, amazingly enough. Even though the faulty science in the animal experiment is only a subplot of the episode, the gratuitous use of animals in poorly designed experiments provides a nice jab at animal experimentation.

## Tortured Baby Cows and Vaginitus

The *South Park* episode "Fun with Veal" targets vegetarianism and the veal industry, making fun of the compassion many people extend to some animals (cute baby cows, for example) but not to others (fully grown cows, for example). On a class trip to a local ranch, Stan, Kyle, and Butters are horrified to learn what veal is "really made from." Cartman, far from suffering moral outrage, asks for a free sample. When they ask why veal is called *veal*, the rancher responds, "Well, if we call it *little baby cow*, people might not eat it." The boys decide to rescue the cute baby cows before they are sent to the slaughterhouse. During their extended standoff in Stan's bedroom—against their parents, the FBI, and Rancher Bob—the boys find that the only adults who empathize with their outrage over the plight of the cute baby cows are the "no-good, dirty, God-damned hippies" (as Cartman puts it). Thanks to Cartman's slick negotiating and highly honed manipulation skills, the boys get the FDA to change the name *veal* to *tortured baby cow*, which effectively devalues the veal industry and saves the cute baby cows in question.

But despite the boys' outrage over the plight of the baby cows, only Stan decides to give up eating meat completely. Unfortunately, Stan then develops the fictional illness *vaginitus*, as anyone who completely gives up eating meat will obviously turn into a "giant pussy." In the end, Stan is ultimately saved from this horrible fate in the nick of time, thanks to medical intervention and an IV-drip of pure beef blood. All's well that ends well, as the boys and their parents go out for burgers.

Other chapters in this book talk about faulty reasoning and the problems that result from holding beliefs based on errors in reasoning.[1] This chapter is about *ethics* (the branch of philosophy concerned with what we ought to do and how we ought to live) in general, and about vegetarian and animal suffering claims in particular. Ethics or *moral philosophy* is the branch of philosophy concerned with "how we ought to live," as Socrates (469–400 BCE) said.[2] Moral philosophers explore questions about how we *should* live, rather than describing how we *actually do* live—which is more the job of social scientists like psychologists or sociologists. Thus, ethics is *prescriptive* (telling us what *ought to be* or what *should be* the case), rather than *descriptive* (telling us what *is* the case). In addition to offering guidelines for acting and for treating others, and an ethical theory should also tell us who should matter in our moral deliberations and who should not.

*South Park* revels in something that really concerns philosophers, the inconsistency of moral beliefs. In the case of "Fun with Veal," it seems that many people are outraged over the treatment of some animals while they happily devour the dead carcasses of other animals, seemingly having no problem with the pain and suffering animals endure before reaching the dinner table. And so while it's terrible to harm cute baby cows, only a giant pussy—or a no-good, dirty, God-damned hippie—would give up eating meat completely. As Stan says, "Guys, I learned something today. It's wrong to eat veal because the animals are so horribly mistreated, but if you don't eat meat at all, you break out in vaginas." Of course, he makes this judgment before the boys meet the Feegans—South Park's life preserver-wearing vegan family in "Broadway Bro Down." If vegetarianism (or not consuming meat) makes you break out in vaginas, imagine what veganism (or not consuming any animal products) will do to you!

The same irony about inconsistent moral beliefs bubbles up in other *South Park* episodes. For example, in "Red Hot Catholic Love," Father Maxi confronts Catholicism's contradictory beliefs, especially those arising in the conflict of Roman Catholic dogma with the cover-up of the sexual molestation of young boys by Catholic priests. In "The Death Camp of Tolerance," Mr. Garrison breaks down at the end and screams at the townspeople for confusing a reasonable moral belief—that people should be tolerant to some extent of different ideas and lifestyles—with a less reasonable moral belief—that condemning or judging anyone for any behavior, even blatantly degrading and harmful behavior, is intolerant. The whole episode, including the title, is a satire of intolerance of the perceived intolerance of others. In "Sexual Healing," we're confronted with the remorseful Tiger Woods and other "sex addicts" who apologize for acts for which they are not genuinely apologetic; they're really only remorseful because they were caught. We as viewers and voyeurs revel in the inconsistency of seeing the downfall of people over acts that we wish we could commit. Lastly, let's note that "Starvin' Marvin" points to a possible moral contradiction in deciding to donate money to famine relief on the condition that you'll receive a free sports watch.

## Kids versus Adults and Cuddly Animals versus Yummy Animals

There are two story threads in "Fun with Veal" that nicely highlight two ethical issues surrounding the consumption of meat. The first issue is the difference between the ways children and adults perceive the killing of animals for food. The second is the unstated moral difference between *cute* and *cuddly* animals and *yummy food* animals.

Most children don't believe the explanations given by adults of what their chicken nuggets or hamburgers "really are," or they get really confused about or upset over those explanations. Why does eating meat bother children, but not adults (except for the hippies, of course)? Why is it that children believe, pretty much automatically,

240 CYNTHIA JONES

that it's wrong to kill animals and eat them, while the overwhelming majority of adults do not?

Perhaps, as adults, we are desensitized by many years of eating meat. After all, the typical person doesn't have to go out and actually hunt animals, kill them, strip them, clean them, or process them.[3] The meat that we eat is, for the most part, purchased from a grocery store and wrapped in plastic; it doesn't resemble an animal at all. Maybe children are just naive or, perhaps, they see a kind of inconsistency most adults miss. We should be nice to others and not harm others needlessly—so we tell our children. Is there a reason why this consideration doesn't apply to animals? Contrary to what some opponents of vegetarianism say, humans don't *need* to consume dead animals to survive or to live healthy lives. We can get all of our nutrition—including protein—from fruits, nuts, grains, soy products, and all kinds of vegetables.[4] And, believe it or not, even though "Medicinal Fried Chicken" ends with physicians concluding that Kentucky Fried Chicken must prevent testicular cancer (since the sharp increase in testicular cancer coincided with changing KFCs to medicinal marijuana shops), the consumption of meat doesn't prevent disease. Given the lack of nutritional necessity and the lack of disease prevention, you could argue that it's acceptable to eat meat only if it's not wrong to torture and kill animals. Or it's acceptable unless we can draw some morally relevant distinction between the animals that are commonly eaten and the ones that aren't or shouldn't be eaten.

This brings us to the second point. Why is it that many people are outraged over the torture and killing of a "cute" animal, but have no problem with the pain, suffering, and death caused to animals like cows, pigs, and chickens that are, admittedly, considerably less cute and cuddly than puppies, kittens, dolphins, and baby cows? If there is a *morally relevant* distinction between these kinds of animals, then these differences in treatment may be justified.

One answer might be that certain animals that we keep as pets, like dogs, are considered quite a bit smarter than animals that we eat, like turkeys (except, of course, for Alinicia, the turkey, who performs great feats, from "Helen Keller! The Musical"). So maybe intelligence is the key. Dogs and cats surely seem to be smarter than cows, chickens, and turkeys. But that can't be all of it. Pigs, for example, are at least as smart as dogs, but most Americans shudder at the thought of eating a dog, while pork is "the other white meat."[5] If intelligence is what we should look to in deciding who or what receives our moral consideration and who or what does not, then we should include pigs (at least) when we draw our line. Further, why wouldn't really smart animals—like the rhesus monkeys routinely used in neurobiological and psychological experiments—deserve more consideration than some humans who have mental impairments so severe that they're functionally less intelligent than the monkeys?[6]

Maybe the line should be drawn between animals that are "useful" for purposes other than human consumption and animals that aren't so useful. Some dogs, for example, can be trained to retrieve victims from disaster areas, assist handicapped people with certain daily tasks, or sniff out drugs in luggage. So, some animals have highly prized abilities that other animals don't. But the standard for line-drawing can't be physical abilities or prowess or anything like that because, if it were, then Cartman would be justified in harming or killing Timmy or Jimmy, both of whom lack the physical prowess and certain physical abilities that Stan, Kyle, Butters, and even Cartman have.

Maybe the problem some people have with eating veal has to do with a disgust factor. Let's face it, it's gross to imagine a chained-up baby cow as your dinner. But the living conditions of other animals people commonly eat are just about as gross and disgusting, so it's hard to imagine that the disgust factor could keep someone from eating veal while they eat other animals bred in similarly gruesome conditions.[7]

Could it be the age of animals that matters? It seems worse to harm a baby animal as opposed to an adult animal, just as it seems worse to harm a child rather than an adult. Many *South Park* episodes play on the moral outrage people feel over harming children. The episodes that deal with child abuse typically face more serious and successful protest and censorship. "Jared Has Aides" is a good example. In this episode, which is also controversial for making light of AIDS, it becomes clear that Butters is being physically abused and beaten by his parents. But when we look at crimes against *people*, as opposed to animals, the difference has to do with innocence and protection. A crime against a child seems worse because the child is innocent. Society has a duty to protect such individuals and watch them more closely because they're not fully equipped to protect themselves. But even if it's worse to hurt a child than it is to hurt an adult, it's still wrong to hurt an adult. People deserve moral consideration regardless of their age. It would be strange to maintain the age of an animal makes a morally relevant difference when it comes to deciding which ones deserve our moral consideration and which ones do not.

And yet we humans do seem to place a high value on "cuteness." Let's say your daughter wants a puppy, a kitten, or a baby brother or sister for her next birthday. When you remind her of the fully grown dogs or cats and the older sibling she already has, she admittedly finds these considerably less interesting. Or, think of all of the smiles and "awws!" when a cute little baby, an adorable puppy, or a fuzzy little duckling makes an appearance in a group of adults. Even a piece of poop with a Santa hat, mittens, and a happy voice is cute to people ("Mr. Hankey, the Christmas Poo"). But we can't imagine "cuteness" as being a morally relevant standard for inclusion or exclusion. If it were, then Nurse Gollum from "Conjoined Fetus Lady" would surely be treated as having fewer rights than the rest of us. Social scientists tell us that beautiful people make more money and are generally viewed as more likable than the average person. But we're not talking about a cuteness rule for animals that makes them more popular, we are considering a criterion that allows us to kill the "ugly" ones without remorse but allows people to pass laws to protect the cute and cuddly ones. This kind of moral criterion is unfounded.

So, why is it that we draw a line between different kinds of animals and conclude that some of them deserve to be protected, while some of them do not? This problem is typical of a much larger issue in ethics: the issue of where we draw lines—that is, of deciding who or what deserves our moral consideration and who or what does not.

## The Line Goes Here, Not There!

An important part of many ethical deliberations is the decision where to draw lines concerning whose interests need to be taken into account in moral decision making. In "Fun with Veal," when Kyle and Butters happily eat beef jerky and fried chicken but refuse to eat veal, they're drawing a moral line. The cute baby cows matter, so we can't eat them. But the adult cows and chickens don't matter in the same way, and so we can eat them. Stan decides to draw his line in a different spot by claiming that all animals matter, so he refuses to eat any of them. Cartman, on the other hand, draws a circle of consideration pretty much just around himself. This makes Cartman an *ethical egoist*, because he would probably argue that he doesn't need to worry about the wishes of others, people or animals, unless those wishes correspond to what he, Cartman, wants.[8] Most of the adults, except for the hippies, would draw a line that excludes most animals from moral consideration, but includes most or all people and domesticated animals like dogs and cats.

Ethical egoism is only one kind of ethical theory. Although it's not particularly popular among ethicists, we've already mentioned what ethical egoists think about line drawing: the line goes around the egoist, excluding everything and everyone else. An ethical egoist is concerned with the interests of others only if they promote or correspond with her own self-interest. Most other ethical theories draw the line differently. Ethical theories like utilitarianism, deontological ethics, and contractarian ethics, to name a few, contain some sort of appeal to *impartiality*.[9] This means that the interests of others should count equally, unless there is some morally relevant reason to exclude them. Generally, we shouldn't exclude some people from our moral consideration because of their gender or race, for example, because these characteristics aren't *morally relevant* characteristics. But this shouldn't be surprising. After all, something very much like this can be found in the American Declaration of Independence: "We hold these truths to be self-evident, that all men[10] are created equal ..." And so all people, at least, matter—unless we can point to some morally relevant reason to exclude them from the same consideration that is afforded to all other people. But this doesn't directly answer the question about whether some animals count and some don't.

## Don't Worry, You Probably Won't Turn into a Giant Pussy

Peter Singer, the best-known contemporary moral philosopher writing about the way humans treat other animals, argues that humans are guilty of "speciesism." That is, most humans draw a line of moral consideration around their own species, while pretty much excluding all other species. Singer compares speciesism to racism and sexism, both of which are full of moral problems because they make distinctions, or draw lines, on the basis of irrelevant characteristics.[11]

Singer claims that the interests of any creature that can feel pain or suffer significantly need to be considered in ethical decision making. In this respect, Singer subscribes to utilitarianism, an ethical theory developed by John Stuart Mill (1806–1873), which claims that the right action to choose in a given situation is the one that brings about the most happiness and the least pain possible for *all* those affected by the decision.[12] And it's been argued that "*all* those affected" would have to include humans *and* non-human animals, since *all* can experience pleasure and pain. Given that utilitarians are concerned about the happiness of all creatures that can feel, Singer argues that animals should be included in our ethical deliberations, especially when we're considering the slaughter of these animals.

At this point, it should be obvious that Singer would disagree with Cartman and the majority of the South Park adults (except for the hippies). We can't draw a line that excludes some animals from our ethical consideration without good reason. Since humans don't need to eat animals to survive ("Medicinal Fried Chicken" notwithstanding), unless we can draw some *morally relevant* line that excludes them, we shouldn't eat them. Cuteness and cuddliness aside, all animals deserve some moral consideration because of their ability to experience pleasure and pain, and especially because they can suffer.

So Singer would agree with Stan's original decision to give up eating meat completely, because eating meat involves causing harm and death to creatures that can feel pain and suffering, and because this pain and suffering caused to animals *does* matter, on moral grounds. Now that we're all vegetarians and giant pussies, what about zoos and aquariums that keep animals captive in small spaces, animal experimentation, and those crazy animal rights activists?

## Fun with Animals and Crazy Animal Rights Activists

From the ALF (Animal Liberation Front) members in "Free Willzyx" to the eco-terrorist pirates in "Whale Whores," and maybe even extending to the vegan Feegans and the hippie vegetarians, *South Park* revels in poking fun at animal rights activism. Utilitarian arguments against killing animals, even the ugly ones, for human consumption can easily be extended to keeping animals confined in zoos and aquariums. This is especially true if confinement causes them serious harm.

The episodes featuring animal rights activists show the activists protesting the captivity of animals. Even though this seems to be a lesser harm than slaughtering and eating the animals, keeping "wild" animals confined in a habitat that is "unnatural" can be harmful. Of course the animals that are prey to other creatures in the wild typically live longer lives in captivity than they otherwise would, but there's still something to be said for the quality of the animals' lives: a longer life may not compensate for low quality of life. The harm caused to a particular animal by caging it depends on the species as well as the condition of the confinement.

The question of where to draw the line in using animals in experiments that stand to cause significant harm or death to the animals is also situation-specific, at least on utilitarian grounds. The scientists in "Pee" and Dr. Mephesto, the Marlon Brando-like evil scientist in "An Elephant Makes Love to a Pig," clearly cross a moral line in their experiments on animals, given the moral claims already discussed, but other experiments that stand to have significant benefit and attempt to minimize the harm caused to the animals may be permissible.

So, now that we're all converted to hippie vegetarianism and crazy animal rights activism, allegiance to feminism must be next. Thankfully, there's an episode for that too ("Eat, Pray, Queef")![13]

## Notes

1. See, for example, chapter 2, by Henry Jacoby, "You Know, I Learned Something Today: Stan Marsh and the Ethics of Belief," or chapter 4, by Robert Arp, "Dude, Listen to Reason! Logic Lessons Inside and Outside South Park."
2. See Plato, *Plato's Five Dialogues: Euthyphro, Apology, Crito, Meno, Phaedo*, trans. G.M.A. Grube (Indianapolis, IN: Hackett Publishing, 2002).
3. The year 2006 marked the 100th anniversary of the publication of Upton Sinclair's *The Jungle*, a story about Lithuanian immigrants who came to Chicago around the turn of the twentieth century to work in the famous stockyards. Sinclair gives a *very* descriptive account of the slaughterhouse process. Read the book, and you may never eat meat again.

4. For example, see the research accumulated by Peter Singer and Jim Mason in *The Way We Eat: Why Our Food Choices Matter* (Emmaus, PA: Rodale Books, 2006).

5. See, for example, Donald Broom, Michael Mendl, and Adroaldo Zanella, "A Comparison of the Welfare of Sows in Different Housing Conditions," *Animal Science*, 61 (1995): 369–385.

6. Rhesus monkeys, and other monkeys, have been used in experiments for years. In most cases, because of the experimenter's radical adjustments to their physiology, they are killed after the experiment. A standard paper illustrating this kind of experimentation would be Thomas Rowell, "Agonistic Noises of the Rhesus Monkey (*Macaca Mulatta*)," *Symposium of the Zoological Society of London*, 8 (1962): 91–96.

7. See Peter Singer, *Animal Liberation: A New Ethics for Our Treatment of Animals* (New York: HarperCollins, 2002) for a discussion of factory farming practices in the United States. An examination of the conditions under which most animals bred for consumption are kept would result in a fairly high "disgust factor."

8. Ethical egoism is a bit more complex than this. For an ethical egoist, the right action is the one that best promotes the interests of the egoist. See, for example, the treatments of ethical egoism in Louis Pojman, ed., *Ethical Theory: Classical and Contemporary Readings*. (Belmont, CA: Wadsworth Publishing, 2001) and Louis Pojman, *Ethics: Discovering Right and Wrong* (Belmont, CA: Wadsworth Publishing, 2005).

9. For more on this, see: James Sterba, *Morality in Practice* (Belmont, CA: Wadsworth Publishing, 2003); James Sterba, ed., *Ethics: Classical Western Texts in Feminist and Multicultural Perspectives* (Oxford: Oxford University Press, 1999).

10. Of course the "Founding Fathers" probably meant *white male landowners* when they said *men*, but it is more reasonably interpreted today to mean "all *people* are created equal."

11. Peter Singer, *Animal Liberation*; also, Peter Singer, *Practical Ethics* (Cambridge: Cambridge University Press, 1993).

12. J.S. Mill, *Utilitarianism* (Indianapolis, IN: Hackett Publishing, 2003).

13. Dr. Jones wishes to thank her brilliant research assistants, Eduardo Flores and Justin O'Donnell, for their tireless efforts in watching *South Park* episodes that contributed to the completion of this chapter.

# Aesthetic Value, Ethos, and Phil Collins
## The Power of Music in South Park

*Per F. Broman*

*We're not the artistic side; we are the thinking side.*
— Eric Cartman, "Wing"

In the fifth-season episode "Kenny Dies," Cartman gives a passionate and sentimental speech to the US House of Representatives, arguing for the legalization of stem-cell research to save his dying friend, Kenny. Unable to get the lawmakers' full attention, Cartman begins to sing Asia's "Heat of the Moment." It turns into a sing-along with tight clapping fill-ins from the audience. Surprisingly enough, every Representative knows this rather rhythmically complicated song. The shared musical experience allows the legislation to move along, despite the fact that the love lyrics have nothing to do with the issue. So from this example, it would seem that music itself has greater value than the content of the lyrics, according to *South Park*. This should not surprise us since music that affects the emotions doesn't neces-sarily need words. Think of the commanding opening of Beethoven's Fifth Symphony, the tear-jerking melody of *Love Story*, or the repetitive power-chord progression found throughout Deep Purple's "Smoke on the Water."

Music's ability to influence people's thoughts and emotions has been an important part of Western philosophy's look at art and beauty, a subfield called *aesthetics*. Philosophers, rulers, and parents have known this and tried, often in vain, to control and censor music.

*The Ultimate South Park and Philosophy: Respect My Philosophah!*, First Edition.
Edited by Robert Arp and Kevin S. Decker.
© 2013 John Wiley & Sons, Inc. Published 2013 by John Wiley & Sons, Inc.

Sextus Empiricus' (160–210) *Against the Musicians* talks about the power of music in poetic terms:

> Pythagoras, when he once observed how lads who had been filled with Bacchic frenzy by alcoholic drink differed not at all from madmen, exhorted the *aulete* who was joining them in the carousal to play his *aulos* for them in the *spondaic melos*. When he thus did what was ordered, they suddenly changed and were given discretion as if they had been sober even at the beginning.[1]

The Greek term *spondaic melos*, refers to a solemn piece of music dominated by long note values. The *aulos* was the ancient double piped reed instrument often used as a Dionysian instrument of exaltation. Think of it as the distorted electric guitar of ancient Greece. Its use was controversial and some writers, including Plato (427–347 BCE), argued that it should be banned.

This chapter is about the power of music, how characters in *South Park* use it in telling stories, and how music conveys ideas in the context of Western philosophy. I can't provide a "philosophy of music of *South Park*" because the series is too eclectic and self-contradictory. But *South Park* does raise questions about music that philosophers—particularly Plato—have dealt with again and again.

## "Maybe I Can Put It Best in the Words of a Timeless Song"

In his *Republic*, Plato echoes the lesson of the Pythagoras story when he describes which of the seven *Harmoniai* were appropriate for performing music.[2] *Harmoniai* is a term similar to today's "modes," or scales, though the Greek modes were different from our modal scales. The Ionian and the Lydian modes, they said, were "utterly unbecoming," as they are "relaxed" and "soft or drinking harmonies." Such modes are to be avoided, even "banished," according to Plato. On the other hand, Dorian and Phrygian *Harmoniai* were acceptable because they were useful during military activities in defense of the Republic. Plato indicates his belief that simply altering the pitch would completely change the impression of the song. This is a suggestion that seems curious, yet German musicologist Hans Joachim

Moser has suggested that today this kind of alteration would be equivalent to changing a minor-mode tango to a major mode, and so taking away its erotic appeal.[3]

Both Plato and Pythagoras emphasize that changes in music can produce an entirely different effect on the listener. For both, listener's souls were affected by music's mathematical properties, the relationship between different pitches, and the correspondence of pitches with the movements of the planets. This occurred more or less automatically: the direct effect of music was subconscious.

Despite their flaws, these Greek thinkers' views were instrumental to asking questions about music's impact (often referred to as *ethos*), its mathematical properties in relation to the universe, and how these two aspects interact with one another. The stories are amazing in their simplicity: the power of music makes it a fundamental part of society.

## Diegesis in South Park

In a 2008 interview, Trey Parker claimed, "My favorite musical? It changes all the time. I'm just a diehard, I'm totally old school, like I'll sit and watch, if they are redoing *Oklahoma* in New York, I will be the first one there."[4] Music is of immense importance to Trey Parker and Matt Stone. Parker started out at Berklee College of Music in Boston before transferring to the University of Colorado, and Stone is also an accomplished musician. Many of the songs on the show were composed by Parker—"Blame Canada" from *South Park: Bigger, Longer & Uncut*, for example. After 14 seasons of *South Park*, their musical *The Book of Mormon* premiered on Broadway (and received nine Tony Awards).

Two types of music play a crucial role in the series. *Diegetic*, or source music, has a source of sound in the narrative. *Non-diegetic* music is part of the background, and isn't perceived by the characters on screen. This kind of music is frequently used to set the mood, and you've heard it in *South Park*'s laid-back chord accompaniment to the hyper-ironic moral of many earlier episodes, "You know, I learned something today." The show has many allusions to existing music, like the rhythmic pulse from *Jaws* heard before the man fishing on the lake in "Grey Dawn" gets hit by an elderly driver in a car; the use of Samuel Barber's *Adagio* in "Up the Down Steroid" after Jimmy's *Platoon*-like violent rampage; or Gabriel Fauré's *Pie Jesu*—Merciful Jesus—when the dying louse Travis is rescued by a fly in "Lice Capades."[5]

Like background music, diegetic music is also a source of cultural reference. The show's range of musical allusions is astonishing, including the musical *Oklahoma* in *South Park: Bigger, Longer & Uncut*, appearances of rock bands and musicians (Korn, Ronnie James Dio, Radiohead, Ozzy Osbourne, Meat Loaf, Blink 182, Metallica, Britney Spears, Alanis Morissette, Jimmy Buffett, Biggie Smalls, Michael Jackson, Kanye West, Puff Daddy, Neil Diamond, and the Jonas Brothers), allusions to nineteenth-century Italian opera (the Dreidl-Song quintet in "Mr. Hankey's Christmas Classics") and the genre of musicals, as characters burst into song in many of the series' episodes. Musicals even form an integral part of some episodes, such as the "Elementary School Musical" episode, "Helen Keller! The Musical," and the Terrance and Phillip film in *South Park: Bigger, Longer & Uncut*.

## Musical Spraying

Controlled sound has a number of surprising uses. A company named Compound Security uses the analogy of "bug spray" for its own brand of teenager deterrent, a device that emits an annoying mosquito-like sound that's *clearly* audible: "Acclaimed by the Police forces of many areas of the United Kingdom, the Mosquito ultra-sonic teenage deterrent has been described as 'the most effective tool in our fight against anti social behavior.'"[6] Similarly, the *Toronto Star* reports that classical music has been used successfully to "clear out undesirables" in Canadian parks, Australian railway stations, and London subway stations. With such accompaniment, robberies in the subway went down by 33 percent, assaults on staff by 25 percent, and vandalism of trains and stations by 37 percent. As a result, "London authorities now plan to expand the playing of Mozart, Vivaldi, Handel and opera (sung by Pavarotti) from three tube stations to an additional 35."[7]

These surprising uses of sound point to the same behavior-changing capacity of music we saw in the Pythagoras story. Several *South Park* episodes draw on the power of music to do just this. In "Die Hippie, Die," when South Park is infested by thousands of hippies holding a music festival, the only way to break up the gigantic crowd is by changing the music. "We use the power of rock 'n' roll to change the world," announces one hippie. Cartman's response is to use even more powerful music—death metal. After having convinced the town that the hippies are bad, a group of town people builds a machine to drill through the masses of hippies to reach the center stage, as in the movie *The Core*. Once there, they play Slayer's "Raining Blood."[8] The hippies disappear quickly, as the music is "so angry," and the town is saved. Strangely enough, the episode begins with actual bug spraying, as Cartman searches through a house, like an exterminator, looking for hippies hidden in the walls and the attic ("giggling stoners").

Another instance of "musical spraying" occurs in "Two Guys Naked in a Hot Tub." During a wild party, the adults attract the attention of ATF agents, who believe that the party guests are members of a suicide sect. To break up the party, a version of Cher's "Do You Believe in Love" is blasted through gigantic speakers. As one officer puts it: "Nobody can stand this much Cher. This is her new album. If this doesn't drive them out, nothing will." But ironically, the drunk party guests appreciate the music!

The difference between music and noise is not as clear-cut as it might seem. *South Park* shows that music has different effects on different people. Cher's music fits into a mode for drinking and carousing (like Plato's Ionian mode), while Slayer's music is in a mode for war (like Plato's Dorian mode). But in *South Park* there is no formula to predict music's effects on everyone. Plato believed the impact of music was universal in scope. This is an unfeasible stance to defend today and a position note represented in *South Park*: Cher and Slayer work differently in different contexts and with different audiences.

In some episodes, music has universal power. In "World Wide Recorder Concert," Cartman discovers the Brown Noise, a sound that causes the bowel to loosen, located "92 cent below the lowest octave of E-flat." On a school-sanctioned trip to perform "My Country, 'Tis of Thee," Cartman alters the score to make the note heard. When the entire four-million-child orchestra plays this note, the consequences are global.[9] Such a low pitch could never be performed on recorders. But the story points to a connection between the magic in music and the how human physiology works: there is plenty of evidence to support the notion that sound waves could resonate and interfere with the electrical waves of the autonomous part of the nervous system, changing behavior.

## Music to Move Plato's Soul

Plato divides the soul into three parts. First is the "appetitive" part, the seat of our most base, irrational emotions and inclinations. Next is the spiritual part, which gives us our vim and vigor, and is supposed to respond to situations where we need to be courageous and moral. Finally, and most importantly, there's the rational part, which is supposed to *direct* the spiritual part while controlling the appetitive part, like a charioteer directs a chariot pulled by two horses.[10] "Bug spray" music and the Brown Noise both "resonate with" (pun intended) the appetitive part of Plato's human soul. In these cases, music directly affects the body in a visceral way.

But music also works directly on the spiritual part of the soul. In "Prehistoric Ice Man," Ace of Base's hit "All That She Wants" is played for the "Ice Man" Steve, unfrozen from the ice after two years. As a baby needs soothing lullaby, Steve needed the familiar music from 1996, his own time, in order to function. In "The Succubus," Chef has fallen in love with Veronica, a woman who draws him to her by singing "The Morning After," an Academy Award-winning song made famous in the 1972 movie *The Poseidon Adventure*. The boys believe that Victoria is taking Chef away from them, and Mr. Garrison tells them she's a female demon that seduces men. They find a definition of "succubus" in an old dictionary: "Succubus: enchants its victim with eerie [sic] melody. This is succubus power. Only playing this melody backwards can vanquish the succubus power." During the wedding of Chef and Veronica, the boys perform the song backwards, and her true diabolical self is revealed before being destroyed by the music. The power of music can create a spell, and the only way to break it is to reverse the order of the notes.[11]

Plato's rational soul must be critical of music's power, however. "Then, when any one says that music is to be judged of by pleasure, his doctrine cannot be admitted," Plato argued, "and if there be any music of which pleasure is the criterion, such music is not to be sought out or deemed to have any real excellence, but only that other kind of music which is an imitation of the good."[12] To make judgments about what's good, we need to rationally consider aesthetic value.

Some music is simply bad. Plato believed the way to good from bad was to consider whether the individual parts of a musical performance were consistent with each other:

> The poets are artists very inferior in character to the Muses themselves, who would never fall into the monstrous error of assigning to the words of men the gestures and songs of women; nor after combining the melodies with the gestures of freemen would they add on the rhythms of slaves and men of the baser sort; nor, beginning with the rhythms and gestures of freemen, would they assign to them a melody or words which are of an opposite character; nor would they mix up the voices and sounds of animals and of men and instruments, and every other sort of noise, as if they were all one.[13]

In his *Symposium*, Plato adds, "You cannot harmonize that which disagrees."[14] Although we don't know what good music sounded like in Plato's time, his argument makes lots of sense today. We may not be able to pinpoint the problem with a particular piece of music exactly, but we have a strong feeling when something is not right.

In their 1997 project "The People's Choice Music," Dave Soldier, Vitaly Komar, and Alexander Melamid tried to show what a deeply flawed musical work might sound like. They placed a poll on the Internet where some 500 visitors responded to questions about musical genres, instruments, and structures. They then used the survey results to write music and lyrics for the "Most Wanted" and "Most Unwanted" songs. The result is a 27 minute composition that alternates between a number of moods, styles, and dynamics, including an opera soprano, rapping, and children singing commercial jingles out of tune.[15] Disliked instruments, including bagpipe, accordion, and tuba, were prominently featured. Few, if any, listeners will find anything to appreciate in this music. The problem is its blend of incompatible elements, just as Plato described. Indeed, it's easier to make bad music than good.

There are no such horrendous pieces performed in *South Park*, but its writers don't hesitate to point out which artists they consider inferior, either musically or ethically. In *South Park*, good music serves the same functions it did for the ancient Greeks: it educates, emphasizes morals, and sometimes is even used to indoctrinate the people.

Added to this is that good music must be authentic: the series takes strong stands against several artists who seem to have no redeeming qualities.

Again, as for the Greeks, music is part of education in *South Park*, but imposed music performances or education are seen as chores at South Park Elementary School. Consider the school orchestra during the Fourth of July celebration in the episode "Summer Sucks." The assignment is forced upon the students and is not artistically rewarding. On the other hand, music is creative and joyous outside of school. The true spirit of music, it seems, doesn't emerge from scholarly activities. A true artist works for him or herself, and true artistry cannot be taught. Consequently, a true artist could be considered a genius, a notion in aesthetics emphasized since the nineteenth-century Romantic era. So, in South Park, a garage band like "Timmy and the Lords of the Underworld" is superior to a school-sanctioned recorder orchestra (even one consisting of four million players). Still, one has to live with the times. In "Guitar Queer-O," Randy Marsh, Stan's dad, fails to convince the boys that a real electric guitar is superior to "playing" a Guitar Hero mock-up. However absurd it seems, being a Guitar Hero virtuoso is appreciated by the community and by music-industry executives, and we see the beginning, peak, and decline of Stan's musical career, following a traditional rock-artist narrative.

## Phil Collins and Aesthetic Value

*South Park* also features strong reactions *against* musical performances. In "Mr. Hankey, the Christmas Poo," the controversy over religious holidays is supposed to be settled by a non-sectarian show featuring Philip Glass's low-key, repetitive music: the "happy non-offensive, non-denominational Christmas play." His minimalist composition "Happy, Happy, Happy, Everybody Happy" upsets the audience, however. Barbara Streisand's piercing voice, similar to the "bug spray" music, makes the boys cover their ears in "Mecha-Streisand." She even uses her voice in the torture chamber to make the boys reveal the location of the Triangle of Zinthar. In "Timmy 2000," during the Lalapalalapaza 2000 festival, the children can only appreciate Phil Collins in concert after taking Ritalin. Kyle says with a blank expression, "His flowing melodies are really enjoyable to us."

It's clear why Philip Glass and Streisand are targets for Parker's and Stone's acerbic wit, but what's wrong with Phil Collins (except for the fact that he won the 2000 "Best Song" Academy Award for "You'll Be in My Heart," instead of "Blame Canada," and holds his Oscar statuette in more than one episode of the show)? Answer: he lacks authenticity and integrity, and fails to inspire artistic devotion. His low-keyed music does not fire the boys' passion, and he appears unfocused on stage.

Music is much more than just the notes: it involves interactions with other art forms. In fact, the Greek *mousiké* included more than just musical pitch and metric organization; it was the art of the Muses, the nine daughters of the titan Mnemosyne.[16] Music was seen as a servant of the greater good. In *South Park*, too, music should engage with society, and a musician should express an artistic persona. But in the hopelessly collectivistic South Park, there is not much room for musical individualism. As one Goth kid expressed it, "To be a non-conformist, you have to dress in black, and listen to the same music we do," or as the boys sing in *South Park*'s version of High School Musical, "You gotta do what you wanna do. Just make sure what you're doing is cool and popular with everyone else."

These ironic dismissals resemble Plato's harsh and uncompromising judgments of some of the *Harmonai* and of the *aulos* instrument. But "Timmy 2000" also criticizes low-key, expressionless music as undermining the very foundational aesthetic of rock 'n' roll and an authentic lifestyle. To the contrary, an active, focused, non-intoxicated intellect is necessary for appreciating music. Mr. Mackey was right, "Drugs are bad, m'kay," and here Plato agrees:

> Thus far I too should agree with the many, that the excellence of music is to be measured by pleasure. But the pleasure must not be that of chance persons; the fairest music is that which delights the best and best educated, and especially that which delights the one man who is pre-eminent in virtue and education.[17]

Plato says that any passive enjoyment of music is problematic. This may appear contradictory. On the one hand music appeals subconsciously, but on the other, it needs to be appreciated with the intellect. But for Plato and in *South Park* alike, music works on a subconscious level *and* on an intellectual one. Remember the episode "Fat Butt and Pancake Head," in which Cartman, without any effort, writes taco-themed songs for his hand puppet Jennifer Lopez? Although he claims that the "style of music is so easy; it doesn't require any thought at all," his intellect has grasped the "creative" technique, and his skills even impress the real Jennifer Lopez's record company. Again, Cartman displays similar skills but with a more scornful twist when he starts a Christian rock group, "Faith + 1," with Token and Butters, to win a bet against Kyle. He takes an existing love song, "I Need You in My Life, Baby," changes "Baby" to "Jesus" and voilà—he has created a hit song. It is, of course, the cynical approach typical of Cartman, who admits that although he doesn't know anything about Christianity, "I know enough to exploit it." Although "Faith+1" have deep impact on their audience, putting new words to old songs to make money is an absolute no-no for an authentic musician.[18] The downfall of the band is rapid and hard when the audience realizes the insincerity.

## Schopenhauer and "Death"

At the very end of *Republic*, Plato recounts the legend of Er, a soldier killed in battle who returned to life telling about the hereafter. The story he tells is one of reckoning, punishment, and accountability for the actions taken in life. But there is also an absolutely stunning description of how music relates to the workings of the universe. At the universe's very center is a spindle turned on the knees of Necessity. The eight Sirens, one for each known body of the solar system, are "hymning" a single tone and forming one harmony at equal intervals. The three daughters of Necessity accompany the harmony. Needless to say, it's impossible to figure how this would sound, but the combination of the circular motion of the rotating spindle and the single chord gives a supernatural sense of a slow, never-ending repetitive music (Philip Glass's music comes to my mind).

The episode "Death" provides a musical image of dying. Stan's grandpa wants the boys to assist him in euthanasia, and so he illustrates how it is to grow too old by bringing Stan into a dark room where he plays a parody of the Enya song "Orinoco Flow" on the cassette player. Stan is appalled: "It's cheesy, but lame and eerily soothing at the same time." Like Philip Glass's music, the emotionless music proves quite upsetting after a while. It's so terrible that Stan agrees to assist Grandpa. Enya, of course, is far from the depictions of hell in later episodes, but the music is a representation of despair prior to death or, in Plato's words, a *mimesis* of dying. The story also brings to mind the pessimistic philosopher Arthur Schopenhauer's (1788–1860) central concept, *Will*.

For Schopenhauer, the Will is the dominating force in humans, and in the universe, above intellect. By itself, the Will is neither good nor bad, but its representation to us in reality is destructive, as it is the central source of suffering in the form of desire and will to life. Satisfied desires are meaningless, leaving us bored and leading only to other desires. Schopenhauer described this perpetual striving quite strikingly as: "constantly lying on the revolving wheel of Ixion, is always drawing water in the sieve of the Danaids, and is the eternally thirsting Tantalus."[19] The Greek mythical references are not coincidences, as Schopenhauer was strongly influenced by Plato. But for Plato, music was just another imitative art, an imitation of the World of Senses, which in turn was an imitation of the World of Ideas: "The imitative art is an inferior who marries an inferior, and has inferior offspring". [20]

Schopenhauer, however, had a completely different conception of music, and maintained that there were striking differences between the arts. "Music answers [the question, "What is life?"], more profoundly indeed than do all the other [art forms], since in a language intelligible with absolute directness, yet not capable of translation into that of our faculty of reason, it expresses the innermost nature of all life and existence". [21] Schopenhauer saw two distinct categories of art: music on one side and every other art form on the other. Music is distinctive since it does not copy anything from the world of appearances, an opinion in complete disagreement with Plato. In fact, music is a copy of the Will itself. Schopenhauer meant that music was the key to suspending the Will for a moment through an aesthetic respite from everyday pain. But this is, of course, not what Enya is doing: Enya is instead aggravating the existential anxiety. Nevertheless, Enya provided a suspension of the will to live and could communicate this to Stan in a most direct way.

## The Only Way It Works Is Through Music

Plato's and Sextus Empiricus's descriptions of the ancient musical modes don't appear timeless. Likewise, *South Park*'s critique of contemporary music also sometimes seems dated, as is the case with "About Last

Night …,” which aired the day after the November 2008 election (and which may appear quite dated in a not-too-distant future). Strangely enough, Pythagoras, the Enya episode, and Cartman's encounter with the House of Representatives are very similar, despite their differences in musical context and ethos. Phil Collins and Asia may not survive history's merciless aesthetic filter, just as the *aulos* instrument vanished long ago, but where the underlying philosophy is concerned, the issues are timeless. Grandpa, Cartman, and Pythagoras were unable to communicate their visions verbally: the only way they could was through music.

## Notes

1. Sextus Empiricus, *Against the Musicians*, trans. Denise Davidson Greaves (Lincoln, NE: University of Nebraska Press, 1986), 131.
2. For Plato's discussion of the tonal modes, see *Republic*, trans. G.M.A. Grube (Indianapolis, IN: Hackett Publishing Company, 1992), books 2 and 7. For historical discussions of the various tonal modes of music, see Cristle Collins Judd, ed., *Tonal Structures of Early Music* (New York: Garland Publishing, 1998).
3. Hans Joachim Moser, *Musikästhetik* (Berlin: Walter de Gruyter, 1953), 151.
4. iCelebz.com. Retrieved from, http://www.icelebz.com/quotes/trey_parker/, accessed Feb. 26, 2013.
5. For an excellent selection of not-so-subtle allusions or parodies, see Sam Greenspan's, available at, http://www.11points.com/tv/11_most_spot-on_song_parodies_from_south_park, accessed Feb. 26, 2013.
6. See the company's website: www.compoundsecurity.co.uk/security-information/mosquito-devices, accessed Feb. 26, 2013.
7. Scott Timberg, “Halt … or I'll play Vivaldi,” *Toronto Star*, February 20, 2005, C05.
8. Cartman is not completely correct here: Slayer's music is typically not categorized as “death metal,” but as another somewhat gentler sub-category of heavy metal, namely “thrash metal.”
9. On the commentary track on the DVD, Stone and Parker claim that there were real attempts to find this frequency to be used in WWII as a weapon. That may or may not be true, but the topic resembles one episode of *Monty Python's Flying Circus*, a series of which Parker and Stone were long-time fans, in a sketch about the world's funniest joke. The joke was so funny that anyone who heard it laughed to death. It, too, was supposedly used as a weapon during WWII.

10. Plato, *Republic*, book 4.
11. The technique, referred to as retrograde, was considered the most eso‐teric of the contrapuntal techniques during the medieval period, as the original melody becomes completely incomprehensible. See, for example, Virginia Newes, "Writing, Reading, and Memorizing: The Transmission and Resolution of Retrograde Canons from the 14th and 15th Centuries," *Early Music*, 18 (1990): 218–232.
12. Plato, *The Laws of Plato*, trans. Thomas Pangle (Chicago: University of Chicago Press, 1988), book 2.
13. Ibid.
14. Plato, *Symposium*, trans. Christopher Gill (New York: Penguin Books, 2003), part 1.
15. See the Dia Art Foundation: www.diacenter.org/artist_web_projects, accessed Feb. 26, 2013.
16. Calliope presides over elegies; Cleo, the stories of heroes; Erato, love poems; Euterpe, flute playing; Melpomene, the tragedies; Polyhymnia, hymns and mime; Terpsichore, choral dancing and song; Thalia, the comedies; and Urania, astronomy.
17. Plato, *The Laws of Plato*, book 2.
18. As popular-music scholar Simon Frith argued: "Rock, in contrast to pop, carries intimations of sincerity, authenticity, art—noncommercial concerns. These intimations have been muffled since rock became the record industry, but it is the possibilities, the promises, that matter." Simon Frith, *Sound Effects – Youth, Leisure and the Politics of Rock 'n' Roll* (Suffolk: St. Edmundsbury Press, 1983), 11.
19. Arthur Schopenhauer, *The World as Will and Representation*, vol. I, trans. E.F.J. Payne (New York: Dover, 1966), 196.
20. Plato, *Republic*, book 10.
21. Schopenhauer *The World as Will and as Representation*, vol. II, 406.

# Contributors

**Robert Arp, Ph.D.,** works as an analyst for the US Army, and is the editor of *South Park and Philosophy: You Know, I Learned Something Today* (Wiley-Blackwell, 2006). Like Descartes and Kyle, he thinks that the "basis of all reasoning is the mind's awareness of itself. What we think—the external objects we perceive—are all like actors that come on and off stage. But our consciousness, the stage itself, is always present to us" ("The Tooth Fairy's Tats 2000").

**Neil Baker** recently completed his B.A. at Hope International University. A former religious fundamentalist turned skeptic, he has found it a bit difficult to continue on his original career path as a Christian minister. He does, however, hope to pursue his interest in the field of interreligious dialogue through graduate study, and perhaps even achieve his ultimate dream of meeting the Super Best Friends!

**Per F. Broman, Ph.D.,** is Associate Professor of Music Theory and Associate Dean at the College of Musical Arts at Bowling Green State University. He writes about twentieth-century music and aesthetics and is the author of *"Back to the Future": Towards an Aesthetic Theory of Bengt Hambræus* (Gothenburg University, 1999), and has contributed to books and journals including *New Music in the Nordic Countries* (Pendragon Press, 2002), *Woody Allen and Philosophy,*

*The Ultimate South Park and Philosophy: Respect My Philosophah!*, First Edition.
Edited by Robert Arp and Kevin S. Decker.
© 2013 John Wiley & Sons, Inc. Published 2013 by John Wiley & Sons, Inc.

*Music, Sound and Filmmakers: Sonic Style in Cinema* (Routledge, 2012), *Perspectives of New Music, College Music Symposium,* and *Journal of Popular Music Studies.* He can't be a non-conformist if he doesn't drink coffee.

**Paul A. Cantor, Ph.D.,** is Clifton Waller Barrett Professor of English and Comparative Literature at the University of Virginia. He is the author of *Gilligan Unbound: Pop Culture in the Age of Globalization* and *The Invisible Hand in Popular Culture: Liberty vs. Authority in American Film and TV.* Under severe questioning, he admitted that he bought his *South Park* essay "real cheap" at the Semiotics section of his local Wal-Mart.

**Shane D. Courtland, Ph.D.,** is an Assistant Professor at the University of Minnesota, Duluth. His publications have appeared in *Pacific Philosophical Quarterly, Reason Papers, Hobbes Studies, Utilitas, Stanford Encyclopedia of Philosophy* and the *Journal of Environmental Philosophy.* During his free time he engages in public activism aimed at informing the public about the illusive (and dangerous) Manbearpig.

**David Valleau Curtis, Ph.D., B.C.B.A.-D., L.B.A.,** works as a behavior analyst for the Columbus Organization in Saint Louis, Missouri and holds the position of Senior Consultant helping special needs individuals develop skills to prevent problem behaviors. He has deemed Cartman a lost cause.

**Kevin S. Decker, Ph.D.,** is Associate Professor of Philosophy and Director of the Philosophy Program at Eastern Washington University near Spokane, Washington. He's the co-editor of *Star Wars and Philosophy, Star Trek and Philosophy, Terminator and Philosophy,* and editor of the upcoming Wiley-Blackwell book *Ender's Game and Philosophy.* Currently, he's writing *Who is Who? The Philosophy of Doctor Who* for I.B. Tauris Publishers. And like Luke Skywalker, Santa Claus, Bugs Bunny, and Superman, he's affected your life in a "more realer" way than most of the real people you know.

**Jeffrey Dueck, Ph.D.,** is Associate Professor of Philosophy at Nyack College. While focusing on philosophical issues in ethics, aesthetics, and the philosophy of religion, he also enjoys writing and performing music and playing with his kids. If he could time-travel into the future, he would forgo the search for the latest video game console and instead embrace the fame and glory stemming from the *South Park* book he once contributed to.

**Gerald J. Erion, Ph.D.**, is Associate Professor of Philosophy at Medaille College, where his research includes work in ethics, philosophy of mind, and the teaching of philosophy. While traveling home from a recent academic conference he fell from a burning bridge, tumbled down a rocky cliff, and was impaled on a tree branch, then attacked by a mountain lion, shot by the Super Adventure Club, and mauled by a grizzly bear.

**Jeffrey Ewing** is a graduate student in sociology at the University of Oregon. In his spare time, he studies Marx, gender, alternative economic systems, and is trying to avoid becoming one of those people who you can never remember whether he was there or not.

**John Scott Gray, Ph.D.**, is Associate Professor of Humanities at Ferris State University in Big Rapids, Michigan. His main areas of research are political and social philosophy, philosophy of sex and gender, and applied ethics. He is the author of a number of articles, including articles related to same-sex marriage in the *South African Journal of Philosophy* and the *Review Journal of Political Philosophy*. John also is the co-author of a textbook titled *Introduction to Popular Culture: Theories, Applications and Global Perspectives*. He also does not tolerate intolerance.

**Jacob M. Held, Ph.D.**, is Associate Professor of Philosophy at the University of Central Arkansas. He is the editor of *Dr. Seuss and Philosophy: Oh, the Thinks You Can Think!* (Rowman and Littlefield 2011) as well as a contributor to other volumes in Blackwell's Philosophy and Pop Culture Series, including *Watchmen and Philosophy* and *Black Sabbath and Philosophy*. His recent research interests include just war theory, critical legal studies, and American Indian Jurisprudence. Although he recognizes he's getting old, he's convinced that the reason most new music sounds like sh*t, is because it is sh*t. Doesn't anyone listen to Dio anymore?

**Henry Jacoby, Ph.D.**, teaches philosophy at East Carolina University. His research interests, when he's not playing guitar or practicing martial arts, include consciousness and the mind-body problem, the nature of moral perception, and the conditions for a meaningful life in a natural universe. He is the editor of *House and Philosophy: Everybody Lies* (now in nine languages), and *Game of Thrones and Philosophy: Logic Cuts Deeper Than Swords*. And yes, the rumors are true: he has become ungroundable.

**Dale Jacquette, Ph.D.**, is Senior Professorial Chair in Philosophy, Division for Logic and Theoretical Philosophy, University of Bern, Switzerland. Most of his research is in philosophical logic and analytic metaphysics, although he published an essay on "Satan Lord of Darkness in South Park Cosmology" for a previous *South Park and Philosophy* volume, and a handful of similarly weak occasional pieces on popular culture. He has adopted his pedagogical methodology from the South Park police department motto: To Patronize and Annoy.

**David Kyle Johnson, Ph.D.**, is an associate professor of philosophy of King's College in Wilkes-Barre, PA. Academically he publishes on philosophy of religion, and has also done a grandiose amount of work on pop culture and philosophy. In addition to South Park, he has written articles on *Family Guy, The Office, The Onion, Batman, Battlestar Galactica*, Quentin Tarantino, Johnny Cash, *The Hobbit, Doctor Who, The Daily Show*, The Colbert Report and Santa Claus. He also edited the Blackwell volumes on the NBC show *Heroes* and Christopher Nolan's movie *Inception*. Additionally, he hosts a pop-culture and philosophy blog, with the Blackwell series editor William Irwin, for *Psychology Today*: "Plato on Pop." Lastly, despite being a card-carrying skeptic, Kyle believes, wholeheartedly, in the Jewpacabra and calls for him every night behind his house. (Kyle is not popular in his neighborhood.)

**Cynthia Jones, Ph.D.**, is Associate Professor of Philosophy and Director of the Ethics Center at The University of Texas – Pan American. She publishes and researches in healthcare and public health ethics, intelligence ethics, ethics and technology, and the moral issues in violence against women in border regions. Whenever she calls her partner, Cartman's "You will respect my authoritah!" alerts him to the call.

**Christopher C. Kirby, Ph.D.,** is Assistant Professor of Philosophy at Eastern Washington University. His general areas of research are in the history of ideas and comparative philosophy. He hopes one day to be able to wield the Sword of a Thousand Truths, or at least to catch the pink dragon. Either way, he'll shout "Looks like you're about to get pwnd!"

**David Koepsell, Ph.D., J.D.,** teaches ethics at the Delft University of Technology in The Netherlands and has written and edited numerous books and articles. including *Who Owns You: The Corporate Gold Rush to Patent Your Genes* (Wiley-Blackwell 2009) and *Breaking Bad and Philosophy: Badder Living Through Chemistry* (Open Court, 2012) co-edited with Robert Arp. Like all his contributions to his various popular culture and philosophy books, the one in this book was really written by manatees.

**Kevin J. Murtagh, Ph.D.,** has taught numerous philosophy courses in and around New York City since 2002. His book, *Corporal Punishment: A Humane Alternative to Incarceration*, was published in September of 2012. He wants to join the Allied Atheist Alliance, but because their membership is limited to sea otters, he has joined New York City Atheists instead.

**Roberto Sirvent, Ph.D., J.D.,** is Assistant Professor of Political and Social Ethics at Hope International University. His primary research interests are hermeneutics and moral reasoning, and he is co-editor of the book *By Faith and Reason: The Essential Keith Ward*. He hopes no one at his church finds out that he saw, enjoyed, or wrote about *The Book of Mormon*. Is he going to hell? Probably.

**Willie Young, Ph.D.,** is Associate Professor of Humanities at Endicott College in Beverly, Massachusetts. He is the author of *The Politics of Praise: Naming God and Friendship in Aquinas and Derrida*, and *Uncommon Friendships: An Amicable History of Western Religious Thought*. He was the proud recipient of the 2010 Biggest Smug Cloud award at the Massachusetts Farming and Technology (MASSFART) Convention. His favorite cake flavor is Ferrari.

# Index

*The Ultimate South Park and Philosophy: Respect My Philosophah!*, First Edition.
Edited by Robert Arp and Kevin S. Decker.
© 2013 John Wiley & Sons, Inc. Published 2013 by John Wiley & Sons, Inc.